# The History
of the
# Royal Bank of Scotland

His Grace the Duke of Buccleuch & Queensberry K.T.
Governor 1914 -
from a photograph by Dorothy Wilding

# The History
## of the
# Royal Bank of Scotland
### 1727-1927

Neil Munro

The Grimsay Press

The Grimsay Press
An imprint of Zeticula
57, St Vincent Crescent
Glasgow
G3 8NQ
Scotland
http://www.kennedyandboyd.co.uk


First printed for private circulation in 1928

First published in this form in 2011
© Estate of Neil Munro 2011

ISBN 978-1-84530-097-5
The Official Website of the Neil Munro Society
is at http://www.neilmunro.co.uk/

All rights reserved. No part of this publication may be reproduced, stored in a retrieval system, or transmitted in any form or by any means, electronic, mechanical, photocopying, recording or otherwise, without the prior permission of the publishers.

# PREFACE

To the Governor, Deputy Governor, and Directors of the Royal Bank of Scotland, the bicentenary of its foundation under Royal Charter in 1727 seems a fitting occasion to publish some review of its history. The story of the Bank, in general outline, is to be found in most of the literature of British banking, but usually unrelated in any way to contemporary Scottish events and leading personalities, and necessarily lacking those intimate details only to be got from access to its archives in St. Andrew Square, Edinburgh.

For the material of this volume the writer has depended mainly upon minute books covering the period of 200 years. From the very outset, the Court of Directors and the Court of Proprietors of the Royal Bank kept careful record of all affairs that came before them, their deliberations thereon, and their decisions. Set down with precision and minute attention to detail, those records fill an amazing number of close-written manuscript volumes. Their conscientious perusal from first to last might well daunt any historian concerned only with the entries of abiding interest.

## The History of

Fortunately for the chronicler in this instance, something like a rubric to the salient entries in those manuscript volumes has always been kept up by the successive scribes, and an exhaustive synopsis of this kind, made by an official of the Bank, the late Mr. H. H. Pillans, greatly facilitated the writing of this book.

Acknowledgment must be made, too, of the valuable aid given by Sir Alexander Kemp Wright, the General Manager of the Bank, who made accessible any old books or documents essential to the elucidation of points arising from references to the more remote period of the Bank's history, and was otherwise indispensable in a consultative faculty. The Secretary of the Bank, Mr. J. B. Adshead, must also be mentioned as helpful in many ways.

Written primarily as a souvenir of the Royal Bank's bicentenary celebrations in 1927, and more obviously for readers interested in the career of that great Scottish Corporation, this is to be regarded not as a portentous professional contribution to the history of Scottish banking, but as a layman's light domestic chronicle of the Royal's career as seen from the inside. Yet to put the domestic annals of the Royal, in old romantic and in modern

## The Royal Bank of Scotland

days, in their right perspective and in their proper relation to contemporary history, it has been necessary at times to encroach briefly on ground already covered by Scottish banking historians or in national history.

The final chapters, treating of the present century and of events still too transitional for an historical setting, and with individuals still alive, are necessarily mere summaries of a period which is left for some future historian of the Royal Bank to deal with more minutely.

N. M.

# CONTENTS

### CHAPTER I

THE DARIEN ADVENTURE . . . . 1

>The beginning of British banking—William Paterson—Chief projector of the Bank of England—His attention turned to Scotland—Founds the Darien Company—Expeditions to the Isthmus of Panama—New Caledonia—Hostility of England and Spain—Evacuation of the new colony—Great loss of life and treasure—Scotland beggared.

### CHAPTER II

UNION OF PARLIAMENTS . . . . 12

>Foundation of the Bank of Scotland—Darien Company also starts a banking business and a bank-note issue—A hopeless project—King William's diplomatic regrets—A discontented, almost rebellious Scotland—Queen Anne's overtures for a Union of Parliaments—Compensation for the Darien losses—Act of Union passed.

### CHAPTER III

THE EQUIVALENT . . . . . 20

>Genesis of the Royal Bank of Scotland—The "Equivalent Fund"—Only in part pays Scotland's National Debt—New coinage—Dubious debentures for six years pay no interest—Diminishing revenues—George I.'s amending Act—The "Society of the Subscribed Equivalent Debt"—William Paterson, Director—Incorporation of the "Equivalent Company"—Royal Bank's first Charter.

# The History of

## CHAPTER IV

THE ROYAL BANK OF SCOTLAND . . . . 34

Appointment of Governors and Directors — Lord Ilay — Capital secured — First Bank premises in Edinburgh — Printing the first bank-notes — Office staff appointed—Business begins—First deposit and first credit accounts.

## CHAPTER V

EARLY RIVALRIES . . . . . 50

The Old and New Banks—A lively competition—Whig and Tory — Royal the favourite of the Government — Exchange of notes — " Mother of the modern clearing-house " — An amalgamation of the two banks proposed — Negotiations broken off.

## CHAPTER VI

THE CASH CREDIT . . . . . 62

Business hours in the Ship Close office—Directors, their fees and duties—Printing the notes—Scotland's small population — Social conditions — An isolated Capital—Royal opens an account with the Bank of England—And initiates the Cash Credit System. The " Option Clause "—Bank-notes largely supersede specie —Some pioneers in note forgery.

## CHAPTER VII

SECOND CHARTER . . . . . 77

Lord Milnton goes to London on a diplomatic mission —A new Charter, with authority to increase the capital — Some country customers — Emergence of " John Campbell of the Bank "— Old Edinburgh's tavern hospitality—The Duke of Buccleuch and the Earl of Breadalbane—Great destitution in the country —Royal comes to the help of the municipalities—Small firms as " private bankers ".

# The Royal Bank of Scotland

## CHAPTER VIII

THE 'FORTY-FIVE . . . . . 91

John Campbell becomes Cashier—Prince Charlie's landing—Marches on Edinburgh—Anxious hours in the Ship Close—£10,600 in notes destroyed by the directors—Cash, books, and securities consigned to the Castle vaults—Highland army enters the city—John Campbell's Diary of the six weeks' Occupation by the Rebels—Prince Charlie marches into England and the Royal resumes " business as usual "—Abolition of the Hereditary Jurisdictions — The forfeited estates and the Royal's interest in them—Highland jaunts for the bank tellers.

## CHAPTER IX

SMALL NOTE MANIA . . . . 108

Start of the British Linen Company — Its country agencies—Glasgow and Aberdeen open unchartered banks—Royal lends £5000 to "improve and ornament the City of Edinburgh "—Modest first schemes for "the Modern Athens "—New bank premises off High Street—An *entente cordiale* between the Old Bank and the New Bank — First bank drafts and guinea notes—Fantastic paper money—Shortage of specie—New Act of Parliament to abolish the "Option Clause " and regulate bank-note issues.

## CHAPTER X

CRISIS OF 1772 . . . . . 131

Provincial banks opened in Dundee, Ayr, and Perth—The failure of Douglas Heron and Co. — Whole foundation of Scottish private banking shaken—Royal gets its third Charter giving it free use and command of the capital of £111,000 of Equivalent Stock—Finances great new national enterprises.

## CHAPTER XI

GLASGOW'S AWAKENING . . . . 141

War with America, France, Spain, and Holland; rebellion in Ireland; India in revolt—But tranquillity and progress in Scotland—New era of private bankers—Glasgow enters on the Industrial Era—Death of John Campbell—Lord Gardenstone's burned bank-notes—David Dale opens the Royal's first branch in Glasgow—A real " City Father "—French Revolution and the crisis of 1797.

## CHAPTER XII

THE PRIVATE BANKS . . . . 160

Changes in the Royal Bank administrative personnel—New Glasgow premises—A flood of unfortunate new semi-private banks—Stamp duties on all bank-notes—Rise of the Commercial Bank—Private bankers on the boards of chartered banks—The case of Messrs. Ramsays, Bonars and Co.—Glasgow branch " flits " again to more imposing quarters—A seventh Charter for the Royal and a capital of £1,500,000—Edinburgh office removes to St. Andrew Square—The " Radical Rising " in the West.

## CHAPTER XIII

FOUNDATIONS OF PROSPERITY . . . 185

Purchase of Dundas House, St. Andrew Square, and another removal—Speculative mania reaches a crisis—Pole, Thornton and Co., London, crash; short panic in the West of Scotland—The Royal sells its Glasgow office to the Glasgow Royal Exchange and builds its present chief office premises there—Lord Liverpool's menace to the One Pound Note—Sir Walter Scott comes to its defence and the attack is routed—Royal's capital increased to £2,000,000 by eighth Charter.

# The Royal Bank of Scotland

## CHAPTER XIV

EXTENSION OF BRANCHES . . . . 200

    Sir Walter Scott and his creditors—A heroic reparation—The tribute of the Edinburgh banks—First Parliamentary Reform Bill leads to rioting—Agitated nights in St. Andrew Square—Royal has more money in hand than it can profitably use—Buys American securities—Opens new country branches—Edinburgh Corporation gets a large loan—Position of Scottish banking in 1837—Royal appoints its first Inspector of Branches—Sir Andrew Agnew and the Sunday mails.

## CHAPTER XV

REGULATION OF NOTE ISSUES . . . 217

    An ex-cashier relinquishes his annuity—Bad trade in Dundee, Shetland, and Paisley—Peel's Act of 1844 to regulate note issues—The railway-projecting mania —French Revolution, and Chartist agitations at home— Profound trade depression in Glasgow—But a speedy recovery.

## CHAPTER XVI

FALL OF THE WESTERN BANK . . . 234

    Equivalent Company dissolved by Act of Parliament —Duty stamps on bank-notes become unnecessary— The last of William Paterson and his "phantom fortune"—Last surviving private bank in Edinburgh disappears—Great extension of the Royal's country branches—Failure of the Western Bank—Three years of unexampled prosperity for the Royal.

## CHAPTER XVII

FIRST LONDON BRANCH . . . . 251

    Dundee Banking Company merged in the Royal Bank —The "Authorised Circulation"—Premises bought

# The History of

in Lombard Street for a London branch—First published Abstract of the Royal's annual balance-sheet—The Royal Bank of Scotland Act, 1873, puts the Bank on an unequivocal footing to start business in London—Abandons the Lombard Street project and opens in premises in Bishopsgate Street—The London branch an immediate success—Another English assault routed.

## CHAPTER XVIII

THE CITY OF GLASGOW BANK . . . 271

"London Tavern" property acquired — Laying foundation stone—Investment in U.S. Funded Loan, 1871—The London Clearing House—Failure of City of Glasgow Bank—Companies Act, 1879—Projected State issue of bank-notes — Successfully opposed by Scottish banks—Staff of the Royal in 1883.

## CHAPTER XIX

CLOSE OF THE VICTORIAN ERA . . . 288

The Baring Brothers Bank crisis—Interest on current account creditor balances abolished—The Transvaal War—Death of Queen Victoria—Consols at their lowest—A Royal branch "held up" by robbers.

## CHAPTER XX

YEARS OF WAR . . . . . 302

Outbreak of the Great War — A moratorium proclaimed, and a long Bank holiday—Five feverish days of mobilising currency—Utility of the £1 note brilliantly vindicated—Complete public confidence in the Scottish banks—Enormous note circulation—Two-thirds of the Royal's staff join the colours—Its contributions to the War Loans and Credits—Armistice, and the building up afresh of civilisation—"Royal Bank of Scotland Act, 1920" receives the Royal Assent—A Granton robbery—War Memorials.

# The Royal Bank of Scotland

## CHAPTER XXI

DRUMMONDS' BANK . . . . . 323

Royal Bank acquires the old business of Drummonds' Bank, London, for its West End branch—The story of Drummonds' Bank—Capital of the Royal increased from £2,000,000 to £2,500,000—A disastrous labour dispute — The brief General Strike and the long-protracted closure of the coal-mines—Bicentenary of the Royal, and its celebration.

## APPENDIX

| | |
|---|---|
| THE BICENTENARY CELEBRATION . . . | 343 |
| LIST OF THOSE PRESENT . . . . | 385 |
| THE BANK'S POSITION FROM 1865 TO 1927 . | 390 |
| THE BANK'S REPORT AND BALANCE SHEET AS AT 8TH OCTOBER 1927 . . . . | 391 |
| GOVERNORS, DEPUTY GOVERNORS, DIRECTORS, AND CASHIERS . . . . . | 397 |
| THE GREAT WAR—ROLL OF THE FALLEN . | 416 |

# LIST OF ILLUSTRATIONS

### PORTRAITS REPRODUCED IN PHOTOGRAVURE

HIS GRACE THE DUKE OF BUCCLEUCH AND QUEENSBERRY, K.T., Governor, 1914–. From a photograph by Dorothy Wilding     *Frontispiece*

FACING PAGE

ARCHIBALD, EARL OF ILAY, subsequently Third Duke of Argyll, First Governor, 1727–1737. From a mezzotint by J. Faber, after the portrait by Allan Ramsay     38

GEORGE DRUMMOND, Lord Provost of Edinburgh, 1725, 1746, 1750–1751, 1754–1755, 1758–1759, 1762–1763, an original Director, 1727–1745. From a mezzotint by A. Bell, after the portrait by J. Alexander     40

"JOHN CAMPBELL OF THE BANK", Cashier, 1734–1777. From a portrait by an unknown painter in the possession of Lieut.-Col. Sir Guy T. Campbell, Baronet     82

SIR LAWRENCE DUNDAS OF KERSE, Baronet, Governor, 1764–1777. From a painting by T. Hudson, in the possession of the Marquis of Zetland, K.T., at Aske, Richmond, Yorks     138

HENRY, THIRD DUKE OF BUCCLEUCH, Governor, 1777–1812. From an engraving by H. Meyer, after a drawing by T. Heaphy     146

WILLIAM SIMPSON, Cashier, 1780–1808. From a portrait by Sir Henry Raeburn, R.A., in the Head Office of the Bank     148

## The Royal Bank of Scotland

FACING PAGE

DAVID DALE, First Agent in Glasgow, 1783–1806. From a photogravure by T. & R. Annan & Sons, Glasgow, taken from the original tassie dated 1792    150

JAMES SIMPSON FLEMING, Cashier and General Manager, 1871–1891. From a photograph by John Moffat, Edinburgh    264

ROBERT WILLIAM DUNDAS, M.C., W.S., Director, 1919- ; Chairman of Directors, 1926- . From a photograph by W. & E. Drummond Young, Edinburgh    310

SIR ALEXANDER KEMP WRIGHT, K.B.E., D.L., General Manager, 1917- . From a photograph by A. Swan Watson, F.R.P.S., Edinburgh    314

ANDREW DRUMMOND, Founder of Drummonds' Bank in 1717. From a mezzotint in Drummonds' Bank by J. Watson, after the portrait by Zoffany    328

### VIEWS OF BANK BUILDINGS IN HALF TONE

FRONT VIEW OF HEAD OFFICE, EDINBURGH, formerly the Mansion-house of Sir Lawrence Dundas    190

PRINCIPAL OFFICE IN GLASGOW    194

BANKING HALL AT HEAD OFFICE    246

BOARD ROOM AT HEAD OFFICE    248

LONDON (CITY) OFFICE, 3 Bishopsgate, E.C.    268

WEST END OFFICE, EDINBURGH    318

VIEW SHOWING DRUMMONDS' BRANCH AT CHARING CROSS (on left of Admiralty Arch)    332

THE WAR MEMORIAL AT THE HEAD OFFICE    416

# CHAPTER I

### THE DARIEN ADVENTURE

WHEN joint-stock banking began in Scotland at the end of the seventeenth century, so closing an age-long era of primitive barter in which an always dubious coinage played but a secondary part as a medium of exchange, it might well seem the most unlikely country in which to establish such an institution. The bank, in the modern sense, was still a novelty even in England, though a familiar feature of commercial life in other parts of Europe during the Middle Ages.

Public banking in Britain began only in 1694 with the founding of the Bank of England, but many of its functions may be traced in the practice of the London goldsmiths who, throughout the seventeenth century, were in the habit of receiving deposits of money, plate, and other valuables, against which they issued receipts that, under the name of " goldsmiths' notes ", passed freely from hand to hand. Sir Walter Scott, in *The Fortunes of Nigel*, introduced us to one of those accommodating gentlemen, to

# The History of

whose coffers resorted James VI.—" Jingling Geordie ", otherwise George Heriot, an Edinburgh man who had followed his Sovereign to London, where, as Court jeweller and banker, he amassed a fortune, most of which, like an honest Scot, he bequeathed for the education of the sons of poor Edinburgh burgesses.

At the end of the seventeenth century England was poor, money was scarce, public credit was bad, and there was little confidence in private integrity. The Bank of England, first projected by Dr. Hugh Chamberlain as a means of raising money for the use of the Government, was started and founded on a plan the entire credit of which was due to William Paterson. He was one of the original twenty-four directors, and saw it fairly started, but owing to some disagreement with the majority of his colleagues, voluntarily withdrew from the corporation in 1695 by selling out his qualification of £2000 stock. Henceforth his attention was to be turned in the direction of Scotland.

There is, in the British Museum, a pen-and-ink portrait of Paterson, the only really suggestive feature of which is its accompanying Latin motto, " Sic vos non vobis ". Was this Virgilian tag his own selection, or an admirer's summing-up of a career in which Paterson usually did the work and others got the credit?

All that is known with certainty of William Paterson's youth and early manhood may be

## The Royal Bank of Scotland

put into a paragraph. He was born about 1658 at Skipmyre Farm in the parish of Tinwald, Dumfriesshire; spent some years in the West Indies, where he acquired a moderate fortune at an early age, and whence he returned to England about 1686, to become a London merchant.

It is only inferred that his education was got in a Dumfriesshire parish school. In any case, it was sound enough to make him in after-life as socially self-assured a gentleman and as competent an English writer as if he had gone through Oxford. There is an ill-accredited story of his having had to flee to a relative in Bristol when seventeen years of age on account of "intercommuning" with Covenanters, and a more fantastic tradition that his first appearance in the Indies was as a missionary who subsequently found a more rapid way to affluence by joining the Brethren of the Coast and flying the Jolly Roger. It was really a shrewd man of affairs with considerable mercantile experience only to be gained in merchant offices, not on pirate ships, who returned to London with his head full of schemes of foreign trade; a quiet gentleman of serious walk and conversation.

Paterson's interest in the establishment of the Bank of England was only a residual product from a brain in which fermented far more romantic and grandiose projects. His fellow-countrymen and fellow-merchants in London were to hear from him a good deal about the Potosi possibilities of foreign lands he had visited, the evils of monopoly, the potential blessings of Free Trade, the arrogance of the London East India Company and, above all, the supereminent appropriateness of the Isthmus of Panama to be a great British *entrepôt*. Had he ever been in Panama, or did his instinctive recognition of it as the fulcrum of his visionary schemes come from the map alone or the common talk on Jamaica quays? In any case, it was as early as 1684 he first conceived the idea of a colony in Darien, a disastrous project which, however, as will be seen, led not indirectly to the formation of the Royal Bank of Scotland.

The London East India Company was of course firmly established in a monopoly of English trade with the Orient, which Paterson and many other London merchants envied, and England's Navigation Laws made any project for even the most circuitous English intrusion upon that monopoly certain of violent opposition. They were mainly London capitalists, however, eager at any cost to have a share in the spoils of foreign trade so jealously guarded as a monopoly of the E.I.C. who, probably on Paterson's suggestion, initiated a project which was eventually to become entirely Scottish, ruin Scotland, and drive her ultimately into the surrender of her Parliament.

# The Royal Bank of Scotland

In 1693, the year after the Massacre of Glencoe, the Scottish Parliament had passed an Act for the Encouragement of Foreign Trade. Paterson, having assured himself of the financial interest of his London fellow-merchants, gave tangible shape to this too vague conception by producing the scheme he had been brooding on for nine years. In June 1695, through the influence of the Earl of Tweeddale, Viscount Stair, Fletcher of Saltoun, and others, King William was induced to give his consent to a Scots Act conveying the power to a Scottish East India Company to engage in an African, American, and Indian trade organised from Scotland, the provision being made that "foreigners" as distinguished from natives of Scotland could take half the stock in the enterprise. "Foreigners", of course, comprised Englishmen. It seemed obvious from the first that so poor a country as Scotland could never wholly finance the scheme, and Paterson was in a position to guarantee that 50 per cent of the stock could be sold by him in London.

King William, busy with a continental war, had not realised what a tumult he would create in England and elsewhere when he authorised his Scots Commissioner Tweeddale to give his assent to an Act he knew little about in its details and implications. It must be confessed that his Ministers in Scotland contributed nothing to his enlightenment till they put on

## The History of

the Statute Book an Act which launched Scotland, with only about £800,000 of liquid resources in her possession, on a career of imperial ambition certain to bring her into conflict with England, France, and Spain.

Paterson quickly got together his company —twenty directors, including himself, half of them London merchants, the others men well known in Edinburgh. The English half of the capital of £600,000 was over-subscribed as soon as the books were opened; it took somewhat longer for the Scots to make up their moiety, but when this was done the storm broke over the land.

English E.I.C. stock fell twenty points in a week. Lords and Commons in Westminster protested to the King that this Caledonian company would destroy England's commerce in America and Asia. The King declared he had been " ill-served " by his Scottish Ministers, and made it plain that in him the new company would have no champion. Immediately all the English shareholders withdrew from the enterprise, and Scotland was, in the vulgar phrase, " left to hold the baby ".

It became a patriotic duty in Scotland now to prove that she could do without English help and could defy the claims of any English trading company to the mercantile sovereignty of the seas. A capital of £400,000 was now the aim. Though Macaulay, in his *History*, says, " From

# The Royal Bank of Scotland

the Pentland Firth to the Solway, everyone who had a hundred pounds was impatient to put down his name ", this is merely rhetoric; there were large tracts of the country to which the ultimate Darien fiasco meant nothing financially. The stock, in blocks of £100 up to £2000, was, in the main, subscribed by the Lowlands; the North was less involved, and the Highlands were too poor to come in.

It took six months to complete the £400,000 —on paper; of this sum only £220,000 was actually paid and lost. "With what great efforts such a sum was raised may be better understood if it be borne in mind that it probably bore as great a ratio to the wealth of Scotland then as twenty-two millions would bear in our day," wrote Mr. James Simpson Fleming of the Royal Bank of Scotland in 1877. The subscribers included nobility, landed gentry, merchants, professional men, small shopkeepers, and nearly every Royal Burgh in the country.

Of Paterson's integrity there has never been any question, but his twentieth-century finesse as financial expert was hardly understood in seventeenth-century Edinburgh. Though he settled down for a time in that city as adviser to the new Board, of which he was a member, he found himself overruled in many respects by others who were without his talent or experience. An unhappy part in his tactics was to

## The History of

keep the essential and primary feature of his designs secret while subscriptions were coming in, but it is unlikely that they would have come in any less satisfactorily had it been known. Public curiosity regarding details was fobbed off with vague talk of a settlement to be made " upon some island, river, or place in Africa, or the Indies, or both ".

From the first, his old dream of the Panama Isthmus engaged his mind exclusively, or, at all events, with an insistency that left him little enthusiasm for these vague East Indian and African elements in the scheme before the public. On his heart was graven " Darien ". In that narrow reef between the two Americas and the two great oceans the far-sighted Paterson saw the fulcrum wherefrom could be levered and directed towards Scotland the commerce of two worlds. He could have no view of a canal, but in every other respect he anticipated by two hundred years the reasoning which in the nineteenth century was to actuate the employers of De Lesseps and result in the Panama Canal. There was, moreover, in his conception, a moral grandeur even yet too generous for universal acceptance.

To a select few of his fellow-directors he laid bare the plans for a Scottish trading colony at Darien, whereat should concentrate the mutual trade of the Atlantic and the Pacific sea-boards; the traffic between Europe, Far Cathay, and

## The Royal Bank of Scotland

the Orient. No greedy spirit of monopoly should, in his conception, keep the world at large from freely benefiting by Scotland's enterprise; not hers would be the Spaniard's policy of excluding all commerce except his own; the ships and merchandise of all nations should be equally free to use the Scottish ports, contributing only their proportion to the costs of the establishment.

By June 1697 London learned the real objective of the forthcoming Scots expedition " under sealed orders "; and the " vested interests " took steps to make it plain that whatever happened to the adventurers, England was in no respect responsible. A year later, three ships and two tenders were bought in Holland for the Company; laden with cargoes whose grotesque and unsuitable nature has occasioned a satirical paragraph for historians ever since; armed for their own defence; and despatched from Leith on 26th July with 1200 men on board.

Paterson, perhaps the only man who could have saved the ill-starred adventure from failure had that been humanly possible, accompanied the expedition as a " volunteer ", taking his wife with him; but his fellow-directors did not appoint him one of the Council of Seven which was to function as central authority when the new colony was reached.

This is not the place to recapitulate at any

## The History of

length the melancholy story of the Darien Expedition, but inasmuch as the origin of the Royal Bank of Scotland is directly traceable to that event, there must at least be a brief epitome of circumstances whose narration has filled many volumes and saddened countless Scottish hearts.

There were really two expeditions. The first, in which Paterson set sail, reached the Isthmus of Panama at Darien, and took possession of the country under the name of New Caledonia. To the vast annoyance of Spain, the adventurers proceeded to lay the foundations of a city to be called New Edinburgh. In the following year, with Scotland still in a frenzy of exalted expectation, four more ships were despatched from the Clyde to the Isthmus, with 1300 men on them, only to find that the pioneer colony had disappeared. Unable to toil in that tropical heat, unaccustomed to tropical food, and scourged by tropic fever, the first Scots settlers had perished in scores, and at last the survivors, disregarding Paterson's entreaty to be left with a few companions to welcome the second contingent, put off for New York.

A pathetic attempt was made by the second expedition to redeem the site of New Edinburgh from the wilderness state to which it had already lapsed, but they, too, died in grievous numbers; dissensions awoke, and final disillusion came

## The Royal Bank of Scotland

with the appearance of a Spanish squadron having the determination and the physical force to compel evacuation. When the last of the adventurers sailed for home they had, in four months, lost nearly a quarter of their number. Paterson's wife, who had accompanied him, was one of the earliest victims of malaria, and died among the first of the pioneers. Broken in heart and health, he had reached this country from New York before the second catastrophe was apprehended.

The loss of life and treasure inexpressibly shocked Scotland; bitterly, too, was felt the conviction that those disasters were in a measure the result of indifference on its Sovereign's part and of the hostility of the English people.

# CHAPTER II

### UNION OF PARLIAMENTS

WITHIN a month after the statutory creation of the Darien Company, and two years before the tragic culmination of that great adventure, an Act was passed " for erecting a publick bank ", which became the Bank of Scotland. The earliest name to be publicly associated with the project was that of a London merchant, John Holland, who drew up its constitution at the request of a London Scotsman.

By Hill Burton and some other historians after him, William Paterson has been tentatively suggested as the Scotsman, but in truth he had nothing to do with a scheme which was in draft before he heard of it, and met with his active opposition. Among the London Scots associated with Holland as original members of the Bank of Scotland were John Foulis, David Nairn, Walter Stuart, and Thomas Deans, all previously having an interest with him in a Scottish baize manufactory originated by Deans. It was one of those—" an honest and ingenious friend of mine, a Scotch gentleman " (as

## The Royal Bank of Scotland

Holland wrote in later years)—who first importuned Holland to think out a scheme for a bank in Scotland, with an assurance that parliamentary powers could be got for it.

Holland was induced to draw up so much of a constitution as would be necessary to appear in an Act of Parliament; he gave his " honest and ingenious friend " the draft of it, and a few days later a formal Bill " drawn up in the Scotch stile " was laid before him.

Professor F. W. Ogilvie of Edinburgh University has recently made a very convincing case for the argument that the " honest and ingenious friend " was Thomas Deans, who was the son of a Bailie in the Canongate of Edinburgh.

The Bank of Scotland got its statutory credentials on 17th July 1695, but it was not till the following year that its modest capital of £100,000 was secured and business commenced. As first Governor of the new bank, Mr. Holland came to Edinburgh, opened its head office in Parliament Close, established branches at Glasgow, Aberdeen, Dundee, and Montrose (only to be closed as unprofitable a year later), and with liquid resources amounting only to £10,000, the product of the first call on shareholders, began to issue notes of £100, £50, £10, and £5 sterling. The practice of receiving money on deposit had not begun, and the clients of the bank were all borrowers on

## The History of

heritable and personal bonds or bill discounters. Not till 1704 did the note issue condescend to a £1 note — or, strictly speaking, a note for "Twelve pounds Scots"—the designation it bore on its face long after Scots money was abolished in 1707.

The Scots Act of Parliament on which the new bank was founded stipulated that no other banking company should be permitted to start business in Scotland for twenty-one years. This, however, did not prevent the directors of the Darien Company from organising in 1696 a banking business as adjunct to their great colonisation scheme. In the Company's charter was no reference whatever to banking, but Paterson, all along, would seem to have what he called a "fund of credit" in his mind as a part of the scheme, and recommended to his confrères on the Board a departure not easily to be distinguished from a flagrant attack on the Bank of Scotland's twenty-one years' monopoly.

The first "call" on the shareholders of the Darien Company had brought in nearly £100,000, of which £34,000 was paid before the date on which it was due—not because Scotsmen are absurdly precipitate on such occasions, but because a discount of 12 per cent was allowed on all prepayments. It was felt that this £34,000 should not be allowed to lie idle, consequently the Company began to treat

## The Royal Bank of Scotland

it as a fund from which the proprietors could borrow money at 4 per cent on the security of their stocks, the same rate of interest at which the new bank was giving accommodation.

There followed a bank-note issue. Copperplate notes were printed in facsimile of the handwriting of one of the Darien Company's best caligraphic artists, with blanks left for filling in the amounts to which the notes were limited, *i.e.* £100, £50, £20, £10, or £5. Agents were appointed in Glasgow, Aberdeen, Dundee, and Dumfries, to place the notes in the hands of the public. It was a project hopeless from the start; the whole of the Company's paid-up capital, with borrowed money in addition, was inadequate to finance its legitimate colonisation scheme, and the convertibility of the notes was always dubious since it was never certain that there would be, at any moment, sufficient " till money " to meet demands for change.

It took five years to convince the directors that banking on these lines was more precarious than profitable; the notes were finally retired from circulation in 1701, when the total issue, from first to last, had amounted to little more than £12,000.

For two reasons the Bank of Scotland took no steps to defend itself against this poaching, save by opening its short-lived branches already mentioned. Otherwise the Darien Company

## The History of

was allowed to carry on its competition undisturbed. It was felt that the clause in the bank Charter which forbade the setting up of " a distinct company of bank " had a textual weakness of ambiguity, despite its clear intention, and left a debatable issue for the Darien Company which would be expensive to contest at law; also that to fight the Darien Company, at the moment beloved in Scotland, would make the bank unpopular. The policy of "wait and see " was amply vindicated in a year or two, when the Darien Company's banking business was too trivial to cause the slightest apprehension.

If the phrase *fin de siècle* had had its modern connotation two centuries and a quarter ago, it could well have been used to express the disillusionment, the spirit of bewilderment, instability, unrest, and fear that filled the Scottish people in the winter of 1699. It was plain that the Darien enterprise was an iridescent bubble burst, and the only hope left was that the second expedition, with its 1300 colonists, might at least come out of the fatal Isthmus without further humiliation or more serious loss of lives. The national depression was lifted for a brief space in the summer of 1700 by the news that Captain Campbell of Finab had defeated the Spaniards, and Edinburgh "mafficked" wildly for a night, but a week later came news of the surrender of the colonists to Spain and the final abandonment of the settlement.

"Nothing", says Sir Walter Scott, "could be heard throughout Scotland but the language of grief and resentment. Indemnification, redress, revenge were demanded by every mouth, and each hand seemed ready to vouch for the justice of the claim." Not only were life and treasure lost, but the national pride of the Scots was tortured by the conviction that their efforts to establish a foreign trade were defeated by the unscrupulous jealousy of England and the unfriendliness of a Sovereign who had never set foot in their country.

Paterson, who was in Edinburgh when the dire news came, must have had the most anguished hours of his life, but he bore himself manfully. He might easily have diverted recriminations from himself by joining in the chorus of execration against England and the King, but he honestly and boldly contended that the main contributing causes of the failure were the lack of foresight in the directors at home, and the ignorance and dissensions among the council they had sent to Darien itself. He never relinquished a hope that England, sooner or later, would make amends for a catastrophe to which she was at least contributory.

King William in October, through his Commissioner the Duke of Queensberry, expressed his diplomatic regrets for what had happened, and his willingness to concur with Parliament in any steps to be taken for aiding and supporting the Company and making good its losses; but this little salved the wounds to Scotland's *amour-propre*, and during the brief period to run of his reign he was far from popular. Queen Anne in 1702 inherited all the embarrassment he had left her in a discontented, almost a rebellious Scotland.

Yet he had left her also the consolatory gift of a project—long cherished by himself though not to be accomplished in his lifetime—for the Union of the Parliaments of England and Scotland. Queen Anne lost no time in taking the matter up with her faithful Scottish Commons.

It is unnecessary to recapitulate all the political *pourparlers*, diplomatic intrigues, dissensions, jealousies, distrusts, and other human passions which made difficult all attempts at a reconciliation and amalgamation of the two old enemies.

It was clear, however, that a Union was the only possible means of allaying the apprehensions of civil war, and Commissioners from both countries, pushed to extremities of diplomacy, succeeded in a treaty which found expression in the Act of Union passed in May 1707. No man more zealously worked for this consummation than William Paterson. Largely through his unremitting advocacy of Union, and of Scotland's claim for reparation for the Darien

## The Royal Bank of Scotland

shareholders, the last Act passed by the Scots Parliament directed that an amount " not exceeding the sum of £232,884 : 5 : 0¾ sterling " should be paid to the Darien subscribers.

# CHAPTER III

### THE EQUIVALENT

To comprehend satisfactorily the origin of the Royal Bank of Scotland, which came into existence in 1727, it is necessary to begin twenty years earlier with the Union of Parliament, for in the Treaty of Union lay, all unsuspected, the germ of the Royal Bank.

It might seem, from the foregoing compression of years of mediation into a few sentences, that all the parleying was frankly in the open and that the pact agreed on was more or less agreeable to high and low in both countries. Not so guilelessly, however, are diplomatics of State conducted; great international bargains still involve something of the craftiness that goes to any business-like deal in horses.

The really influential men in Scotland responsible for the Treaty were numerically less than an infantry platoon, and were not infrequently in London where all the arguments of a " sweet reasonableness " could be imparted to them over a dinner-table. Politically and ecclesiastically they were more or less at war

## The Royal Bank of Scotland

at home in Scotland, but these were stringent times for empty pockets, and if their individual interests were safeguarded, they could not shut their eyes to the alluring nature of the prospects which the Union offered.

Something less than £600,000 represented the total National Debt of Scotland, even when the £232,884 lost in capital and interest by the Darien Company was included. The balance was more conventionally a National Debt, as it was due by the Government to private individuals—its own officials, tradesmen, Army, and pensioners as pay deferred. Those latter unhappy, inarticulate creditors, it was decided, should have to wait with patience till the more picturesque and clamant demands of the Darien Company proprietors were satisfied. Among the Darien stockholders were most of the aristocracy and upper bourgeoisie of Scotland, and tactfulness dictated their immediate appeasement if the Union project was to have any chance of success.

Then came the delicate problem of adjusting other terms between the parties to a matrimonial alliance in which Scotland had little " tocher " and yet was manifestly entitled to some rights by marriage settlement. As citizens of Great Britain, the Scots, having equal trading rights with the English, must now pay proportionately equal duties and excises, and so contribute to the payment of England's

## The History of

National Debt, in whose creation they had had no concern. The public revenue of England from custom and excise was about £2,300,000; that of her neighbour scarcely came to £65,000, and some new impositions were imperative if even this humble figure was to be maintained.

Before the burgh towns and the remoter glens of Scotland were fully aware that a treaty was finally in prospect, its terms were cut and dried. As compensation for the drain England henceforth was to make on her new partner's annual revenues, a pecuniary equivalent was to be handed over. The sum agreed upon was £398,085 : 10s., together with a proportion of what increase of revenue might be realised in after years. This *quid pro quo* was ear-marked for the following purposes: To compensate the Darien stockholders to the extent already mentioned; to reimburse all private individuals who might incur loss through the re-coinage of the Scots currency; to pay the real Scots National Debt of deferred pay and pensions; to pay £2000 a year for seven years towards the encouragement of woollen manufactures, and a like sum in after years for the development of fisheries and other industries.

"Equivalent", on the face of it, was a misnomer; it would little more than pay the debts of the Scottish Treasury, even if the claims of the Darien shareholders, first to be

## The Royal Bank of Scotland

dealt with, had been out of the question, and the " charges " of the Commissioners of the Union, which came to the sum of £30,000.

The official expenses of Her Majesty's Lord High Commissioner swallowed up about half of this £30,000, and other Scottish Ministers had little difficulty in disposing of the rest among themselves. Scotland, when she heard of it, swore she had been sold for money down in bribes to her own noblemen; the truth has never satisfactorily been " redd up "; but, in any case, more elemental reasons than the pecuniary needs of a handful of noblemen made the Union inevitable.

The Queen appointed twenty-five Commissioners to administer this Equivalent fund, four of them being Englishmen, of whom Sir John Cope was the most distinguished. The money was deposited in the Bank of England, and by agreement was to be handed over on the 1st of May. In a singularly perfunctory manner, however, the payment was postponed for over two months for what seemed the most trivial reasons, and such was the irritation and distrust aroused in Edinburgh that some hotheads began publicly to call for the abrogation of the Treaty. Finally, however, on 8th July, the money was despatched from London in twelve waggons, each with six horses, and an escort of thirty troopers, an official of the Bank of England being in charge of the convoy. It took four weeks to accomplish the journey to Edinburgh; no doubt in English inns *en route*, and English hamlets, the passage of this imposing cavalcade was a day's sensation, and the yokelry of the shires had ironic comments to make on the monetary cost of Scotland's friendship.

Arrived in Edinburgh, the waggons were driven straight to the Castle, where the precious freight was formally handed over to the Commissioners by Mr. Thomas Whitehall, the Bank of England official. When it was discovered that only £100,000 of the Equivalent was in specie, and that the remainder was in Bank of England notes and Exchequer bills payable on demand four hundred miles away in London, there was the utmost dissatisfaction. It was plain to the Commissioners that they had underestimated the Scotsman's preference for money that really talks instead of merely rustling, and they had hurriedly to send to London for £50,000 more in coin. It came in " one of the Queen's carriages " guarded by seventy mounted Grenadiers to Berwick, whence a relay escort saw it safely to the capital.

From the old Darien Company office in Milne Square the Commissioners began at once to distribute the money among the numerous claimants. It was found that, with very few exceptions, the original stockholders in the Darien Company had either died or assigned

## The Royal Bank of Scotland

their scrip to others, or had had their property arrested by their creditors. To verify the claims of unknown assignees and claimants involved protracted investigation and vexatious delay; the Commissioners were pestered by actions at law in the Court of Session by impatient individuals shrewdly suspicious that the Castle vaults held less than would satisfy all the claims, and that the last to be settled with would come off worst.

Having settled with the creditors of the Darien Company, and satisfied the claims of the Commissioners, the next task was to rectify the coinage. There was a Mint in Edinburgh, a handsome building in the Cowgate, dating from 1574, somewhat poorly equipped for putting a new face on all Scotland's pocket-money, but not from the hands of the Master of the Mint, Mr. George Allerdyce, had all the coinage come that was now in circulation in a nation that made its shillings go a long way. Of gold coinage there was probably no more than £30,000. Of foreign silver money £132,080 turned up for re-minting; of Scottish coins later than 1673, £96,856; of older hammer-struck coins, £142,180; and of English coin, £40,000. The foreign coins were quaintly cosmopolitan; the English coins in some cases were as old as the dynasty of Plantagenet, and there was little coinage of any origin that was not "clipped" or pared at its edges, the frugal resort of the unscrupulous before milled edges came into fashion.

The magistrates of the principal burghs were authorised to receive, examine, and assure themselves of the face value of all coins brought to them, and give the possessor a certificate of what loss he would sustain by their transformation into coins of English standard and value. The coins and the certificate were then taken to the Equivalent Commissioners, who paid from the money received from London a sum sufficient to satisfy the owner he was not a loser by this new fad for English insignia on everyday cash.

The loss on melting down and re-minting this heterogeneous specie, consisting mainly of dollars, ducatoons, merk pieces, threepenny bits and forty-shilling pieces, came to about £50,000. To assist Mr. Allerdyce, the Duke of Queensberry arranged with the Government for the services of some "moneyers" from the Tower Mint, London, who were paid 9d. on each pound of silver refined and coined.

As might be expected, the surplus left after the Commissioners had dealt with the allowance for the Commissioners, the Darien creditors, and the re-coinage, was so small that the real National Debt to the public, amounting to over £200,000, could not be paid. It was presumed that the public revenue would increase as a result of the Union, and it was from this

## The Royal Bank of Scotland

hypothetical increase, pledged to the creditors and called the Arising Equivalent, that payment of the debts was expected. Unhappily the revenue declined seriously after the Union, and though in 1711–12 an increase took place, it was not maintained, and in 1714 it was lower than seven years previously.

In a manuscript based upon close research into the whole intromissions of the Government and the Equivalent Commissioners, the late Mr. H. H. Pillans, for many years an official of the Royal Bank of Scotland, throws the most lurid light on the shameful treatment to which for seventeen years the poorest creditors of the Union were subjected. It is a document no national historian should henceforth overlook, a marshalling of facts that have hitherto been entirely left out of account or ignored as insignificant. Collated they go far to explain the detestation of the Union which was felt in Scotland for at least a generation.

No annual subsidy was forthcoming for the woollen and other manufactures as promised; nor was anything left to settle what, as the real National Debt, should have been a first charge on the Equivalent — the deferred wages and accounts of Army officers who had had to clothe their regiments at their own expense; the salaries, and fees long overdue, of humble State officials; tradesmen's bills for work contracted for by Government departments;

## The History of

indemnifications for losses by war for which the Scots Government had admitted liability; a whole Civil List of pensioners, mainly the widows of officers, clergymen, and civil servants.

To placate this horde of unfortunates, debentures were issued to them by Act of Parliament, to the amount due in each instance, the said debentures to bear interest at the rate of 5 per cent from June 1708, " to the day to be intimate for payment out of the Revenues of the Customs and Excise and other Arising Equivalent due to Scotland, mentioned in the 15th Article of Union ". The value put upon these debentures, so delightfully vague about the date for paying interest and so non-committal regarding any prospect of ever re-paying the capital, may be estimated from the fact that William Paterson, who was awarded £18,000 of them by special Act of Parliament, could only raise a loan of £3000 on them in his hour of necessity. The Duke of Athole, who obtained a debenture for money due to him for clothing his regiment, asked Campbell of Monzie what value it had. " I declare I cannot tell, but I think worth very little money," was Monzie's reply.

Six years after those dubious bonds had been distributed, six years during which no payment was made of either principal or interest, the debentures were called in by Act of Parliament and renewed, plus the six years'

## The Royal Bank of Scotland

interest, with a promise of 5 per cent interest on the total. Shortly afterwards a sum of £15,822 was provided for the payment of one year's interest, but only £5000 of it reached the hands of the debenture-holders, a nobleman with a quite sound claim for £10,000 having come early in the morning to the payout counter to avoid the crush of widows and orphans from every part of Scotland.

Distracted by perplexities for which they can scarcely be regarded as blameless themselves, and alarmed by the growing discontentment of the people, the Commissioners sent Campbell of Monzie to London at his own expense to put the position of affairs before the Members of Parliament. It was assumed that the Treasury must now be deriving from the Scottish customs and excise (including new taxes imposed since the Union) sufficient at least to make the Arising Equivalent a tangible thing and warrant the settlement of that quarter of a million debt outstanding to the poorest section of the nation's creditors. In reality, the revenues of Scotland were diminishing.

Mr. Campbell found it a thankless mission; Government officials met him with the " rudest and most unmannerly things on the subject of Scotland and its claims ", and even the Members of Parliament representing Scotland appeared to have little interest in the claims and sufferings of their countrymen. There was an ironical humour in the honorarium now given to him by the Government for his trouble over the Equivalent—a present of the " Dead Stock " of the Darien Company! This meant the material wreckage salved from the Company's expeditions — old sails and cordage, muskets, nails, candlesticks, and other junk. From the Equivalent Commissioners he got £200 cash down, and the promise of £200 more on the following year, or alternatively a debenture for £300 without delay. No great munificence could be expected from that source; the Commissioners themselves were by this time working for nothing and maintaining office staffs at their own expense—a ludicrous state of affairs that went on for at least seven years.

In the fifth year of the reign of George I., 1719, an Act was passed making provision for a yearly fund of £10,000 to be paid out of Scotland's customs and excise as interest on £248,550 debentures. This, as it happened, meant little relief for Scotland; under pressure of want the debenture-holders had long since sold out at a serious discount, and £170,000 of debentures out of the total of about quarter of a million were now held in London. Those English debenture-holders found it inconvenient to send for their interest to Edinburgh, where it was payable, and they accordingly incorporated themselves into a " Society of the Subscribed Equivalent Debt ", in London;

## The Royal Bank of Scotland

collected their interest in a lump sum and divided it among themselves afterwards.

William Paterson was a director of the society, as was also Campbell of Monzie; one of its objects was the further purchase of debenture stock, and it granted its members loans on the security of their holdings. A similar society was, soon after, formed in Edinburgh, promoted by such notable men as the Earl of Ilay, Sir Hew Dalrymple, Duncan Forbes of Culloden, Campbell of Monzie, and Haldane of Gleneagles. Besides purchasing debentures, the Edinburgh society proposed to lend or employ all or any part of the money subscribed to it in bills, heritable bonds, wadsetts, and the purchase of lands, and hopes were entertained of an amalgamation with the Bank of Scotland. Twenty per cent of the proposed capital of £75,000 was to be the first call; a considerable number of debentures were transferred to the society, but little serious business was transacted. The Bank of Scotland could not be tempted to an amalgamation of any kind, and proposals to merge with the English society also came to nothing.

That both societies would prove supererogatory whenever the question of Scotland's public debt was settled—a consummation now regarded by the sanguine as imminent—was a serious thought for the Edinburgh society, and even for the London one. The latter thought

## The History of

to engage its capital in a banking business, but the Bank of England's monopoly by charter was an obstacle not to be overcome.

In 1724 the English society, which had been paying 7½ per cent, was wound up, and the holders of debentures were incorporated by Act of Parliament into what was called the Equivalent Company, which became the immediate and legitimate parent of the Royal Bank of Scotland. Its capital was the exact amount of the debentures—£248,550 : 0 : 9½, and the £10,000 per annum to be taken from the Scottish customs and excise as stipulated in the Act of 1719 was to be paid to the proprietors as dividend. As most of the debentures were held in London, though the income of the Company was wholly derived from and payable in Scotland, the head office was situated there, and a subordinate office was opened in Edinburgh in the premises in Milne Square, for the convenience of the Scots debenture-holders, whose holdings amounted to little more than £28,000. The Company had a board of thirteen directors, two of whom were resident in Edinburgh—Monzie and Sir Hew Dalrymple, Lord President of the Court of Session. Its first proceeding was to pay the arrears of interest due up to 29th September 1724.

Merely to act as recipient and dispenser of a fixed amount of annual interest and carry

## The Royal Bank of Scotland

through transfers of stock when necessary was not satisfactory to the new Equivalent society; the London directors were desirous of extending their activities by "keeping other people's cash as well as their own", in other words, doing a little banking. No English company could encroach on the monopoly of the Bank of England, but the Equivalent was—as now decided—a Scottish incorporation, and on 31st May 1727 a Charter was got under the Great Seal of Scotland, sealed 8th July, for banking in Scotland only. The Bank of Scotland's twenty-one years of exclusive monopoly guaranteed by Parliament had ended in 1716, when no application had been made for its renewal.

## CHAPTER IV

### THE ROYAL BANK OF SCOTLAND

THE name " Equivalent " had so many disagreeable associations for Scotland that the new Charter wisely dropped the word out of use altogether. It was, unequivocally, a Charter " incorporating the Royal Bank of Scotland ". There are now four chartered banks in Scotland (not including the Bank of Scotland, which, though popularly called "chartered", is, strictly speaking, a Parliamentary Corporation); but the first Charter of the Royal Bank is unique in its antiquarian interest, in its recapitulation of its old historic origins in redundancy of terms that to-day have a quaintness which no discerning reader with a fancy for the past would modify by a single change *brevitatis causa.*

It began with an impressive recitation of the Act of 1719 dedicating £10,000 annuity to the soothing of Scottish creditors of the State; reviewed the powers and privileges of the Equivalent Company in a paragraph as long as a modern newspaper column, without a full

# The Royal Bank of Scotland

stop, and as breathlessly proceeded to lay down the constitution of the new bank.

The capital fixed upon was £111,000, with power to increase by £40,000. His Majesty nominated, authorised, and appointed James Campbell, Paul D'Aranda, John Drummond, Edward Harrison, Daniel Hayes, Benjamin Longuet, John Merrill, Bulstrode Peachy Knight, Christopher Tilson, Robert Williamson, Esqrs.; Sir Hew Dalrymple, Baronet, Lord President of the Session; Patrick Campbell of Monzie, and Patrick Craufurd, Esqrs., or any three of them, " to take and receive at Edinburgh, all such voluntary subscriptions as shall be made on or before the 29th. day of September, 1727, by any person or persons Members or Proprietors of the said Equivalent Company who have or shall have credit for stock in the books of the said Company at Edinburgh at the time of such subscription of all or any of such part or share of the stock of the said Equivalent Company as he, she, or they shall think proper, for and towards raising a fund for the more effectually carrying on the trade and business of banking there and the uses herein after mentioned ".

The subscribers of said Equivalent Stock were thenceforth to be and be called one Body Politic and Corporate of themselves in deed and name by the name of *The Royal Bank of Scotland*, having perpetual succession and the use of a common seal. They could sue in any court of Scotland, purchase and enjoy lands and hereditaments, and "sell, grant, demise, analzie or dispone" the same. Their liberty of banking was confined to Scotland, and within these limits they could lend money on personal and real security and on pledges, keep money on deposit, borrow, owe, and take up money on their bills or notes payable on demand. Trading with the stock or money of the Bank in buying or selling goods was prohibited; dealing in bills of exchange and buying bullion gold or silver was confined to Scotland only. Goods pledged and not timeously redeemed, or lands or hereditaments purchased, could be sold when the necessity arose.

The Charter stipulated for the appointment of " Our right trusty and right well-beloved Cousin and Counsellor Archibald Earl of Ilay " as first Governor, and " Sir Hew Dalrymple, Lord President of Our Session", as first Deputy Governor. There were to be nine Ordinary Directors and nine Extraordinary Directors appointed periodically to manage the affairs of the Corporation. The first nine Ordinary Directors were to be:

ANDREW FLETCHER, Esq., Lord Milnton, one of the Senators of the College of Justice.
GEORGE DRUMMOND, Esq., Lord Provost of Edinburgh.
PATRICK CAMPBELL of Monzie, Esq.

# The Royal Bank of Scotland

RICHARD DOWDESWELL, Esq.
JOHN PHILP, Esq.
JAMES PATERSON, Esq., one of the Commissaries of Edinburgh.
HUGH SOMERVILL, Writer to the Signet, Esq.
PATRICK CRAUFURD, Sen., Esq., and
GEORGE IRWINE, of Newton, Esq.

The first nine Extraordinary Directors were to be:
MATHEW LANT, Chief Baron of Our Court of Exchequer in Scotland.
JAMES ERSKINE, Esq., one of the Senators of the College of Justice.
Sir JOHN CLERK, one of the Barons of Our said Court of Exchequer.
HEW DALRYMPLE, Esq., one of the Senators of the College of Justice.
GEORGE BAILLIE, of Jerviswood, Esq.
CHARLES CATHCART, Esq., Our Receiver-General for Scotland.
GEORGE ROSS, Esq., one of Our Commissioners of Excise in Scotland.
CHARLES ARESKINE, Esq., Our Solicitor-General for Scotland, and
JAMES NIMMO, Esq., Cashier to Our Commissioners of Excise in Scotland.

A general Court of the Proprietors was to be held four times a year, and no proprietor having less than £300 of the capital stock was to have a vote. The possession of £600 stock qualified for two votes; of £1200, three votes; and of £2000, four votes, the maximum voting power of any individual, irrespective of what stock he held over £2000. A Governor must have at least a £2000 qualification, a Deputy Governor £1500, an Ordinary Director £1000, and an Extraordinary Director £500; they were elected for one year, and were ineligible for any office in the Bank.

The Earl of Ilay figured as first Governor, doubtless on account of the supereminent influence of his name in Scotland, and in recognition of the invaluable service he had given to the promoters in getting their Charter. The President of the Equivalent Company, writing to the Edinburgh directors from London on 20th July 1727, said, significantly: "We cannot conclude this without taking notice of your attributing more merit to us than we really think we have deserved upon this occasion, for though we have done our part with true zeal and application, we are obliged in justice to my Lord Ilay to declare that the success in general and the dispatch of this important affair in particular has been greatly owing to his Lordship's diligent and powerful assistance".

Archibald, Lord Ilay, born in 1682, brother of that second Duke of Argyll,

> . . . the State's whole thunder born to wield
> And shake alike the senate and the field,

had, like his brother, fought in the campaigns of Marlborough, and inherited much of the

Archibaldus D. Argathelia

Archibald Earl of Islay and Third Duke of Argyll
Governor 1727-1757

state-craft genius of his family. In 1705 he was made Treasurer of Scotland, and made so great a figure in Parliament as to be chosen one of the Commissioners for the Treaty of Union in 1706, when he was created Earl of Ilay, Lord Ormisary and Dunoon, etc. In 1708 he became an Extraordinary Lord of Session, and was elected one of the sixteen Scottish peers to the united Parliament, to which he was ever after chosen. At the outbreak of the Rebellion of 1715, though retired from the Army, he took the field in defence of the House of Hanover, and was of signal service to the cause. When his diplomacy and influence were engaged in the creation of the Royal Bank of Scotland he was Lord Register of Scotland, and Keeper of the Privy Seal. Almost universally admitted to be one of the ablest politicians and statesmen of his time, and peculiarly representative of the loyal element and most progressive ideals of Scotland, he had, till the day of his death (with a qualification hereafter to be explained), the utmost confidence of Sovereign and Parliament, and practically held the reins of Scottish administration up till his death in 1761, when he had been Duke of Argyll for eighteen years.

At the first meeting of the " Court of Proprietors " held in Edinburgh on 28th November 1727, Campbell of Monzie presided. He had been a director of the Darien Company, a commissioner of the Equivalent, a friend and champion to many of his countrymen who had compromised themselves in the affair of 1715. He was able to inform the meeting that up till 29th September £106,747 : 14 : 9⅛ of the stock of the Equivalent Company had been subscribed and transferred to the capital of the Royal; that banking premises were now secured; that the plates for printing bank-notes were ready or in the engravers' hands; that the paper for printing the notes and a printing-press were ready, as well as the official seal of the new incorporation, and that the officers and servants of the new bank had been chosen and elected.

The first premises occupied by the new bank were on the north side of High Street. Lord Provost Drummond and Lord Monzie, who had been deputed to look out for a convenient office, had, on 17th August, decided that "the large house at the foot of the Ship Close", then in the joint occupancy of two tenants, Mrs. Cotton and Mr. Marishall, Limner, was suitable, " being in a central place and detached from other houses, which guards against fire ". On 1st September Mrs. Cotton was reported to the Board as willing to remove elsewhere for "a compliment of £50"; and Mr. Marishall was equally agreeable to " flit " for a compensation of £25. They removed at Michaelmas, Mr. Marishall by agreement leaving seven

George Drummond six times Lord Provost of Edinburgh
Director 1727-1745

## The Royal Bank of Scotland

carts of Dryden coal, which he had in his cellar, for the use of the Bank. For the coal the Bank paid £2 : 2s.

The premises were taken by the Bank on a three years' lease at a rent of £65 per annum, payable quarterly to Mr. Hamilton of Bangour's factor. For over two months after the premises had been vacated, Mr. James Smith, mason, was employed in constructing a vault fifteen feet in length and ten feet in breadth; repairing the coal-house, hearths, the close pavement, and garden dyke, etc.

To begin with, cash and valuable securities were entrusted to somewhat crude iron chests or "strong boxes" with complicated locks, specimens of which survive that are creditable to the elegant art of the locksmith of the times, though a burglar of the twentieth century would find them pathetically responsive to a drill, an oxygen flame, or a pinch of gelignite. By and by a sort of strong-room was evolved for the further security of valuables, such as the pledged jewellery of "my Lady Glenorchy", and the liability of the Old Town to the ravages of fire and the ingenuity of the wicked suggested other precautions.

From the original ledger recording the charges of management one gets a fair conception not only of how the Bank premises were furnished, but of day-to-day expenditure on establishment and what to-day would be called the petty cash. The earliest entry is on 16th June 1727—£5 : 5s. to " Mr. Thomas Rudiman for translating the Warrant of the Charter into Latin ", and £2 : 2s. to John Smith " who attended him and wrote the Scroll of the Charter ". Obviously the Royal meant to have this classic job well done. Thomas Ruddiman (as he himself spelled his name), was the author of *Ruddiman's Rudiments*, published thirteen years before this, a Latin grammar which was to be found in Scottish schools as late as 1860. The son of a Moray farmer, he had as a youth been a brilliant student in Aberdeen University, where Simon Fraser, Lord Lovat, was one of his class-mates. At the time when the translation of the Royal's Charter brought him a fee, he was librarian in the Advocates' Library, a post in which David Hume the philosopher succeeded him, with a salary of £40 a year.

In November five guineas were paid to David Beatt, writing master, for designing the first notes, which, of course, were reproduced in a facsimile of his handwriting.

Stocks of stationery were ordered at frequent intervals from William Monro—ledgers, foolscap, account paper (ruled by hand), standishes (inkstands), quills by the quarter-hundred, killavine pens (lead-pencils), less than a dozen at a time, a few sticks of wax, ink in sixpenny bottles, and " pownce " (the fine sand used to

## The Royal Bank of Scotland

dry up wet manuscript before the age of blotting-paper) in an unspecified quantity priced at fourpence. The first six months' bill for necessities of this kind amounted to less than £26.

Postages in the aggregate were not a serious item, though no letter seems to have cost less than sixpence, and the heavier ones might be as much as six shillings.

Coals were, as we should think to-day, of an agreeable cheapness—" 198 Loads at a shilling a load "—whatever a " load " might be. Candles were the only illuminants; they were stored in the "candle chest"; cost £4 : 8s. a stone for the ordinary kind and £5 : 4s. a stone for cotton wicks. A year's candle consumption ran to about £180 : 10s.—but these were pounds Scots; in sterling the bill came to £15 : 0 : 10.

For more than a year after the premises were entered, they must have been to an embarrassing degree in the hands of tradesmen —masons, wrights, and blacksmiths. William Richardson, master smith, for months was busy on the metal work of the strong-room, which had an iron door of twenty-nine stone weight, and on the provision of iron bands on chests; chains, locks, and window stanchions.

When the Bank doors opened, eight "officers and servants" formed its establishment, with

## The History of

an aggregate salary of £476 : 13 : 4. The entire staff and its emoluments were:

| | | | |
|---|---:|---:|---:|
| Allan Whitefoord, Cashier (besides the dwelling-house) | £100 | 0 | 0 |
| Daniel Campbell, Secretary, for himself | 90 | 0 | 0 |
| Daniel Campbell, for a clerk | 30 | 0 | 0 |
| Thomas Thompson, Accountant, for himself | 90 | 0 | 0 |
| Thomas Thompson, for a clerk | 30 | 0 | 0 |
| Alexander Innes, Teller and Receiver under the Cashier of all moneys due by Bonds, Bills, and other ways | 60 | 0 | 0 |
| George Andrews, Teller and Keeper of the Cash of such as lodge moneys with the Bank | 60 | 0 | 0 |
| William Brown, Messenger and Porter | 16 | 13 | 4 |
| | £476 | 13 | 4 |

Mr. Whitefoord, the first Cashier, held the office up till 1745, when he retired, to die twenty-one years later at Fountainbridge, leaving no marked evidences of an outstanding personality as a banker. For eleven years at least, the records would suggest that John Campbell the lawyer, then his assistant, was relieving him of a good many of the cares and responsibilities of his office, and was *persona grata* with the directors. The name Campbell, for various reasons, was probably an asset in itself for a bank which plumed itself on being

## The Royal Bank of Scotland

always on the loyalist side, or, as it was called at that period, Hanoverian, and this particular Campbell had the luck to have as patrons and friends some of the most influential territorial magnates in Argyll and Perthshire, not only customers of the Bank, but high in Government confidence. Apart from that, however, he was a gallant and outstanding figure, whose mien, character, and accomplishments inspired respect and admiration. We shall have much more to say of John Campbell later on; meanwhile it is enough to say that he emerges first in the records of the Bank in 1732, when he was promoted from the Accountant's office to be assistant secretary in room of his deceased clansman Daniel, a post abolished two years later, when he became Mr. Whitefoord's "second cashier" at a salary of £60 per annum. Four prominent clansmen were his security to the amount of £5000—Lord Breadalbane, Lord Glenorchy, Campbell of Achallader, and Campbell of St. Germaine. His cashiership was of course merely a part-time occupation; like most of the officials he had other irons in the fire.

During the preliminary arrangements for opening the Bank a sum of £20,000 was paid to Scotland by Government to be laid out at interest for improving the fisheries and manufactures—a belated settlement of the old obligation incurred under the Treaty of Union. This money was, in its entirety, deposited with

## The History of

the Royal at 5 per cent interest, the Chairman and the majority of the Trustees and Commissioners of the Board of Manufactures being Equivalent proprietors; consequently the establishment in Ship Close started business quite unembarrassed by any shortage of liquid resources.

No time was lost in instituting a note issue. The first notes, of the denomination of £100, £50, £20, £10, £5, and £1, were bound up in books " with check, to be cut out and issued as occasion serves "; they were printed on paper specially made for them at the paper mill of Richard Watkins at Yester, Giffordhall, in close enough propinquity to the High Street of Edinburgh to give the Bank staff a frequent excuse for visiting it to consult over experiments in new forgery-proof textures for the raw material of their " Promises to Pay ". Those spacious times permitted a certain degree of human cheer to such business engagements, and a visit to the " Mill " had its allotted though not extravagant expenditure in " drink-money ".

Not till 10th January 1728 were the Cashier and tellers in daily attendance at the Bank " to prepare for the ensuing term of Candlemas and to lend out or make advances to such parties as they think expedient, and who may require it at the term ", but as early as 13th November the Cashier had given his receipt for the first

## The Royal Bank of Scotland

deposit—a sum of £700 paid in by Mr. James Corrie, ex-Provost of Dumfries.

On 12th January 1728 the first advance was made—£1000 to Mr. George Drummond, ex-Provost of Edinburgh, on "his bond with Sir James Campbell of Aberuchall, Baronet, and James Baillie, Surgeon in Edinburgh, conjunctly and severally granted to Sir Hew Dalrymple, My Lord Monzie, and Patrick Craufurd, and by them assigned over to the Royal Bank dated the first of August last". The interest was at the rate of 5 per cent. Of ex-Lord Provost Drummond, Ordinary Director of the Bank, more shall later be recorded.

Among the first customers of the Royal, the Equivalent Company naturally took a prominent place, the Bank being in very truth a child of its own creation. For its trouble and expense in engineering the passage of the Charter in London, the Equivalent Company sent in a bill for £300—a sum so modest that it exonerates everyone engaged in the preliminaries from the slightest suspicion of ulterior motives. This bill was accompanied by an assurance of the Equivalent Company's readiness at all times "to assist and support their Bank—the Royal Bank of Scotland". As it happened, however, on many occasions, it was the Bank that came to the assistance of the Equivalent Company, the quarterly payments of the Scottish Exchequer's interest of £10,000 on the Equivalent debentures not always being settled on the proper dates, in which case recourse was had to the Bank for a loan so that the dividends to the individual stockholders should be punctually paid.

It has been assumed by some banking historians that the Royal Bank of Scotland now entirely superseded the Equivalent Company and that the latter ceased to exist. As a matter of fact, though closely connected in their business transactions, they remained distinct corporations up till 1851.

There were only about half-a-dozen holders of Equivalent Stock in Scotland yet unwilling to transfer to the Royal Bank, but still the annuity raised in Scotland by its customs and duties on salt, hides, leather, soap, and candles had to be collected in the Equivalent's Edinburgh office, and the proportion to meet the dividend due to the English proprietors was regularly remitted to London by the Royal Bank's draft on the Bank of England.

For many years the Cashier or Secretary of the Bank acted as a sort of honorary Edinburgh agent for the Equivalent Company, and a chamber of the Bank—at one period an attic—was set aside for the Equivalent books and business. How little real business was involved was reflected in the annual " allowance " made by the Equivalent for looking after its Edin-

## The Royal Bank of Scotland

burgh affairs—a sum of £25 conscientiously earned for many years by Mr. John Symer, one of the Bank clerks, who earlier had been in like service with the Darien Company itself. Naturally, the Company's quarterly instalment of the annuity was paid into the Bank, as were also later on all remittances of Scotland's public revenues to the Treasury in London. The Barons of Exchequer in Scotland had decided that this would " be the safest and easiest way for the regular and punctual remitting of the Public Money in time coming ".

# CHAPTER V

### EARLY RIVALRIES

For some years after the Royal Bank opened, and most violently in the first year of its existence, war waged between it and the Bank of Scotland—the Old Bank, as it came to be called in common parlance, the term New Bank being inevitably used to designate its young rival. Into their competition with each other the two concerns brought much of the fierce reprisal spirit of an old clan feud, tactics that to-day would seem dictated as much by personal animosities as by the struggle for survival, craftiness which resorted to the most infantile expedients, that must in later years have seemed laughable even to the gentlemen who adopted them. Before long the rival partisans, now doubtless cutting each other haughtily in the High Street, and fulminating at their respective Boards over the perfidy of each other, were to be the best of friends and doubtless take their " meridian " wine together, having realised that there was ample room in Scotland for both of them, and that they were both pathfinders

## The Royal Bank of Scotland

through moneyed realms hitherto unexploited and unexplored.

The Bank of Scotland, as we have seen, when founded in 1695, with a capital of £100,000 sterling, of which only £10,000 was called up, was guaranteed a national monopoly in joint-stock banking for twenty-one years. That period had elapsed in 1716, and no renewal of the privilege was sought for, the comforting but delusive theory being held that in Scotland, as in England, it would be utterly impossible to maintain two banks, and that no one was likely to test it. A reasonable period of monopoly was doubtless imperative in the case of a portentous new institution on its trial, but Scotland has ever had reason to be thankful that it was not too long perpetuated.

During those thirty-two years of monopoly remarkable prosperity attended the Old Bank. On two occasions only a great and unexpected demand upon its funds compelled a brief stoppage of its payments. The first was in 1704, when a scarcity of coin occasioned by its concentration in London for England's foreign costs of the wars of Marlborough made specie scarce. The crisis was met by a further call of 10 per cent on the nominal capital; of the solvency of the concern there was never any serious question; its assets exceeded its liabilities by about one-fourth.

This chastening experience coincided with,

but was unrelated to, the first issue of £1 notes denominated £12 Scots. When the Old Bank started, it had confined itself to lending out of its capital on heritable and personal bonds and bills of short usance, and took no deposits; its loans were given in notes of £100, £20, £10, and £5 sterling. The absence of any paper money smaller than a £5 note restricted its use, and for the everyday disbursements of the populace coin remained the popular medium. The crisis found the Bank for the moment with nearly £51,000 of outstanding debt, consisting mainly of notes, and only £1600 of old silver merks in hand to meet it, the great bulk of its other assets being inconvertible heritable and moveable bonds.

Deposits were first openly accepted in 1707, doubtless in the hope of increasing the working fund by securing some of the money which came to Scotland from England under the Treaty of Union. Not always was interest allowed on those deposits, and little of the Union payments found its way to the Old Bank, for the Darien proprietors secured the bulk of them, as we have seen, in the form of debenture stock, upon which the Royal Bank was ultimately to be founded.

After the Treaty of Union there survived for many years a governmental suspicion of the Old Bank's political integrity; its Tory directors had objected to the Treaty; its treasurer

## The Royal Bank of Scotland

was a Jacobite. The directors were probably actuated less by Jacobite sympathies than by an intuition that the Whigs of the Darien and Equivalent Companies were serious potential rivals. During the Rebellion of 1715 another awkward run was made on the Bank for coin in exchange for its notes—a run which the directors were surmised to have encouraged lest their specie should fall into the hands of the rebels. They had at the moment £30,000 of Government money in their repositories, and it was sent to Edinburgh Castle for security. When the specie in hand was exhausted, the Bank doors were closed for nearly four months, but such notes as were left in circulation were retired in the following year, with interest on them from the date of stoppage.

It is quite unprofitable to speculate now upon whether the gentlemen directing the Bank of Scotland in those troublous years were anti-Hanoverian or not. Who can say with certainty of any of them what the dominant political preferences were at a period when waverers were to be found in every class of Scottish society, and cautious men evaded as much as possible any frank discussion of their " patriotism ", a term capable of more than one definition in the circumstances? Nevertheless, the ascription of Jacobite sympathies to the Bank of Scotland was widely current in 1715, when no rival concern existed to give utterance to it, and the Crown was influenced by these rumours, which unquestionably made it easier to secure a charter for the Royal twelve years later.

One result of the 1715 affair was that the Bank of Scotland, for the second and last time in its history, paid no dividend. The stockholders, however, had little occasion to grumble, for their dividends all along had been of the most substantial character, though curiously erratic in amount, ranging from 6 per cent to 30 per cent.

The knowledge that such satisfactory profits were being made by the Bank brought several proposals to it for extension of its capital and amalgamation with other concerns, but these were emphatically turned down. The Bank's paid-up capital remained at £20,000 from 1704 till 1727, when the alarming prospect of a competing bank compelled a recognition of the fact that the liquid reserves had been cut much too fine, and a further call for £10,000 was made on the stockholders.

Early information of the Equivalent's Scottish banking project reached the Old Bank proprietors; they lodged a *caveat* against any new charter, and petitioned the King—not very hopefully. As a measure of precaution they stopped all further loans till they saw " how the cat would jump ". Again the old innuendoes regarding the Bank's political heterodoxy went

## The Royal Bank of Scotland

round; much was made of its stinginess in granting loans, refusing loans on pledges, and refusing to deal in exchange or foreign bills.

As might be expected, the partisans of the Old Bank attributed those vexatious reports to the projectors of the Royal, and retaliated by pooh-poohing the imminent opposition as having no capital at all but a national debt. The new bank's Charter revealed how foolish was such a conception, the tangible capital being £111,347 sterling of Government stock, with 20 per cent additional as a banking fund, the proceeds of calls on the proprietors; to which was added the Government's £20,000 for behoof of Scottish fishing and manufactures.

With the opening of the Royal Bank premises in Ship Close, mere skirmishing and reconnoitring ceased, and at close quarters opened a brisk duel in which the combatants used each other's notes as missiles. The late Mr. William Graham, in his admirable and entertaining *History of the One Pound Note*, states that the first notes issued by the new bank, dated 8th December 1727, were " apparently in exchange for as much of the Bank of Scotland's paper as could be got for the money—the Old Bank at once endeavouring to make a similar collection of its rival's notes. The modern exchange clerk might naturally suppose that his occupation then began, as indeed it did in the truest sense; but nothing was further from the Old

## The History of

Bank's notions of banking propriety than that its notes should be returned to it in thousands by a rival institution and peaceably paid for, as is done in our enlightened times. In those days it was regarded as an offensive innovation which was not to be tolerated. Unfortunately for the Old Bank, the Royal Bank proved to be more than its match. The new bank was the favourite with the Government as well as a considerable portion of the Edinburgh people; and, above all, it had the support of the Glasgow merchants, who hoped to extend their credit by its aid."

It has been suggested that the Royal made no haste to present its rival's notes for payment, but accumulated them till there were sufficient to embarrass considerably the Old Bank's tellers when their equivalent in specie had to be provided from a meagre coin reserve. If this tactic was contemplated by the Royal Bank management, the fact never emerges in their minutes, which in all other respects are frank enough. How the position looked to the General Court of Proprietors of the Royal is indicated in a minute of 5th March 1728, which says: " It was observed that difficulties do arise in the circulation of the Notes of this Bank, by the industrious pains taken by its Enemies to pick up their notes out of the circle of commerce and lodge them in the hands of such as value themselves above drawing cash

## The Royal Bank of Scotland

out of the Bank for these Notes ", and it was agreed " That for the better preventing thereof, all the Proprietors by themselves and their interest do support the circulation of the Notes of this Bank, by throwing in their cash upon a cash account with the Bank, or on the Cashier's Receipts, to put the practice now complained of, out of the power of their Enemies ".

As Mr. Graham has pointed out, tactics apart, the Old Bank was bound to find unusual numbers of its notes pouring back upon it when a rival note issue came into being; and whatever the motive that might have actuated the Royal Bank in presenting Old Bank notes for payment, its action " was at once correct in law and economics, and it is extremely interesting to see in this the true initiation, even though perforce, of the system of note exchange —the mother of the modern clearing-house— which has done so much since then to regularise the note issues of Scotland and the commerce of the world ".

For three months only did this internecine campaign last, the larger circulation of the Old Bank being steadily reduced as Royal Bank notes took its place, until, as in 1704, the till was absolutely drained, and on 27th March 1728 the Old Bank's doors were closed again. Mr. Andrew Cochran, Lord Provost of Glasgow, on that day had presented £900 of its notes for change; there was none to give him, and payment had to be deferred. The lesson of 1704 had been forgotten; two-thirds of the called-up capital and all the notes were sunk in heritable and personal bonds.

For the first time in the minutes of the Court of Directors of the Royal Bank we have on 27th March, the day of the Old Bank's closing, any reference to the topic of notes. "The Bank of Scotland having stopped payment of their notes," says the minute, "it was reported by the Accountant that there was of the Bank's notes on hand £9,374."

A special meeting of the Royal directors was called for the following day, when it was "resolved to give relief to the possessors of Old Bank Notes under certain conditions". Those conditions, so far as the large notes were concerned, seem from a minute of a few days later to have been "that such as lodge Old Bank notes with this Bank may either take the Cashier's receipt for them bearing the Bank to be bound to pay the produce thereof, or may have them entered in the Inner Column of their Bank Books as Bills of Exchange to be credited when 'made effectual'".

How this worked in practice may be gathered from the case of Malcolm MacLaren, drover, who, on 1st April, got £200 in notes of the Royal Bank in return for £200 of Old Bank notes and his bill at two months date. The drover was on his way to "Skye and other

## The Royal Bank of Scotland

places to buy cattle ", and his Old Bank notes were " now of no use in these parts ".

On the other hand, the Cashier was authorised (30th April) " to receive from Mr. Murdoch, Glasgow, £652 in Old Bank notes and credit him with it in *cash* ".

The Old Bank's £1 notes were more freely accepted by the Royal up till 13th May, when it was decided to advertise that from the 20th no more notes of the denomination would be " changed " or " received in any payments ". Up till then they were interchangeable in specie.

This prompt recognition and acceptance by the Royal of its rival's paper promises to pay was a courageous and far-seeing policy; it steadied the nerves of the national money market, averted panic, and was immensely reassuring to the masses who had still to be convinced that their notes for £12 Scots (£1 sterling) were as sacrosanct as if they were for £100 sterling. The immediate result was that all over the country Old Bank notes were accepted on their face value even though the Bank was shut, and on 27th June the Old Bank reopened and was able to resume payment of its own twenty-shilling notes.

While the Bank of Scotland, though quite solvent, was still closed, and its management was still embarrassed by the lack of liquid funds to meet immediate demands, the feeling that, after all, one bank might be better than two came uppermost again. On 10th April a union of the two Banks was proposed at a meeting of the Royal's directors, and a special meeting was called for the 16th, when a committee was appointed "to meet and treat" with the directors of the Bank of Scotland to this end. Whatever negotiations took place, on 10th June the treaty was broken off. The Old Bank advertised that it was prepared to pay 5 per cent interest on all its notes till it was in a position to exchange them—in other words, it took up the position that a bank-note, though ostensibly payable on demand, could not have its promise strictly enforced by any existing law. The Bank itself had, under the Bank Act of 1696, power to sue summarily and " put to the horn ", *i.e.* arrest, the person of anyone failing to pay a debt upon *Bills* or *Tickets* drawn upon it, or in favour of it, and by implication such power of summary execution could be used against the Bank if it defaulted. It was the argument of the Bank that this did not apply to notes issued by them as a company, as these were not referred to in the Act, but only to bills for money borrowed as private individuals.

This " distinction without a difference "—whose recognition by law would have the most disastrous effects upon paper currency—was upheld by the Court of Session in a petition for " letters of horning " presented against the

# The Royal Bank of Scotland

Bank by Provost Cochran of Glasgow, whose demand for specie for £900 of its notes had precipitated its closing down.

There remained to Cochran, and others in his position, the expedient of demanding " inhibition and arrestment "—that is to say, an interdict on any sale of the debtor's heritable estate or property or increase of burdens thereon and the attachment of sums due to him. Again the Court of Session found against the petitioners, refusing such inhibition, and an appeal was made to the House of Lords, which reversed those decisions, and so doing, permanently established the responsibility of all banks for the literal interpretation of the promises on their paper money, and their liability to all the actions at default by ordinary law that apply to individual debtors generally. The Bank of Scotland by this time had paid the sums sued for; this decision of the House of Lords now saddled it with the costs of litigation.

## CHAPTER VI

### THE CASH CREDIT

THOSE were busy and anxious days for all associated with the Royal Bank. The office in Ship Close was open for business from 8 A.M. till noon, and from 2 P.M. till 6 P.M. during the months from March till September, and from 9 A.M. till noon, and 2 P.M. till 5 P.M. from October till March. A small committee of its ordinary directors was in attendance on Monday, Tuesday, Wednesday, and Thursday for two hours each afternoon. An ordinary director's fee was £10 : 16 : 8 per annum. Saturday was a half-holiday.

A court of directors had to be called to decide on all loans above £800. No loan upon real security could exceed £5000, and the borrower was obliged to redeem it in annual instalments of 10 per cent. The maximum loan on a personal bond was £1500; on a bill £300. At no time had the Cashier more than £10,000 in hand to accommodate the tellers from time to time.

Richard Watkins' paper for the notes cost

## The Royal Bank of Scotland

2s. 4d. per hundred sheets; the first order was for 44,400 sheets; a printing-press was housed in a cellar of the Bank, and printers were taken in to strike off, in presence of the directors, fresh notes when necessary from the plates prepared by Joseph Cave, engraver to the Mint, or by Richard Cooper, who could do a very neat note for a fee of £1 : 10s.

The notes were at first bound up in books with a scroll counterfoil, like a modern cheque-book, but there were no perforations, and each note had to be cut out with a knife or a pair of scissors. They remained in circulation only about nine months, and then their condition made their destruction necessary. Notes of the larger denomination survived the wear and tear of usage from two to six years, and a £100 note struck in February 1728 was cancelled only seven years after. It could hardly have, by its possession, gratified many people in that time; even the £50 note was soon discontinued.

Compared with the ingenious, elaborate, and often beautiful Scots bank-note of to-day, those first bank-notes seem primitive and almost to invite imitation by a clever penman, having that specious look of blunt, blank innocence which, in the Bank of England note, always surprises a Scotsman. Watkins' paper was of very special and excellent quality, but for the unscrupulous caligraphist of skill, a facsimile of the free cursive script, in which the promise

## The History of

to pay was written for the engraver, must have looked temptingly easy. A mezzotint little portrait of George I. on the top left-hand corner was all of deliberate art or safeguard, in a monochrome engraving.

The wording of the twenty-shilling note, which was typical of the others, ran:

No. $\frac{48}{75}$ *Edinburgh, 8th December* 1727.

*The Royal Bank of Scotland is hereby obliged to pay to.......................or the Bearer on Demand* TWENTY *Shilling Sterling.*

By Order of the ⎰Tho: Thomson, *Accountant.*
Court of Directors⎱Allan Whitefoord, *Cashier.*

It was but slowly business expanded in Scotland throughout the first half of the eighteenth century. Edinburgh, including its port, Leith, increased its population from 30,000 at the beginning of the period to about 50,000 in 1750. Glasgow, at the Union a pretty town of 12,500 inhabitants, more than doubled its population in the same period. Over the whole country the population rose from something over a million to one and a quarter million. But Leith had little more than 2000 tons of shipping in the year, and Glasgow only about 5000.

"Men of rank", says Professor James Mackinnon, "kept a lumbering coach, imported from Holland and drawn by six horses, to convey them when on a journey over deeply rutted roads, with two footmen standing behind armed with long poles to prise it out of the ruts, and one to go in front to give warning of any obstacle." Lairds went on horseback with their ladies behind them a-pillion. For " gentle and semple " everyday wearing apparel was of native homespun, though for festal occasions English broadcloth was coming into vogue— like tea, which Forbes of Culloden denounced as a vile drug.

While there was much social and convivial intercourse among the upper classes, it was considerably governed by political considerations; the terms Whig and Tory differentiating individuals as rigorously as if they were Indian castes. The " merchant " might be the humble brother of a laird, a baronet, or even a lord, though his business might be only the retailing of chandlery. In the Highlands, shopkeeping was still regarded as beneath a gentleman's dignity, though keeping a wayside inn or cattle-dealing was not derogatory even to the sons of chiefs. To be a soldier of fortune in a foreign army was the brightest prospect open to ambitious Highland youth. A great many of the landowners were in the position of the Fifeshire laird who had " a pickle land, a mickle debt, a doocot and a law-suit ". Gold was practically never seen; coinage from Holland, Spain, and France eked out the national silver

## The History of

currency; a doctor for his fee of a guinea was content to have five ducatoons or a jacobus.

The lack of communication tended to prolong this old-world social life well up to the middle of the century. Even so late as 1740, London was less quickly reached from Edinburgh than Canada is to-day. It took Lord Lovat eleven days to drive in his chariot from Inverness to the Scottish capital. There was only a monthly stage-coach between Edinburgh and London, which did the journey in from twelve to sixteen days. Letters by post took six days to cover the same distance, and sometimes the mail-bag held but a single letter.

The remoteness of Edinburgh from London is reflected in many ways in the first few years' records of the Royal Bank. As a rule, its more urgent correspondence with England was by "flying pacquitt", the flattering designation for a post-boy with a portmanteau on his saddle. Yet, from the start of its activities, the Royal had occasion to carry on a fairly brisk correspondence with the southern metropolis. It was only a few weeks open when it resolved to open a deposit account with the Bank of England, after having made a second call of 10 per cent on its subscribed capital. A sum of £4000 was lodged to its credit with the London bank, the intermediary, it would seem, being Mr. George Middleton, the London goldsmith who had transferred £9611 of his

## The Royal Bank of Scotland

Equivalent Stock to the Royal, and who was to prove a very useful friend in time to come.

The £4000 was borrowed, on the Cashier's bond, from John, Lord Glenorchy. It was to be repayable in a year with interest. The first transaction on this credit was a bill, dated 29th February 1728, payable at sight drawn on the Bank of England by Allan Whitefoord, Cashier, payable to Provost M'Aulay, for £65. At this time the exchange between Edinburgh and Glasgow was 1 per cent.

Friendly relations thus initiated, the Royal's "Committee of Co-operation in London"— which meant Benjamin Longuet, John Merrill, James Campbell, and Paul D'Aranda (chairman of the committee), with the backing of the Governor, Lord Ilay—opened negotiations with the directors of the Bank of England for a more expansive association between the two Banks, which would "govern the rate of exchange". Satisfactory conditions seemed not difficult to arrange (Royal Bank Stock already was selling at £105 per cent). On 23rd April the four gentlemen named signed a bond to the Bank of England for £30,000 at 4 per cent to be taken up at such times and in such proportions as the Royal should think fit, and an advance of £10,000 was given on the same day.

Half of this sum was repaid with interest on 3rd October and the balance on 21st November.

## The History of

The Royal Bank's account with the Bank of England thus opened is understood to be the oldest private account (as distinguished from the Government account) in its books; it has been continuously open for two hundred years. The Royal has also acted as agent or correspondent in Scotland for the Bank of England for a very long period.

A dividend at the rate of 2 per cent had been declared on 24th January 1728; a similar dividend was declared every six months after till the end of 1730, when it was raised to $2\frac{1}{2}$ per cent. The first recorded balance-sheet was for the period ended 27th March 1729.

Edinburgh Town Council from the beginning favoured the Royal Bank, and showed "anxious care" in supporting it by facilitating the circulation of its notes, so there was a ready acquiescence by the directors to a request by the magistrates in February 1728 for a loan of £1500 on the city's bond at $4\frac{1}{2}$ per cent till the following Whitsunday. In response to a request from the same quarter in May following, the Bank ordered £2000 of new copper money from the Mint. Counterfeit pence and halfpence had become a serious nuisance all over the country.

During those troubled early years the Royal made a new departure which might have seemed hazardous even in a brighter period, yet was destined to become a permanent and

## The Royal Bank of Scotland

potent feature of Scottish banking for all time to come. This was the principle of cash credit. A merchant or trader of good standing, on the security of his personal bond, backed by two or more responsible friends as co-obligants, could draw upon the Bank up to a given amount decided by the directors, without any cash being to his credit, or even any collateral security. There was thus provided for him a convenient augmentation of his working capital, upon which he could draw from time to time as he required it, and which he could reduce or pay off wholly as his circumstances permitted. Interest was charged, not on the principal sum of the bond, but on the sums actually borrowed for the period they were enjoyed. It was a propitious time for introducing such a principle. The Scottish world of capital and commerce was not then so panoramic and complicated as it is to-day; the Bank directors and officials were in a position to know something of the personality, standing, and business prospects of every applicant for such accommodation, and even if the chief signatory to the bond failed them, it was unlikely that the two others would do so simultaneously. Vistas of profitable business expansion, opportunities for developing many new industries hitherto unexploited in Scotland, were turning up every other week; there was plenty of native shrewdness, ingenuity, and enterprise among the frugal Scots to warrant the confidence that with capital they could vitalise the country's trade, but very often the men most obviously fitted to take advantage of the situation could not produce any tangible security for the borrowed capital requisite to start with.

To them the Royal Bank's new cash credit system came as a providential aid; it enabled them to bourgeon out in business; their profits increased; they were soon able to repay their creditors and accumulate private wealth. The wealth of the country grew with every increase in national industry so fostered by the unostentatious but puissant directorate in the Ship Close, who by the innovation found the issue of their notes considerably augmented. This cash credit principle, cautiously experimented with at the start, and conceded only to firstrate " prospects ", afterwards to be universally adopted by the Scots banks, was of pre-eminent influence in the development of Scotland throughout the eighteenth and nineteenth centuries.

The first to take advantage of it was William Hogg, junior, merchant in Edinburgh, who was granted such a credit on 31st May 1728, and afterwards became a private banker on his own account. Operations on the credit account were limited to sums of not less than £10. There was, in the hands of the Royal Bank, a large new capital, mostly lying idle, and

## The Royal Bank of Scotland

those cash credit transactions could be financed without falling back upon deposits with the Bank, which, as yet, were hardly existent.

Deposits at interest were accepted to a limited extent by the Bank of Scotland as early as 1707, in the hope of attracting what English money might come over the Border under the Treaty of Union, but not till the Royal's lively rivalry compelled a retort to the cash credit system was the principle of deposits seriously exploited. The Old Bank in 1728 had no such agreeable reserves of inutile capital to work upon, so it accumulated as much as it could from depositors before launching out into emulation of its rival's cash credits in 1729. It took cash on deposit on a " Treasurer's Bond ", paying interest at 5 per cent per annum. The Treasurer's bond was, in a sense, the forerunner of the deposit receipt, which did not come into existence till 1810, and the modern deposit receipt, according to Mr. William Graham, "owes its non-negotiability to its descent from the old 'Treasurer's Bond', which, being practically a personal bond, could only be legally transferred to a third party by a formal deed of assignment followed by intimation and did not pass by a simple endorsation ".

After two or three years' experience of deposits on Treasurer's bond, the Old Bank took another step and began to accept those deposits for a fixed period, instead of payable on demand. This was suggested, no doubt, by the success which had attended its efforts to keep its bank-notes in circulation as long as possible. During the run of 1728 its tellers sometimes resorted to the crude bucolic device of discouraging any run for change by cashing notes in sixpences. By the time hundreds of pounds' worth of sixpences had been counted and recounted, the customer (who might or might not be an emissary from the Ship Close) was apt to be sick of the whole transaction, and other exasperated customers with notes to change might find the hour for closing the bank had come before they could be attended to.

The " Option Clause ", introduced into the Bank of Scotland £5 notes in November 1730, was designed still further to keep the notes as long as possible in the owner's pocket. It was " payable to bearer on demand, or £5 : 2 : 6 six months after being presented for payment, in the option of the Bank ". Two years later the option clause was extended to £1 notes, the interest of sixpence in the pound being added as solatium to the possessor for having to wait six months for his cash.

Many small private banking concerns quickly adopted the option clause, but the Royal did not do so till about 1761, compelled thereto in self-defence against heavy demands for immediate coin for the notes held by other banks.

## The Royal Bank of Scotland

Coin, in those early years, was, as it happened, far from profuse, even in bankers' tills. Except for *menus plaisirs* and higgling business, the currency had quickly become the bank-note, and the total amount of coinage in use was, in the aggregate, a mere bagatelle; so the till money of 1730 was mainly in paper. If not at this time, certainly some years after, half a pound note would satisfy a Scottish "merchant" in lieu of ten shillings, or a quarter-note could buy five-shillings-worth of Canongate conviviality. A pretty job of jigsaw-puzzling bank directors must have had when the day of destruction came for their mutilated notes retired! Possibly, however, they did not insist on a mosaic perfection in the fragments condemned.

The Royal Bank's notes had been in circulation for seven years before any case of actual forgery or any attempt at theft came before the directors. In 1734 a man casually employed in cleaning the office purloined several sheets of twenty-shilling notes, and having forged the signatures of the Cashier, Secretary, and Accountant on one of the notes, uttered it as genuine. The flash note was detected as soon as it came back to the Bank; the culprit confessed and declared he had burned all the other notes. It was decided to prosecute him before the Court of Justiciary, but there is no evidence in subsequent minutes that this was done.

## The History of

We may as well here deal with all such eighteenth-century delinquencies and be done with them, though their narrative for a moment upsets our strict chronology. Seven years later—in 1741—a night attempt was made to break into the Bank premises, and a man called Peter Swan was arrested, tried, convicted, and sentenced to banishment. Until an opportunity occurred for shipping him to the American plantations, the Bank, as was the rule at the period, had to pay sixpence a day for his maintenance in gaol, as well as the cost of his deportation.

A few months later the Cashier had to go to Kilmarnock to make inquiries about a forged twenty-shilling note which had turned up there. Two men, Robert and John Wallace, were suspected, and the former " fugitated ", otherwise fled the country. They had forged six twenty-shilling notes; John Wallace was captured in Edinburgh and transported.

There were no more forgeries till 1749, when a soldier named William Parker from the barracks at Fort Augustus was arrested for forging and circulating two twenty-shilling notes in Inverness-shire. Taken to Edinburgh Tolbooth, he promised " a confession of his accomplices; the Lord Justice Clerk and Lord Advocate to make terms with him ". His forgeries were entirely done by the pen, and the directors for the first time considered the

## The Royal Bank of Scotland

advisability of making their notes less easy of imitation. An accomplice, Sergeant Young, was later arrested in Newcastle, and sentenced to death many months afterwards.

There is a significant note in a directors' minute of 23rd November 1750 which says: " The Court, suspecting that application is to be made for a pardon to Sergeant John Young . . . resolved to take steps to prevent this being done ".

As for the less-accomplished Private Parker, who was able to " make terms " with the Lord Advocate and Lord Justice Clerk, he languished over a year in the Tolbooth, then chose, as an alternative to continued incarceration, a transportation for himself and his wife to Boston, the Bank paying his passage. It had also to pay the Tolbooth jailer £70 : 14 : 6 for the board of Parker and his accomplice (there were two), and thirty guineas of a gratuity. The Parker prosecution alone cost the Bank £400, with a gratuity of £40 to an Inverness lawyer " for his trouble in detecting the forgers ".

The air of Boston apparently did not agree with Private Parker; in October 1752 he was back in Edinburgh, re-apprehended, and ordered to be " whipped the first mercate day of every month till he be transported ". Half the cost of the re-transportation had to be paid by the Bank.

More obscurity surrounds the fate of the

# The Royal Bank of Scotland

son of a St. Andrews professor, also of an Edinburgh lawyer and his wife, who, in November 1751, were suspected of forging notes of both the Bank of Scotland and the Royal. The two Banks took joint action for a prosecution. The professor's son was apprehended and let out on bail; thereafter the clerk of the minutes would seem to have lost further interest in him.

# CHAPTER VII

### SECOND CHARTER

IT became apparent in March 1731 that urgent questions of exchange between the Edinburgh and London banks could never be satisfactorily settled by correspondence, and one of the Royal directors, Lord Milnton (Andrew Fletcher, Lord Justice Clerk), was sent to London (but not till nearly a year later) to negotiate with the English bank for a standing credit to the extent of £50,000. He was empowered to purchase India bonds to the extent of £15,400, and deposit them with the Bank of England as a "fund of credit" for the Royal. He really lodged £16,700 of India bonds with the London bank, but the new cash credit system of Scotland was elsewhere regarded askance. He reported to his fellow-directors that he could not prevail on the Bank of England " to keep a cash account of credit in the same manner as the Royal Bank do, no such thing having been practiced by them, or anybody else in London ", but that such sums as should be necessary from time to time would be transferred from the Royal's account of credit to its current account. Thereafter one of the cashiers of the Bank of England, Mr. Thomas Gregory, was given power of attorney to act for the Royal in all dealings with its London account.

Lord Milnton, at the same time, had other missions in London in the interests of his Board. He got into treaty with the Paymaster-General of His Majesty's Forces, and succeeded in making an arrangement that all Army pay for the troops in Scotland should be lodged with the Bank of England for transmission *via* the Royal Bank.

A more momentous part of his embassy, however, was to sound the authorities in London regarding a new Charter for the Royal Bank.

At least £111,000 of the Royal's capital was, as we have seen, in the form of stock in the Equivalent Company. This stock might be redeemed by the Government at any time, and conceivably imperil the very existence of the Royal, hitherto so much dependent on the annuity it involved. What was wanted for the assurance of the directors was a new Charter ratifying and confirming the privileges, authorities, and rights conferred by the first one, and removing all doubts concerning the continuance of the Bank in case of a redemption of Equivalent Stock by the Government.

At the same time, it was felt that the Royal

## The Royal Bank of Scotland

was hampered by too small a capital, and that any new charter should give authority to augment it by £40,000.

Lord Milnton's business it was to put all this before influential quarters in London; no doubt he went as far as discretion allowed, but judicious advisers in London thought the time inopportune, and nothing practical came of it at the moment. Again the Royal fell back on its trusty old friend and Governor, Lord Ilay. In April 1733 a memorial was sent to him urging the desirability of asking Parliament to declare the Bank a perpetual corporation. Still the proposition hung fire, and nearly a year later Ilay, with "friends in London", was considering a draft "signature" to the King, drawn up by the Lord Advocate.

It was November 1738 before all this preliminary skirmishing came to a head, and the new Charter was secured and passed the Seal. This second Charter authorised the enlargement of the original capital by a sum not exceeding £40,000, "either by taking subscriptions of other Equivalent Stock not already subscribed into the Bank, or by taking in subscriptions of certain sums of money upon land security or any other ways and means thought safe and beneficial".

For "the better encouragement of the said Royal Bank", the Charter declared "that in case the Parliament of Great Britain shall at any time or times think proper to redeem the said Equivalent Stock, or such part thereof as has been, or shall be subscribed into the said Company of the Royal Bank of Scotland, that the said Corporation or Company of the Royal Bank of Scotland notwithstanding thereof shall and may after such redemption as aforesaid continue for ever and have perpetual succession and enjoy all the privileges benefits and advantages whatsoever given and granted to them by the said recited Charter or Letters Patent, except the share or interest in the said annual fund of £10000 as aforesaid as if no such redemption were had or made ".

The Royal began to accept deposits early in its career, but not with such simple formalities as are associated with a deposit to-day. Deposits at interest were called " obligements ". The person making the deposit had first to make a proposal to the directors wherein he had to state when he would require repayment, and if partial payments would be expected. If the prospective depositor's overtures were approved of, the directors granted warrant to the Cashier to receive the money and grant a receipt, which was a lengthy document containing the names of the writer and a witness to the Cashier's signature.

Cash credit accounts, as has previously been mentioned, were introduced about 1728. The customer got a pass-book and a quantity of

## The Royal Bank of Scotland

"cheque paper" on which all drafts on the account were to be written. Twice a year the account was balanced and interest charged—the amount that had been drawn not exceeding the sum agreed upon.

Country customers of the Bank had often some difficulty in transmitting their money for lodgement at the Ship Close. Lord Breadalbane, for instance, when his Martinmas rents were collected at Taymouth, had to send the cash through snow-bound valleys to Edinburgh under convoy of armed men of his clan, though Highland "depredations" were usually confined to cattle, and some illogical Gaelic sense of the personality of money possessed made highway robbery in the most unsettled parts of the north a rare thing.

Of the Highland chiefs to have relations with the Bank, Breadalbane was the most conspicuous. Mr. John Campbell, who was promoted to be second Cashier of the Bank in 1734, was Breadalbane's doer or legal adviser, and private friend. He was a son of the Hon. Colin Campbell of Ardmaddy and the grandson of the first Earl of Breadalbane; was brought up by the family at Finlarig, got a liberal education, and became the best-known man in Perthshire. Though he chose business as his career instead of the sword, and lived the greater part of his life in Edinburgh, his touch with the land of Breadalbane always remained intimate and affectionate, and he was liaison officer between his kinsman and chief and the world of law and commerce.

There is extant in Easdale a water-colour portrait of "John Campbell of the Bank" as he is still known to Highlanders, through a song made in his honour by Duncan Ban MacIntyre, the Robert Burns of Gaeldom. The picture shows us the handsome head of a gentleman of *prestance*, with keen intelligent features and a look of race, unbewigged and natural in an age of perukes,—something of an exquisite as we have evidence from the contents of the "portmantel" that usually hung to his saddle during his frequent visits to Breadalbane: a gold-laced hat, a scarlet vest trimmed with silver (possibly the one gifted by Lady Dunstaffnage), scarlet breeches, two wigs, and a razor for every day in the week. Yet Taymouth Castle and Easdale often saw John Campbell even more the chevalier than this wardrobe suggests. The Gaelic song of the bard speaks of an equipment which included pistol, sword and targe, and curveting horses.

John Campbell was by way of being a poet himself, to judge from the confessions of his diary; a poet like *Donacha Ban* could take delight in him, though bankers and lawyers were scarcely in the world of heather and deer his fancy ordinarily haunted. In the Gaelic poem we are shown a man handsome of figure,

John Campbell of the Bank
Cashier 1734-1777
from a painting belonging to Sir Guy T. Campbell Bart.

## The Royal Bank of Scotland

gay, kindly, eloquent, witty, sagacious, and the fine flower of clanship, who loved the bagpipe and the violin, and in his own home or elsewhere was the soul of conviviality. " Fit to be a King!" is the bard's conclusion to his panegyric.

Taymouth Castle saw a good deal of John Campbell every summer. There was his lordship to consult on local affairs of trespass or deerslaying, law pleas merrily going on in Edinburgh (for Breadalbane was a notorious litigant), or the Charter chest to rummage and re-arrange. Easdale, though remote from Taymouth, was Breadalbane property also, but the banker's periodical visitations there were mainly personal affairs; he was a partner in the Nether Lorn Marble and Slate Company, one of the various private enterprises of his that promised more fortune than they ever gave.

From those Highland excursions, John Campbell invariably came back to Edinburgh *via* Crieff, where he spent a night or two with his old kinsman, client, and friend, Patrick Campbell of Monzie, one of the directors of the Bank. Monzie, one of the most prominent Scotsmen of his time, had been a director of the Darien Company and a commissioner of the Equivalent. He had—like all of Clan Campbell, though the fact is not usually recognised in history—been friend of many Jacobites who were compromised in the affair of 1715, and, like the Duke of Argyll and Lord Ilay, at some risk to his own standing among the Whigs, favoured a lenient treatment by the Government of these misguided fellow-countrymen. Agriculture and silver mining at Hopeton and Leadhills had engaged a good deal of his interest up till his elevation to the bench as Lord Monzie, but with little success; at his death in 1751, John Campbell became one of his executors, and at the sale of his effects acquired a large proportion of his silver plate, his library, and his wines.

For "John Campbell of the Bank" was a redoubtable and discriminating *viveur*. His own wine-cellar in the Bank House, or at Restalrig, where for a period he resided, was always plenished with care. He notes the bottling of half-a-hogshead of wine from Lisbon, the laying down of a quantity of Calcavella port, the bottling of Tayside "aqua"—otherwise whisky, and the provision of London porter. His household hospitality was on the most generous scale, but, according to the custom of the times, not a little of his business entertaining was done in taverns—Turnbull's, Fortune's, Mrs. Clerk the Vintner's, or Cleland's. The Bank directors had a tavern fund, as it was called, and it was their custom to entertain their business friends from London—such as Mr. Mathias of the Equivalent Company or Messrs. Coutts the bankers—convivially in those old hostelries, patronised by the very best people in Edinburgh. The directors and their Cashier

## The Royal Bank of Scotland

let few occasions pass that might give an excuse for a simple meal and the flowing bowl; they "adjourned" *nem. con.* after general meetings of the proprietors, or after a day of destroying cancelled notes—even to discuss affairs of the Church of Scotland's annual General Assembly, of which John Campbell was frequently a member. Ex-Provost George Drummond, whose remarkable diary is in the Edinburgh Advocates' Library, was at one of those directors' *noctes ambrosianae* on 6th January 1738. "This evening", he wrote in his diary, "the Directors of the Royal Bank had their anniversary entertainment. My cold got me the privilege of drinking sack and water only, and getting home early. May the Lord pardon me the guilt of others! Closed the day with God."

Of Lowland notabilities associated with the Royal in these early days, the closest at hand was the Duke of Buccleuch, whose rents it handled and remitted for him to England at $1\frac{1}{4}$ per cent exchange. There were, as the ledgers show, fairly modest loans to gentry whose names are now historical, and the moderation of whose demands would amuse their successors. Upon the heritable security of a lordship and barony, £2500 could be borrowed from the Ship Close. A lodgement of the family plate with a promissory note was good for a few hundred pounds. The Bank

The History of

by its Charter was of course empowered to lend money on pledges of goods, wares or merchandise, or other effects whatsoever at " any interest not exceeding lawful interest ".

Apparently the directors had more confidence in the securities of established trading companies and corporations than in those of individuals. During periods of great destitution throughout the country the Bank came to the aid of many municipalities faced with the problem of communal poverty. The town of Irvine in 1735 got a cash credit on the personal bond of the Provost and Magistrates and the assignation of its duties in coal and ale. The early 'forties were years of even greater hardships. Edinburgh had to borrow £2500 for six months to buy meal and corn for the poor; Glasgow needed £4000 for the same purpose; Sir George Gilbert Elliot of Minto £1000 for the poor of the county of Teviotdale; the Earl of Ancrum, Lord Rosse, and others, £700 for the poor of the county of Edinburgh; the town of Irvine another £500; the Incorporation of Baxters £2500 for the same beneficent ends.

Among the Bank's own shareholders was occasionally a customer operating on the security of his stock alone, and in 1738 one knight of ancient lineage, who played a prominent part in Highland politics, was informed that unless he paid up the balance against him diligence would be taken and his

## The Royal Bank of Scotland

stock disposed of by roup or sale. He failed to pay up at the time appointed, and accordingly his £300 of capital stock was sold by public auction, fetching £438. The value of Royal Bank stock had been steadily rising; seven years before it was changing hands at 122 per cent, and was only procurable by " such parties as are likely to advance the interests of the Bank ". Creditors of the Bank, as early as June 1730, were being informed that unless they agreed to 4 per cent interest instead of 5 per cent they would be paid off.

In July 1731 the Bank of Scotland again attempted to establish a system of branches in Glasgow, Aberdeen, and Dundee, only to discontinue them over two years later. In such communities small joint-stock firms, and even individual merchants of no great financial standing, undertook many of the functions which to-day would be entrusted only to the professional bank. They dealt in bills of exchange and received money from small traders and others on deposit, for which interest was allowed on no fixed scale, but as decided after considerable haggling. Occasionally they advertised that side of their business in the local newspapers. Till well into the nineteenth century those private firms (not designated " bankers " till much later), were to play a considerable part in Scotland's financial history. The goldsmiths and merchants of Edinburgh—the former in their booths clustered round St. Giles' Church, the latter concentrated round the Cross—were granting loans, discounting bills, and dealing in inland and foreign exchange long before Scotland's first bank was chartered, and giving the use of their repositories for money or valuables.

The most outstanding mercantile exchange firm of this character in the country in the early eighteenth century was the house of John Coutts and Company of Edinburgh. It was, to begin with, a concern doing business in corn and buying and selling other commodities on commission, and the somewhat speculative corn-dealing element of it persisted up till 1761 at least, when Sir William Forbes, then senior partner, terminated it. John Coutts (whose uncle Thomas was one of the London merchants to establish the Bank of Scotland) was always ready to negotiate bills of exchange in Edinburgh for merchants of Aberdeen, Perth, Dundee, Montrose, or elsewhere who exported to or imported from Holland, France, Spain, or other continental countries. From this exchange business he ventured into other avenues of banking, which ultimately became vastly more important than the purely mercantile part of the business, and was finally, through many permutations of the firm's "style", to culminate afar from Edinburgh in the great London banking house of Coutts and Company.

## The Royal Bank of Scotland

When the Royal Bank started, John Coutts was a man of weight in Edinburgh, and in 1730 he became a Town Councillor of the city—the first merchant ever to be accorded such an honour.

In Glasgow, before or soon after the Union, the number of joint-stock mercantile firms thus trading in money and bills apart from their more ostensible business was considerable. The " tobacco lords " or " Virginia Dons ", Glasgow's merchant princes who ruffled it in bushy wigs and scarlet cloaks on the sunny side of the Trongate and kept humbler folk to the other side of the thoroughfare, did not confine their speculation to cargoes of the " divine weed " from Virginia, but usually had a hand in many new manufacturing businesses coming into existence on Clydeside. The firms with which they were associated did semi-banking business " on the side ", and from early in the century up till near its close sometimes issued on their own responsibility notes for small sums, which were for a time more often to be seen in the West than the notes of the two Edinburgh Banks.

The two attempts of the Bank of Scotland to establish a Glasgow branch failed, mainly, it is said by Dr. John Buchanan, because its directors would not deal in bills of exchange, the exchange business being regarded as improper.

## The Royal Bank of Scotland

Meanwhile the Royal contentedly confined its active staff to Edinburgh. Its stock was always rising in value; by the end of 1741 it was standing at 140 per cent, and on the eve of the Rebellion of 1745 it was at £143. The dividend was now a cautious 3 per cent. By this time the personnel of the Board had changed considerably. Lord Ilay had retired from the Governorship in 1737, to be succeeded by Mathew Lant, Lord Chief Baron of the Court of Exchequer, and at the same time Lord Milnton had been elected Deputy Governor.

# CHAPTER VIII

### THE 'FORTY-FIVE

On 19th July 1745 Mr. Whitefoord, the Cashier, resigned his appointment on account of poor health, and thereafter confined his activities more strictly to the duties of his Government appointment as Receiver-General of Land Tax. He was at the same time made an ordinary director of the Bank.

Mr. John Campbell, the second Cashier, was elected his successor, while Mr. George Innes, Deputy Receiver of the Land Tax, was appointed to the vacancy left by Mr. Campbell's promotion. Mr. Beaumont Hotham, Commissioner of Customs, was now Governor. There was no political disquietude in Edinburgh at the moment — nothing to suggest that within a few weeks the country would be in a state of war. A dividend of 3 per cent had just been declared, and the architect Adam had been engaged to design a new office for the Bank " at the back of the Cross ", on ground acquired the previous year—a project postponed indefinitely on account of the Rebellion.

## The History of

At the battle of Fontenoy, in May, the Duke of Cumberland, with his English and Hanoverian troops, had suffered a serious reverse, and the capture of Tournay by the French, which followed, had results that made the subsequent campaign in Flanders disastrous to the allies. That the French would probably seize the opportunity to embarrass Britain further by their old tactic of stirring an insurrection among the Jacobite clans of Scotland was instinctively apprehended in the Highlands; all that summer there were, in the glens, persistent rumours of an imminent descent by the " auld allies ". Nothing was heard of them in Edinburgh till the beginning of July, when Duncan Forbes of Culloden, Lord President of the Court of Session, reported these rumours to Sir John Cope, Commander-in-Chief of the forces in Scotland. The rumours were not regarded very seriously; Cope informed Lord Tweeddale, the Secretary for Scotland, one of the Ministers acting at the moment as a regency for George II., who was away, as too frequently, in Hanover, where his Electorate seemed to occupy more of his interest than his island kingdom. Nothing special was done.

The intuitions of the Highlands, however, were not mistaken; on 23rd July the " Young Chevalier ", Prince Charles Edward Stuart, was landed with a small entourage off the French ship *Dutillet* on the little island of

## The Royal Bank of Scotland

Eriskay, near Barra, and a few days later was on the Highland mainland, gathering clansmen round him. It was 8th August before this sensational intelligence reached the authorities in Edinburgh, and not till 9th August was the fact known by the Government garrison at Fort William, less than twenty miles from Glenfinnan, where the Prince had raised his standard.

It may be taken for granted that "John Campbell of the Bank" was one of the first men in Edinburgh to learn of this alarming story from the Highlands. How he rose to the occasion may be seen from *Leaves from the Diary of an Edinburgh Banker of 1745*, in which he set down from day to day his own share in stirring contemporary events during two months in which it looks as if he thoroughly enjoyed himself despite the responsibilities of his post.

We need not follow the gallant but misguided Young Chevalier through his Highland Odyssey; for the purposes of such a history as this it is better to keep an eye on John Campbell, who, in his own experiences and reactions, quite adequately represents the Edinburgh of his time. It is to be noted that in his diary neither alarm nor party rancour finds the slightest expression; he seems to have regarded the Rebellion as *damnum fatale*—the act of God, and strictly attended to business so far as it could be done.

## The History of

Prince Charlie (with £30,000 " on his head ", the reward of his capture alive or dead), had eluded General Cope and got, with his forces, down as far as Blair-of-Athole on 1st September. At the meeting of Royal Bank directors on that day the insurgent advance on Edinburgh was noted; a decision was come to regarding certain measures to be adopted for the safety of the cash on hand, and it was arranged that the directors thereafter should meet twice a day—at 10 A.M. and 3 P.M.

Next day they destroyed £10,600 in notes.

Not till the 13th, however, did the rebels cross the Forth at the Fords of Frew, with the Prince wading it like his men; on the following day they were in Stirling and Falkirk, and preparing to go on to Linlithgow. That evening all the gold and silver coin, notes, and everything of value in the Bank were packed up and in part transferred to the security of Edinburgh Castle. The remainder was taken there on the following day, a Sunday. The same steps were taken by the Bank of Scotland. Ex-Lord Provost Drummond, as a captain of volunteers for the city's defence, was busy otherwise. On the Monday morning Mr. Campbell revisited the Castle to get £100 in half-guineas from his balance chest at the request of his Deputy Governor, Lord Milnton, who was discreetly preparing to retire to his country house. A deputation of the magis-

## The Royal Bank of Scotland

tracy went out to Bellsmilns to negotiate with the Prince as to the surrender of the town, without effect; on Tuesday, 17th, the Highland "army" of 1200 men was in possession of the city, and Prince Charlie slept in the old home of his fathers, Holyrood House.

Four days later the rebels fought Cope's troops and routed them at Prestonpans, or "Gladsmuir or Tranent" as Campbell calls it, and returned to Edinburgh, where they remained till 31st October.

For a few days after the battle of Prestonpans the communication between the city and the unsurrendered Castle remained open, and Mr. John Campbell and his directors were at liberty to go there and change or withdraw money. The Highlanders had posted a guard at the Weigh House, an old building situated in the centre of Edinburgh's main street, which led up to the Castle, about four hundred yards from the fortress itself, and they allowed at first all kinds of provisions to pass in for the use of the garrison. This amiable understanding between the Castle commander, General Guest, and the placid besiegers terminated when the Highland guard fired off their pieces one day to discourage some people who were bringing provisions to the Castle, and Guest considered himself justified in firing on the guard. By proclamation of the Prince, therefore, the blockade of the garrison was made absolute, and all intercourse

The History of

with it was prohibited. On 4th October the Castle all day fired down the streets, killing a few people.

The distress which this occasioned roused such a revulsion of feeling against the Prince that he saw the advisability of cancelling the proclamation the following day, and thereafter provisions were conveyed to the fortress without molestation.

John Campbell skipped round the city imperturbably, and was, besides the man of business, a sort of war correspondent. He had to keep Lord Monzie, Campbell of Achallader, Lord and Lady Glenorchy, and others in the country apprised by express of the latest news of Prestonpans, etc. A great many of his acquaintances had left the city for quarters less disturbed, but his friend and patron the Earl of Breadalbane, aged and invalid, luckily for himself no longer reasonably to be expected to take sides in the broils of princes, was in residence in Holyrood.

During the six weeks in which Edinburgh was in the hands of the Highlanders, and Charles Edward held court in Holyrood, Mr. Campbell kept in touch with Breadalbane, and dined with him occasionally at the Abbey. If he witnessed the Prince's entrance to the city, or indeed saw him under any circumstances, the fact is not mentioned in his diary, in which it is noted that the Young Chevalier, on one

## The Royal Bank of Scotland

occasion at least, made an evening call upon the patriarch from Taymouth.

Among the rebel chiefs were of course many well known to Mr. Campbell; between Breadalbane and them he seems never to have been at a loss to secure protections and safe-conducts for his friends suffering inconvenience from the investment of the city.

Prince Charles judiciously took early steps to assure the burghers that so long as they behaved discreetly they had nothing to fear from the presence of his mountaineers. He issued proclamations expressing his anxiety that business should go on as usual, and formally granted protection to the inhabitants and the country people around "from all insults, seizures and injuries". To the clergy of the city a request was sent that they should conduct public worship as usual, but they had all departed for more pacific scenes, and it was obviously with a genuine sense of deprivation that John Campbell noted, on Sunday, 22nd September, "No Sermon in the Churches".

While Charles did all he could to restrain the predatory instincts of his camp-followers, he exercised his power to augment his own exchequer after the usual fashion of conquerors by refitting out his army in tents, boots, and a vast variety of other equipment, which cost so much that there had to be a call of half-a-crown assessment on each pound of the city's rental.

This meant a levy of £8 : 2 : 6 on the Royal Bank, which Mr. Campbell manifestly grudged sincerely.

On the evening of 1st October Mr. Campbell found himself confronted by a demand for change in current coin of the realm for £857 Royal Bank notes presented by Murray of Broughton, an old customer of the Bank, Prince Charlie's secretary. Unless the cash was forthcoming within forty-eight hours, it was indicated that the estates and effects of the directors would be confiscated.

" I answered ", says the diarist, " that by reason of the Commotion in the Country, the effects of the Bank were lately carried up to the Castle, for the Security of all concerned, for as the directors acted, in a manner, as factors for their Constituents the proprietors, it was judged reasonable, and what everybody in their circumstances would have done, to Secure the effects of the Company, that none might be sufferers in the Issue; that Matters were in the Situation at present that there was no access to the Castle at any rate, for that Mr. John Hamilton and Mr. John Philp, two of the directors had essayed to get in on Saturday last with the Accomptant and tellers and myself in order to do Business, but that Access was refused, tho' they continued at the gate for about an hour."

Secretary Murray's reply was that he would,

## The Royal Bank of Scotland

in the name of the Prince, grant a pass and protection for going into the Castle. To precipitate action he there and then " took instruments " of protest against the Cashier in the hands of a notary public, having thoughtfully taken such an officer, with a witness, to the interview.

After consultation with the only two directors accessible, whom he found at " Mrs. Clerk's, vintner ", Mr. Campbell called a meeting of ordinary and extraordinary directors for the following day at noon; five turned up, and it was agreed to cash the Prince's notes if access could be got to the Castle.

Information to that effect was sent to Murray of Broughton, who returned the messenger with the further disconcerting intimation that he had quite a number more of Royal Bank notes to liquidate—£2307 worth, as it turned out some hours later.

Meanwhile there had been got from Cameron of Lochiel a convoy with a white flag, who carried to the fortress portals an intimation from Mr. Campbell for its custodian General Guest that the visit of himself and his directors was to be expected. Murray's pass into the Castle was found to be for three ordinary directors and the Cashier, and was valid only up till ten o'clock that night. It was decided to postpone the Castle visitation till the following day, and Mr. Campbell thereupon proceeded to Lucky Clerk's hostelry and informed Lochiel of the change of programme. "The gentle Lochiel" was there; and after a parley with him and Peter Smith the Jacobite W.S., matters were put in train for the great adventure on the following morning at nine o'clock.

Six doubtless agitated gentlemen breakfasted at eight o'clock next morning in the Bank House—Messrs. Hamilton, Shairp, and Philp, directors; Mr. William Mitchell, Accomptant; Mr. A. Innes, Teller; and their host the Cashier. They had now a passport valid from 8 A.M. till 3 P.M. Making their way to the blockade post at the Weigh House, they were passed on by the officers of a guard of Camerons.

"I then hoisted my white flag," writes Mr. Campbell, "and ushered the rest of the Gentlemen, saluting the rest of the Centinells with it as we past, and as we approached the Gate wav'd it often, at last the Centinells there called to us to come forward, and on our arrival at the bridge, telling who we were 'twas lett down."

From nine till nearly three in the afternoon, during which time citadel and town kept up a brisk exchange of firearms, Mr. Campbell and his company "executed the affairs we came about according to particular Memds and Minutes yrof apart".

What they actually did, as more frankly recorded in the directors' minute book, was to burn £60,000 of Royal Bank notes and

## The Royal Bank of Scotland

tear into small pieces a large number more; give General Guest £2000 in specie for the public service on his receipt, and take with them £6000 in gold and £6000 in silver to meet the demands made, and still to be made, in the city.

Hoisting the white flag of truce again, they retired in good order and proceeded to dine in Mrs. Clerk's. That evening £3076 in gold was handed to Lumsden (Murray's depute secretary) in exchange for the equivalent Royal Bank notes; this coin was counted out three times by the parties present (a slow process which was lubricated by a bottle of wine), and Lumsden, with the bullion in a sealed bag, started off for Holyrood in a sedan chair.

A fortnight later, Mr. Campbell, ex-Provost Coutts, director, Mr. David Baillie, Accomptant, his clerk, named Ewart, and three tellers got access to the Castle vaults again and "settled and balanced the State of the Cash since 11 September". All the notes previously torn were now burned, and the teller's balances, bills falling due, foreign bills, etc., were taken down to the Bank House.

The persistent Peter Smith, "brother to the late Smith of Melvin", made subsequent calls for change in specie for Murray of Broughton, for whom he acted as "deputy secretary"— one for £400 and one for £174, and was duly accommodated.

## The History of

In the final days of the Highland occupation Mr. Campbell, as he confided to his diary, solaced his evening hours by writing poetry, and kept it up even after the cloud was lifted from the city. A characteristic record for a day is : " Din'd at home s. (solus). Begun to compose some Lines. Paid a visit to Mr. Kinloch's. Finish'd my composure."

On Thursday, 31st October, the Prince left for Pinkie, Lord Tweeddale's house; on the following day his troops took the route for England, where we need not follow them; on Sunday, 3rd, Mr. Campbell was able to hear a sermon for the first time in seven weeks, and dined and supped with Breadalbane at the Abbey, whence he returned home in a chair. Ten days later 2000 Government troops, dragoons and foot, entered the city, still somewhat distracted by its dramatic experience, whereupon the judges and other important personages who had fled at the first rumour of the crossing of the Fords of Frew returned in state, and Edinburgh by and by resumed the even tenor of its way.

Before we get out of the mid-eighteenth-century period, when Scotland was providing romantic history for future poets and novelists, it may be interesting to cull a few correlative notes from the contemporary records preserved by the Royal Bank.

It was, as we have seen, with specie squeezed

## The Royal Bank of Scotland

reluctantly on his part out of John Campbell that Prince Charlie largely paid the day-to-day expenses of himself and his mountaineers on their trip to Derby and back again. From the same source came the cash that kept General Guest and his troops going during the *opéra bouffe* blockade of Edinburgh Castle, and £100 of a gratuity to the regiment of foot levied in the city to " protect and preserve the peace ". All the Royalist troops in Scotland for years before and after the Rebellion got their pay in Royal Bank notes, and the making of the military roads through the Highlands was financed from the same quarter.

In March 1748 the Scottish hereditary jurisdictions were abolished. There were over a hundred courts of Regality in Scotland in which the great owners of land presided as hereditary barons or sheriffs. When the Government deprived the barons of their juridical powers, transferring them to the country's senators and law officers, and abolished their feudal claims to the labour or property of their tenants, the nobles thus affected claimed compensation to the extent of £602,127. They had to be satisfied with £152,000, which by Act of Parliament had to be lodged in a Scottish bank. Always alert to any chance of securing business, the Royal Bank directors sent their colleague, ex-Lord Provost George

Drummond, to London to secure as much as possible of this windfall for their books, and part of it at least was lodged in the Bank of England to the credit of the Royal.

Estates forfeited on account of the participation of their owners in the Rebellion were not sold, as was the procedure after the affair of 1715, but became the property of the Crown, whose agents were encouraged to supplant tenants of Jacobite predilections by others of sound Hanoverian sympathies. There were great claims by creditors on those confiscated properties, which Parliament settled—£20,000 in the case of James Drummond on the Duke of Perth's estate, and £38,553 in the case of Lord Lovat's creditors. The money for payment of those debts on confiscated estates was lodged to the credit of the Royal at the Bank of England, and the creditors were paid from the Edinburgh office. It was obviously the influence of Mr. Beaumont Hotham, now Governor, which secured this business. Lovat had been an old customer of the Bank. As far back as December 1733, the cash accounts of his lordship and that other notorious Jacobite, Drummond of Balhaldie, were superseded. But two years later Lovat was getting considerable loans on various securities.

Within a few decades of the Rising of '45 the economic conditions of Highland estates were to be entirely changed, and values were

## The Royal Bank of Scotland

many times multiplied. Greater sums came at term-time into the Bank from Highland landlords. Not always from Highland estates; the Duke of Athole, for instance, owned the Isle of Man, from which his rents, collected in specie, were lodged at the Royal Bank in Edinburgh, who gave him for it bills on London as required.

An Edinburgh bank teller's life at this period must have had much of the spice of adventure in it. By agreement between the two Banks the tellers' hours at the offices on winter afternoons were reduced to two—from two to four instead of two to five—to obviate any risk of taking in dubious specie in candle-light. There were delightful jaunts at other seasons of the year; Tellers Innes and Shairp would set off in October to Crieff with £3000 in paper to return with its equivalent in gold. At Crieff were held the great cattle "trysts" or markets, when hundreds of thousands of Highland cattle were sold to English drovers at an average of £1 a head. Stirling market gave a like opportunity to the tellers for securing gold for their notes.

Long after the Highlands were disarmed and the clan was no longer an entity, troops garrisoned the Great Glen fortresses — Fort William, Fort Augustus, and Fort George. The soldiers' pay was taken up to these forts periodically by a teller who carried about

## The History of

£2000 to £3000 in half-guineas, silver, and notes. Bounties to the extent of £8800 in Royal Bank notes were in the valises of Ship Close employees who rode to Inveraray for the national encouragement of the fishing industry by Loch Fyne "herring-bushes".

In those now untroubled Highlands there was already established, by an English company, on the books of the Royal Bank since 1728, a great lumbering industry which in every respect anticipated modern lumbering practice in Canadian wilds. This "York Buildings" Company, established as far back as 1700 "to raise the Thames water in York Buildings, and for the better supplying of the inhabitants of this part of London and Westminster", wandered, in the course of time, very far from its original purpose. After the abortive rising of 1715 it raised £1,200,000, by subscription, for the purchase of estates forfeited; not only ran English and Scots estates and did "realtor" business, and dabbled in iron-works, salt-pans, and coal-mines (rather unsuccessfully), but leased great stretches of primeval forest in the North; erected sawmills, cut the timber, rafted it down to the sea and there built ships with it, or forwarded it to England. The wages of those lumberers, the sites of whose camps and whose pits of sawdust may still be seen in great lonely Speyside forests that have grown again, were

# The Royal Bank of Scotland

paid from the tills of the Royal. For a hundred and fifty years the "York Company" had great Scots commitments that benefited the country, though the "adventurers" came badly out of the enterprise in the end.

## CHAPTER IX

### SMALL NOTE MANIA

IF any of the early jealousies between the Old Bank and the Royal had so long persisted, they were set aside during those weeks when bagpipes screamed through the old capital, and the whole national edifice looked like tottering. Indeed they were never renewed; henceforth all embittering harassments of each other were abandoned, and a more creditable form of rivalry ensued. By and by the prospect of a third competitor entering the field was to make even closer a friendly understanding between the two establishments.

That the Banks came through the crisis with public confidence in them unimpaired was shown in the fact that, in the following year, Royal Bank Stock was at $144\frac{1}{2}$ per cent.

On 16th April 1746 the Rebellion was crushed at Culloden, and, though the *moral* of Scotland was sadly shaken for a long time thereafter, that end for ever to Jacobite troubles, the conclusion of the Austrian War of Succession, and the Treaty of Aix-la-Chapelle, gave a

## The Royal Bank of Scotland

period of peace which soon encouraged the further development of our national industries. The Banks became more useful and indispensable than ever.

For years the linen trade, of considerable importance to the country, had been languishing; now it began to extend surprisingly, and even while Prince Charlie was still being hunted for through the heather, George II. gave a charter for the formation of the British Linen Company, which, a century and a half later, was to become the British Linen Bank. Incorporated in July 1746, with an authorised capital of £100,000, of which only half was offered for subscription at the outset, it got its money in Edinburgh and London, and opened an Edinburgh warehouse with Ebenezer MacCulloch and William Tod as managers. On 19th September it applied to the Royal for a cash credit of £3000, which was granted. Its more obvious business was to foster the linen trade by the importation and distribution of flax, and the collection and sale of the manufactured product. This necessitated agents all over the country with a certain amount of ready money at their command. In a very short time those agents were provided with British Linen Company promissory notes for £5, £10, and £20, payable on demand, and for £100 bearing interest at $3\frac{1}{2}$ and 4 per cent. Those notes the agents used in paying for goods received, and the Royal Bank, with whom the British Linen Company kept its account and had a substantial credit, retired them as a matter of course.

This British Linen Company's network of agents throughout the country laid, as Mr. William Graham suggests, the foundation of the widespread system of branches which has given such an impulse to Scottish banking. Almost inevitably the agents were utilised for other purposes than giving credit in the shape of flax and paying the workmen for their labour on the return of the finished goods; they discounted bills, and notes or bills were regularly sent to them for circulation or negotiation.

Up till 1749, by far the greatest part of Scotland's banking business, in the strict sense of the term, was confined to Edinburgh. The merchants of Glasgow, Aberdeen, Dundee, and elsewhere were entirely dependent on the two chartered Banks for accommodation; and no regular facilities existed elsewhere for monetary transactions. A few shopkeepers in those towns would give cash for bills on London, or sell bills on London, to persons wishing to make remittances to other parts of the kingdom, but the facilities thus offered were of a limited and precarious kind.

The merchants of Glasgow had dealt with the Royal Bank from its first institution. Trade was now beginning to boom on Clydeside; it

## The Royal Bank of Scotland

was inconvenient to have no bank more close at hand than fifty miles off, and Glasgow merchants invited the two Edinburgh Banks to establish Glasgow branches.

The Banks did something less courageous, being timid as the result of previous attempts at provincial branches, and followed a course they must have regretted afterwards. In 1749 the Bank of Scotland " promoted ", according to Mr. Kerr, the establishment of a banking company in Glasgow, under the designation of the Ship Bank, the firm being Dunlop, Houston and Company. In the following year the Royal Bank initiated the Glasgow Arms Bank, with Cochran, Murdoch and Company as its representatives. Aberdeen merchants, in a more independent mood, had already decided to keep their " ain fish-guts for their ain sea-maws ", and support a local firm called Livingstone, Mowat, Bremner, and Dingwall under the " style " of the Banking Company of Aberdeen; this (started 1749) was the first private banking company to issue bank-notes in Scotland, and was the first provincial bank.

In the archives of the Royal Bank can be followed the effects of repercussion of those upstarting youths on Edinburgh banking. The Aberdeen bank—the real innovator—was not seriously regarded as a rival, and, as it happened, it had to give up business in five years, mainly on account of the scarcity of coin in the country, helped perhaps, as Mr. Kerr suggests, by the assiduity with which local agents of the Edinburgh Banks kept pestering its tellers for change for its notes in specie or their own bank-notes. It was a victim really to the delusion that notes to the full amount of the subscribed capital could be safely issued though much of the capital was unpaid. When Aberdeen notes began to pour into Edinburgh merchants, who promptly passed them on to the two established Banks in the absence of any local agent to retire them on behalf of the issuers, the Bank of Scotland and the Royal Bank, in defence of themselves, appointed an agent in Aberdeen, and sent their gatherings of Aberdeen notes to him for presentation to Livingstone and Company.

Mr. Kerr's statement that the two Edinburgh Banks literally " promoted " or " initiated " the new Glasgow ones is probably correct, though the minutes of the Royal seem to contradict it. In October 1749 it was reported to the Royal directors that the Glasgow Company was erecting a bank and had employed an engraver for making notes. Letters were thereupon written to Lord Milnton and Lord Monzie suggesting that an action of declarator should be raised to prove that no private companies had the privilege of banking " without publick authority ". It was resolved at the same meeting " to have a conference with the directors of

## The Royal Bank of Scotland

the Old Bank on the above affair, and to endeavour to procure them to concur in a joint measure in case it shall be thought proper to raise the Declarator against the Bank at Aberdeen, so as to have the effect of stopping the project of Banking at Glasgow ".

Some weeks later it is reported to the directors that the Old Bank directors had met and considered the matter, and that to them " it did not appear to be an affair of such consequence as to engage them to lay out their money, or venture their interest as to the legality of such erections ".

That the two Edinburgh Banks gave cash credits to the Glasgow " interlopers " is true. So far as the Royal is concerned, it was complacent enough to the Glasgow Arms Bank to allow its officials to see the forms of bookkeeping observed in the Ship Close, on the request of its old friend Provost Cochran of Glasgow, one of the partners in the new concern. It did more. It gave the Glasgow Arms Bank a cash credit of £6000, which was considerably added to a few months later; and agreed to an amicable exchange of bank-notes.

It is clear that the Edinburgh Banks at first regarded those new western banks as agencies likely to be useful to them rather than as dangerous rivals. They were soon to change their minds on this point. In August 1751 Old Bank and New Bank decided that the whole credits or cash accounts to persons within the towns of Glasgow and Paisley should be stopped, " as also the Credits to the two Banking Companies in Glasgow ". The civic sentiment of Glasgow naturally revolted at this, and rallied to the support of its own two banking concerns. Mr. Trotter, formerly a partner of Coutts and Company, was sent to Glasgow to act as agent for both Banks. The two cities thereupon for a while played battledore and shuttlecock with each other's notes; the strife drifted into legislation, but the Glasgow banks doggedly pursued their way.

There came from the City Fathers of Edinburgh to the Royal a proposal for a loan of £5000 " for carrying out the scheme for improving and ornamenting the City of Edinburgh ". It was granted, with a rebate of £250 on whatever interest might accrue. The amount of this credit can hardly be regarded as excessive considering that what was involved was the first step in the creation of the " Modern Athens ", though Lord Provost Alexander and his council could not possibly have visualised the ultimate results of their schemes for improvement and decoration.

For a century, Old Edinburgh, confined to the narrow ridge of rock on which human storms had stranded it, had contemplated a descent on the plain at its feet. From the Castle Hill to Holyrood stretched the High

## The Royal Bank of Scotland

Street and Canongate—a thoroughfare drenched in history, still with a half-wild mediaeval aspect, the wonder and admiration of the stranger. On both sides of it stretched tenements of fantastic form and elevation, their ranks unbroken, pierced by narrow wynds and innumerable "closes"—constricted passages that gave access to the stairs of flats piled on each other to the height of fifteen or sixteen stories in some cases. "The visitor", says Mr. John Geddie in his *Romantic Edinburgh*, "might well fancy he had wandered within the walls of some high fortification—some rock-cut Eastern city, from which egress was possible only to those who held the clue to its labyrinth of straitened passages."

Towards the south it had spread laterally beyond its walls in a maze of squalid and struggling streets, but the Burgh Loch and the Burgh Muir were obstacles to its progress further in that direction. To the north the tenants, perched on the giddy verge of slopes precipitous, looked from their lofty chamber windows over wide prospects of plain and sea. In this direction lay the destinies of the New Town, still hazily and humbly previsioned. Immediately underneath the Castle Rock—basaltic brother of the Bass, of Stirling, Dumbarton, and Ailsa Craig—was the marsh that not long before had been the Nor' Loch; beyond it stretched bare and wind-swept fields.

Only in that direction seemed there room for development and ornamentation. To cross the swampy hollow of the winds by throwing over it a bridge was, in itself, a great adventure; not for many years after Provost Alexander got his credit was the bridge completed.

He got it at a time when the Royal Bank directors were engaged in a flitting of their own. As we have seen, the Bank was dissatisfied with its Ship Close premises. For ten years before the Rebellion a removal to some other part of the city was frequently discussed by the directors. Several different sites for a new office were tentatively approved at various times—the Poultry Market, for instance, and Niddry's Wynd. Properties were actually purchased with a view to their demolition and rebuilding; they were afterwards sold or excambed, but eventually, on 9th June 1750, plans and estimates were passed for the erection of a new office on an area " south of the Cross ", the whole expenses of building and finishing being £2823 : 8 : 3¼, " the building to be carried on with all dispatch ".

It was a site on the south side of the High Street, now occupied by the City Police Chambers—not an ideal one, by any means, but the best procurable at the time. Adjacent ancient edifices of a highly inflammable character were in too close proximity to the new office (consisting of two stories and attics),

# The Royal Bank of Scotland

which had to have iron shutters on all its windows to the west facing Parliament Close buildings. Furthermore, the Fish Mercat Close was not favourable to the amenities. William Mekison, cobbler, got permission to "erect his moveable shop at the outside of the East Entry to the Bank, he promising to keep the Bank Court and entrys free from the disturbance of Fish-wives, oyster-wives, boys and others".

When the Royal took up its new quarters, the Duke of Montrose was Governor. He had bought from the Bank £1000 of stock at 150 per cent in January 1750, and was elected Governor in the following March. "The increase of business and the state of the Bank's affairs" were considered to warrant the augmentation of the annual allowance of the Deputy Governor to £51 : 6 : 8, and the fees of directors attending the weekly meetings were raised to 10s. a day, or £43 : 6 : 8 yearly. Lord Monzie was dead.

Between the Old Bank and the New Bank, now, was a pact, the existence of which was not made public. In joint session they had, in March 1752, agreed that "they were established for the benefit of that part of the Nation"; and

That from long experience it appears that both Banks might lend out as much money as will enable them to make their present dividends a sum equal to their charges of Management, and as much more as will make a reasonable saving to guard them in case of losses.

That it also appears that it is not for the interest or credit of either, or for the service of the country that there should subsist any difference or variance betwixt them, because that through those misunderstandings other Societies, without any legal authority, have associated, and thereby endeavoured to benefit themselves and gain credit in the Country.

That in order to remedy what's past, and to prevent the like inconveniences for the future, a mutual confidence and good understanding should be established between the two Banks.

That the number of Private Banks set up in different corners of the Country, without the sanction of public authority, or depositing a fund or stock of cash appear to be taking an unreasonable credit, and may be attended with great inconveniences to the country and greatly affect paper credit in general.

That the measure begun and continued till lately by the Glasgow Banks, of having agents at Edinburgh for changing their Notes was the most likely to get them into the Circle (*i.e.* circulation).

That the two Banks established by public authority may be of the more use, and better able to answer the ends of their erection; It is proposed that a Mutual friendship and harmony be cultivated, thereby to support maintain and defend each of them their own and the others interest against all attacks that may be made by the other Societies that pretend to carry on the business of Banking in other parts of Scotland other than Edinburgh, without lawful authority.

# The Royal Bank of Scotland

That they shall continue to receive at their respective offices the notes of the other Company, but that they shall not use any private methods to gather in the notes of the other Company. That at the end of each month or oftener these notes shall be exchanged.

That upon all emergencies, if one of these Companies shall need the aid of the other in any respect, particularly in the supply of current Specie, it shall be advanced by the one to the other free of interest to the extent of £10,000.

That the Credits already given to such Companies, or to such private persons as are likely to use them for the support of the Private Banks, be recalled; but in order to avoid a clamour, this measure shall not be put in execution immediately.

That the British Linen Company be not comprehended in this, in regard they make no loans, and therefore cannot interfere or do any prejudice to either Bank.

This is a document of no little historical importance for Scottish bankers; it represents the dawn of common sense in business rivalry, though rivalry inspired it; the start of the Clearing House; the system of friendly exchanges which has, with modifications, persisted to the present day, and secured for Scottish banks the utmost confidence in the convertibility of their paper issues. These have, since, always stood at par, even in times of great financial crisis.

In March 1753 the Royal introduced what was virtually the equivalent of the modern bank

## The History of

draft, to enable its customers to remit money by post without the necessity for sending banknotes. Five years previously Edinburgh merchants had pointed out the hazards of loss or larceny attending the transmission of actual cash by mail, and for their security under such circumstances the Bank engraved and printed what was called a post bill of exchange, payable by endorsement at Edinburgh after an interval of six days from the date of issue. The post bill had this serious disadvantage that it must be for £25; no provision was made for the remittance of sums either below or above that figure.

A few years' experience having shown that its usefulness was limited, it was withdrawn, and its place taken in 1753 by a form of promissory note, as follows:

*No.......* {*Royal Bank of Scotland Promissory Note.*} *Edinburgh.*

*I promise to pay to .......................... or Order on Demand at the Royal Bank Office here, the Sum of ................................ Sterling for value received.*

*By Order of the Court of Directors.*

*Entered........* } *............*

Sums of £10 and over, with shillings and sixpence when desired, could be filled into the blank space in this document, which passed

## The Royal Bank of Scotland

by endorsement simply. These promissory notes were procurable at the Bank only on Tuesdays and Thursdays to begin with, but two years later they could be got on any day.

The Earl of Queensberry's mines at Wanlockhead in Lanarkshire were taken over by a company (1755), and having the appearance of proving a successful undertaking, were granted a credit of £5000. The fact is worth mentioning only for the sake of the reasons given in the minutes of the Bank for a cheerful acquiescence in the loan. " It may be the means of throwing a great deal of the Bank's notes into the circle, and dispersing and diffusing them in a more advantageous manner than any other circulation." Mr. Ronald Crawford, W.S., Edinburgh (one of the adventurers in the mining company), had observed in the country adjacent to Wanlockhead a great deal of specie, both gold and silver, and few notes of any kind in the circle; he therefore proposed to pick up such specie by substituting Royal Bank notes and pay the same into the Bank office in Edinburgh.

More and more was the quantity of floating specie diminishing in the country; there was an incessant drain of silver into England to assist in meeting war expenditure abroad, while in the intervals of peace English investments in Scotland were withdrawn for employment at home. Gold had almost entirely disappeared. The two Banks had experienced great difficulty in maintaining their reserves. English bullion jobbers drew fictitious bills on London, at thirty days' currency, which they sold in Edinburgh at a premium for notes payable on demand. These, in turn, being converted into specie, the proceeds were sent to London to meet the bills when they fell due.

To provide a currency for the payment of workmen's wages and the like, private companies and private individuals in many parts of the country issued notes for trivial sums—in one case at least for one shilling Scots, which is to say a penny sterling. To such an extent did the use of those trumpery paper promises by individuals of no substance extend, that the Scottish sense of humour found release in printing and distributing parodies of them as squibs. The so-called Wasp Note for "One Penny Sterling, or in the Option of the Directors, three Ballads six days after a Demand", elegantly printed in Glasgow, with an ornamental border of wasps, the motto "We Swarm", and the signature of "Daniel Mcfunn" is the best example of those satires.

It was to preserve its silver specie by adding an odd shilling to the currency that the Royal, in 1758, decided to issue a guinea note. There had been an English guinea, made from New Guinea gold, since the reign of Charles II., its value ranging from 30s. in 1695 to 21s. in 1717.

## The Royal Bank of Scotland

It was probably rare in Scotland at this time; in any case, Scotland was to have now thrust on it a currency denomination which persists till to-day, when a single-piece guinea is unprocurable. The Royal decided on a guinea note on 3rd March 1758; on 19th May, Robert Cooper was instructed to make plates for it after this form:

*The Royal Bank of Scotland (pursuant to Act of Parliament and Letters Patent under the Great Seal) is hereby obliged to pay to....................or Secretary, or the Bearer on Demand, One Pound One Shilling Sterling*

      EDINBURGH 24*th day of March* 1758.
      *By Order of the Court of Directors.*

The words in parenthesis were an innovation, designed no doubt to bring home to the public the difference between the paper issue of a chartered bank and the " scrap of paper " of a private bank.

It was ten years before there was any reprint of those guinea notes struck in 1758, though the British Linen Company and many of the banks soon followed the Royal's lead. In 1768 the senior Banks stopped issuing £1 notes entirely, replacing them with the paper guinea.

How eager became the scramble for specie finds expression in the minutes of 1761–62. The Bank of England had given warning that its supplies were short. Mr. John Fordyce, merchant, was authorised to collect £10,000 in London as best he could and bring it back to Edinburgh. Dealers in exchange and merchants having large credits with the Bank were summoned to a meeting at which William Alexander and Company, Coutts Brothers and Company, William Hogg and Sons, Adam and Thomas Fairholm, Gibson and Hogg, John Fordyce, Mansfield Hunter and Company were represented. It was decided that they and others should immediately bring from London £20,000 gold specie " by shares in proportion to their several credits ". It may have been as a result of their activities that £15,000 in gold was lodged in the Bank's vault six weeks later. £5000 of this was loaned to the Bank of Scotland later on for three months.

Holders of cash accounts in the provincial towns were urged to send in all the specie they could to Edinburgh, the charge of conveyance being at the Bank's expense. Another intimation went to dealers in exchange and others buying London bills and paying the amount in specie besides an " exorbitant exchange ", that unless this was discouraged credits on cash accounts would be stopped altogether. In the meantime they were reduced to three-fourths of the sum in the respective bonds.

Further, to check the flow of coin across the

## The Royal Bank of Scotland

Border, owing to the high exchange demanded for London bills, the two Banks agreed to give 5 per cent for money deposited for six months and 4 per cent on deposits repayable on demand. Both Banks called upon shopkeepers having credits with them to come under obligation not to employ " any English merchants or tradesmen who send down their clerks and riders here, as they carry back a great deal of specie ".

William Alexander, merchant, Edinburgh, made a proposal to furnish the Royal with what specie it required for the space of six years upon a yearly premium of £1600, and the offer was accepted on 9th October 1761. Upon how Alexander was to accumulate this cash, no light is thrown; he was probably an optimist; in February 1762, when the Royal and the Bank of Scotland found he was also supplying specie to the Glasgow banking companies, they warned him to desist.

This incessant strain upon the supply of specie compelled the Royal, following the lead given by the Bank of Scotland years before, and afterwards followed by all the private banking companies, finally to issue optional notes for £5, £10, £20, £50, and £100, and cancel all others in circulation as they came in. In five weeks' hard work in 1762 at the Bank's printing-press, 172,000 new notes were struck accordingly. In the original minute is no allusion to a £1 optional note, but a note of

## The History of

this denomination was certainly included, and its terms may stand as typical of the others:

£12 *Scots. No.* .... *Edinburgh 5th April* 1762.

*The Royal Bank of Scotland, pursuant to Act of Parliament and Letters Patent under the Great Seal, is hereby obliged to pay to* ................ *or the Bearer,* ONE POUND STERLING *on Demand, Or in the Option of the Directors, one pound, Sixpence Sterling at the end of Six Months after the day of demand, and for ascertaining the demand and Option of the Directors, the Accomptant and two of the tellers of the Bank are hereby ordered to mark and sign this Note on the back of the same.*

*By Order of the Court of Directors.*

ALEXANDER SIMPSON, *Accomptant.*
JAMES INNES, *Cashier.*

In the same year the British Linen Company's notes had the optional clause added, for the same reason, that the Edinburgh Banks were being obliged to find specie for the notes of all the other concerns in the country as well as their own. The British Linen Company notes continued always to be acceptable at the Royal, the Company retiring them weekly.

A committee of the Royal and the Bank of Scotland directors, on 25th August 1763, decided that no person whatsoever should be allowed credit on a cash account by either of them for the next three months, and at the same time to lay before the Ministry

## The Royal Bank of Scotland

a memorial craving an Act of Parliament to remedy the growing evil of too many banking companies.

In the inland exchange, that with London was always against Edinburgh, and this of itself was sufficient to attract specie from Scotland to London in the absence of sufficient bills in London to settle adverse balances. Every attempt to remedy this deficiency of coin by printing more bank-notes only aggravated matters by raising the exchange still further in favour of the metropolis and attracting more coin south, where English merchants, in the event of their not getting its bullion value, melted it down, and exported it to France in return for continental gold.

To reduce and keep within moderate bounds the exchange with London, the two Banks, on the recommendation of their representatives in London, set about between them to establish a credit on current account for £200,000 with the Bank of England. But the project would seem never to have materialised. More relief was to be expected from the Government taking the sensible course of dealing directly with the chaos of Scottish note issues. In the beginning of 1763 two of the directors—Mr. Young and Mr. Grey—went to London to press for an Act of Parliament. How long they were there is now undiscoverable, but their report came before the Court only in the following

December, when its most consoling feature, so far as the minutes bring out, was the statement that they had "brought down with them a large sum in specie, whereby the Bank had a considerable saving in commission and carriage". Their bill of expenses was £430, and the fees of a solicitor they had engaged came to £31 : 18 : 4. But there must have been something more agreeable in their report than the minutes disclose, for they were warmly thanked, and each got £200 as an honorarium. The Court was in good trim that week; Christmas was at hand, and the cobbler who had a stall by the Bank gate was voted a guinea for keeping the court clean and clear of children and vagrants.

Parliament in February 1765 at last determined to do something; a bill was to be introduced dealing with the banking irregularities of those vexatious Scotsmen. Mr. Young was engaged to return to London with a watching brief for the Royal Bank, and a power of attorney.

In the following year Act 5 of George III. c. 49 was passed through the insistence of the two Edinburgh Banks, ably seconded by the good offices of Lord Advocate Miller of Barskimming. It only partially remedied things. Nothing was to be done to improve the coinage, nor to interfere with the rights of Tom, Dick, or Harry to issue notes. But from and after

## The Royal Bank of Scotland

15th May 1766 it would be no longer lawful " to issue any note, ticket, token, or other writing for money, of the nature of a bank-note, circulated, or to be circulated as specie, but such as shall be payable on demand in lawful money of Great Britain, and without reserving any power or option of delaying payment thereof for any time or term whatever "; also it was decreed that the optional notes still in circulation should thenceforward be deemed payable on demand, and that summary execution might proceed on all bank-notes not paid on demand—one protest being allowed to include any number of notes. Finally, it was enacted that from and after 1st June 1765, no bank-note should be issued for any sum of money less than 20s. sterling, and that those issued up to that date might be allowed to circulate for one year thereafter.

The imminent certainty of having their note issues hurled back on them with a demand for instant payment in specie alarmed those erring banks whose available specie was the tiniest fraction of the value represented by the notes in circulation. Some of them decided to reduce their business and in future to discount no bills excepting those payable in London, Edinburgh, and Glasgow. An almost immediate effect of the Act was that exchanges rose slightly and the drain of gold ceased. The Royal, as we have seen, had long

## The Royal Bank of Scotland

anticipated the suppression of the option clause it had so reluctantly been compelled to adopt, and was in less anxiety than most other banks as to its metallic reserves. But the deficiency of coin in the country generally remained as grave as ever.

## CHAPTER X

### CRISIS OF 1772

THE Royal Bank and its neighbour had consistently given credits to the private bankers of the country, much though the latter harassed them, as it seemed the quicker and more profitable way of doing business to deal in large sums rather than directly in small sums with the public. There was a soothing illusion, too, that the general trade of the country could thus be most quickly helped and expanded. Most of the private bankers, however, used those credits in a speculative way, and looked for most of their profits from buying corn from the farmers to be sold at the highest possible figure to the consumer.

More ostensibly for the promotion of local industries, the Dundee Bank Company of George Dempster and Company had begun business in August 1763 with a paid-up capital of £12,600. George Dempster of Dunnichen at the time was M.P. for the Forfar and Fife district of burghs, a seat which had cost him £10,000 and led to the sale of his estates in

Monikie and Monifieth. He was the "true-blue Scot" of Burns's Address to the Scottish Representatives. We shall hear more about the Dundee bank later; here it must suffice to say it developed into a real banking concern of moment to the country, and after flourishing for a century was ultimately to be amalgamated with the Royal Bank.

In the same year was established the Ayr bank of Messrs. John Macadam and Company, to be purchased eight years later by Douglas Heron and Company. The year 1766 saw the formation of the Perth United Company which, under another proprietary, amalgamated with the Perth Banking Company in 1787, and in 1857 was absorbed by the Union Bank of Scotland.

In 1767 the merchants of Aberdeen made up for their abortive scheme of 1749 by establishing the Banking Company of Aberdeen, which was destined to be a great success. It was managed with conspicuous ability throughout most of its career, and over a series of years its dividends averaged 8 per cent per annum, with occasional large bonuses. In the same year small traders on the Clyde set up the Merchant Banking Company of Glasgow. Contemporaneously were heard the first rumblings of the financial storm which came to a height in the crisis of 1772. The fall of Douglas Heron and Company, trading as the Ayr Bank, was a

## The Royal Bank of Scotland

consequence of financial mania almost as remarkable as that displayed in the Darien disaster.

On 6th November 1769 there was opened at Ayr the head office of a banking company called Douglas Heron and Company, with a capital of £150,000, of which £96,000 was subscribed. Among the original shareholders were two Scottish dukes, two Scottish earls, the Honourable Archibald Douglas of that ilk, Patrick Heron of that ilk, and many men of rank and fortune, lawyers, merchants, shopkeepers, etc., but no bankers. Branches were soon after opened in Edinburgh and Dumfries, with independent powers, under separate boards; agencies were established at Glasgow, Inverness, Kelso, Montrose, Campbeltown, and elsewhere. A fortnight after the opening of the Ayr office the Earl of Dumfries, president of the new Company, wrote to the Royal Bank inquiring if it would accept Ayr notes for the purpose of exchange. A polite reply was made that on principle and to " prevent all suspicion of taking up notes for unfriendly purposes " the Royal did not receive in payments any notes but those of the Bank of Scotland. Twenty months later, however, the Royal and the Bank of Scotland agreed to " take the notes of all the different Banking Companies in Scotland of reputed credit ". At the time, the Ayr Bank had a credit of £10,000 with the two Edinburgh ones.

Among the partners of the Ayr concern were many members of trading firms who immediately secured for the new bank an extensive advance business. The coffers at Ayr were soon emptied, and when the capital and deposit money were exhausted, paper money was launched extravagantly, to come back almost immediately to tills bare of specie. A call of 20 per cent on the shareholders, and the influence of a wealthy and titled proprietary which secured the easy renewal of London bills, tided over the difficulties for a time. A dividend was declared in May 1771; the business of the Ayr Bank was bought that year for £18,000; the Company was represented to be flourishing.

But in June 1772 the bills on London had accumulated to the amount of £400,000; there was £200,000 in notes in circulation, but insignificant available funds to meet them besides £300,000 of deposits. On 12th June a horseman rode into Edinburgh, having come from London in forty-three hours, with the dire news that the banking house of Neale, James, Fordyce, and Doune had failed and dragged down other firms with it. It was a shocking blow for Scottish private banks, to none more than to the bank in Ayr. Douglas Heron and Company immediately sent a memorial to the Royal and Bank of Scotland, in which they said they had the satisfaction of

## The Royal Bank of Scotland

informing them that " they are entirely covered in their engagements which are to the extent of £22,000 with the houses that have failed in London, having actual value in their hands for all these Bills. But as it is of the utmost consequence to prevent any further consequences from the general discredit, they are willing to interpose their credit effectually to stem the evil and make the following proposal to the Banks, which will enable them to supply every aid the country can want in this emergency.

" They propose a loan for six months of £20,000 from each of the Banks, and so as to secure every good effect from this measure it should be immediate. They propose to give a Bond for the amount signed by the Cashier with a Corroborative Bond signed by a quorum of the Directors, and as Douglas Heron and Company propose to return to London a part of the large sum of specie they have brought down to pay the balances to the Banks, they further request that the Banks will allow £10,000 of their notes in the hands of each to lie at interest and take the balance of their daily exchange if in their favour in London bills at four and six months."

The conjoint answer of the two Banks was: " They are of opinion that it would be improper for them to agree to the proposals made in the Memorial. At the same time they will cheerfully do their best upon this occasion to support such private persons as may apply to them for assistance."

Ten days later Douglas Heron and Company issued the following circular:

"The Company of Douglas Heron and Company, Bankers in Ayr, taking into consideration the present state of the Credit of this country and the uncommon demands for specie owing to causes sufficiently well known, have come to a resolution to give over for some time paying specie for their notes, but as the country who have received the most liberal aids from this Company cannot entertain the smallest doubt of the solidity of its foundation, it is hoped that on the occasion of a national emergency the holders of their notes will not be under any alarm." Interest at 5 per cent was to be paid to holders of such notes.

That the failure was disastrous could no longer be concealed. There were liabilities of almost a million and a quarter sterling, £300,000 in deposits, £220,000 in note circulation, £600,000 in drafts on London outstanding, and £104,000 of the partners' paid-up capital.

The total loss to the partners, 225 in number, was £663,396 : 18 : 6, and titled shareholders had to burden their estates with redeemable annuities to the extent of £457,570 got on preposterously extortionate terms. They were

## The Royal Bank of Scotland

able to disburden themselves of the yoke of these annuities two years later, when the Royal helped them to redeem them (23rd November 1774) by a loan of £20,000 on a bond backed by the personal security of Buccleuch and Queensberry and others.

In September following, the bank reopened its doors, after advertising the notes to be payable in gold at Ayr only, and that it would give £1 notes in exchange for large ones; but voluntary liquidation took place in August 1773. A few days before, its directors intimated to the Edinburgh Banks the intention of dissolving the business, and asked them to accept their notes to the amount of £130,000, which was estimated to be all that were in circulation. Beyond the security of the notes themselves, the Royal and the Bank of Scotland were offered a further security from Douglas Heron and Company for reimbursement within a reasonable period of what sums these Banks advanced as well as a corroborative bond in security from individual members of the embarrassed Company.

The Royal and the Bank of Scotland accordingly advertised on the following day that they would pay all notes of the bankrupt firm, and sent £16,800 in their own guinea notes to the bank at Ayr as the most expeditious way of bringing that firm's degraded paper out of circulation. £63,250 of Douglas Heron's notes had accumulated in the Royal Bank vault by May 1774.

The crash at Ayr shook the whole foundation of Scotland's private banking. In Edinburgh the only private bankers to weather the storm were Mansfield, Hunter and Company, William Cumming and Sons, and Sir William Forbes and Company. Glasgow was luckier; its own destined disaster was still to come, but its bankers and merchants had fortunately kept clear of those bill entanglements into which their fellows in the east were lured by specious prospects of easy money in home and foreign speculation, and the readiness with which " capital " could be raised by chains of bills on London.

The Royal and the Bank of Scotland had long foreseen and prepared for the catastrophe; their notes and credit stood firm through the period of chaos; *bona-fide* traders and the public found them as able and willing as ever to grant accommodation, and the crisis left them for sixty years thereafter unvexed by the rivalry of unbusiness-like banking merchants.

At the period of the crisis Sir Lawrence Dundas was Governor, having succeeded John Edwards of London in 1764, and Andrew Pringle, Lord Alemoor, was Deputy Governor. They had got for the Bank a new warrant—its third Charter—on 16th May 1770, giving to it the free use and command of the capital of

Sir Lawrence Dundas of Kerse Bart
Governor 1764-1777
from a painting by T. Hudson belonging to The Marquis of Zetland

## The Royal Bank of Scotland

£111,000 of Equivalent Stock, with power to assign and transfer the same or as much of it as should be necessary "to any person, bodies public and corporate, notwithstanding that the same is incorporated as the stock of the Royal Bank of Scotland. Moneys arising from such transfer and assignments to be deemed part of the stock of the Royal Bank."

Considerable credits were granted in those few years of stress to borrowers having in view the starting of great national works or the extension of others.

The Carron Iron Works, started in 1760 by Dr. Roebuck, an Englishman, for the mining, smelting, and manufacture of iron ore, was flourishing and giving employment to a great body of workmen, whose wages weekly had been paid in Bank of Ayr money. The Carron firm transferred its business to the Royal and drew the wages there each Friday upon three-months' bills. Its development into the greatest iron work in Europe before the end of the century was greatly due to the opening of the Forth and Clyde Canal, from Grangemouth to Bowling, near Glasgow, begun in 1768. In 1771 the "Navigation Company", as it was called, got cash credits for £30,000, on the obligations of Sir Lawrence Dundas, his son Mr. Thomas Dundas of Castlecary, the Duke of Queensberry, the Earl of Abercorn, and George Haldane of Gleneagles.

## The Royal Bank of Scotland

The Bank had £111,000 (in Equivalent Stock) locked up in London, for which it was getting only 4 per cent. It grudged, therefore, paying £5 per cent on the £40,000 it had from the Trustees of Fisheries and Manufactures in Scotland, but did not get the interest reduced till 10th July 1776 to $4\frac{1}{2}$ per cent. Its stock, hitherto valued as security for loans at £120 per cent, was on 12th February 1772 revalued at £150 per cent. At the end of 1771 a committee of the Court was of opinion that the annual dividend might safely be increased to $7\frac{1}{2}$ or even 8 per cent, leaving a considerable " sinking fund to be added to the capital yearly ".

# CHAPTER XI

### GLASGOW'S AWAKENING

HARDLY had the stable banks of Scotland got out of the financial cyclone that left such wreckage round them than another storm arose, involving the whole kingdom, and continuing without intermission for almost a decade. America fought us for her independence; we had grave reverses in India at the hands of Hyder Ali; sedition and open rebellion were rife in Ireland; our armies were engaged in France, Spain, and Holland. National expenditure assumed enormous proportions; the tax-collector became an incubus.

It was England, with her now great foreign trade crippled for the time being, who suffered most, though Scotland had to bear her share of the damages arising from a turbulent foreign policy which, a century earlier, would have been little concern of hers. Her soldiers fought with lustre to themselves an empire's battles far from their native hills and valleys, but at home there was tranquillity unusual to Scotland, and full advantage was taken of it to press forward every national interest that made for industry, human well-being, and that ultimate universal peace whereof civilisation has not yet got the secret.

The value of Scottish land went up considerably as its culture was improved, for wars are always a benefit to the farmer or the laird so long as it is not his own acres that are trodden underfoot by Mars. Capital for investment became more abundant. The banks gave more generous credits where such credits do most national good, though the accusation was sometimes made that too great a proportion of their funds was being sunk in British Government securities and Bank of England Stock bought at low prices and " put away " for the inevitable hour of peace and appreciation. The Royal Bank was certainly putting away, as shrewdness and prudence dictated, fairly considerable reserves in such gilt-edged securities as Navy Bills and East India Bonds, Bank of England Stock and 3 per cent annuities.

A new era of private bankers soon rose in Edinburgh on the ashes of the old concerns that were the victims of ignorance and inexperience rather than of maleficence. The private banker henceforth better knew his business, and as a rule did well for himself and for his clients till the time came when the private bank was to be no longer a feature of Scots finance. Such private banks, free from

## The Royal Bank of Scotland

the defects which ruined their predecessors, were started in the provinces too, in Ayr, in Stirling, and Aberdeen. There were seven in Edinburgh and four in the country issuing their own notes. For ten years after 1772 the casualties among Scottish private banking firms in general were two, the failure of an Edinburgh agent for country banks, and the temporary suspension of the Merchant Banking Company of Glasgow, to whose aid the merchants of the city rallied, and whose creditors were paid in full.

A third and successful effort to establish branches was made by the Old Bank in 1774. There was a rumour at the time that its directors in an underhand way, through the agency of a private bank, were seeking to secure a secret influence on the management of the Royal. There is no hint of such a thing in the Royal's records, though some years after, tactics of this sort are referred to. Nor is there any allusion to a rumour of the same period that the two concerns were contemplating an alliance. Both Banks were doing remarkably well as they were. From its branch deposits the Old Bank found itself in a position to advertise loans on heritable security, and the Royal might have been well advised to embark on a branch system at the time, but though this was not done, the figures show that it was enjoying a decade of extraordinary prosperity.

## The History of

In 1775, by an Act of Parliament passed in 1773, the gold coinage of the kingdom, worn thin to illegibility, was withdrawn from circulation, paid for by the ounce, with a loss of a million sterling to the holders of it. Through the influence of Sir Lawrence Dundas, the Royal's Governor, the collection of this light gold of Scotland was entrusted by the Treasury to the Royal Bank, and also the distribution of the new coinage to take its place. All guineas minted prior to 1st January 1772 of less than 5.8 weight, half-guineas less than 2.16, and quarter-guineas less than 1.8 were put in the melting-pot. The validity of light coin was to terminate on 19th August 1776; for outlying parts of the country it seemed that in the absence of local arrangements for collecting and weighing, many people would find themselves on that date with guineas negotiable only for what change a crafty pedlar cared to offer. On a petition from the Commissioners of Supply for Orkney the Royal appointed a Kirkwall merchant, Mr. Robert Laing, their agent to collect defective coin and pay for it in notes.

The degraded gold, as it was collected, was sent to London; the Secretary of the Bank and the teller, during the last weeks of its collection, were despatched there with £30,000 worth for the Bank of England.

Glasgow's shipping trade suffered a tempor-

## The Royal Bank of Scotland

ary eclipse till the future of America was settled, but its people found plenty of scope for the extension of their commerce otherwise, and in those years when her tobacco trade, a virtual European monopoly, was being permanently lost to her, there were taking shape other industries and enterprises whereon was to be based her future eminence as commercial Capital of the country. New capital was required for the mills and machinery that were henceforth to be Glasgow's business, and in June 1775 the following appears in the records of the Bank: "It having been suggested to this Court that a loan of a considerable sum of money would be of great service to the trade of the town of Glasgow, the Court ordered Mr. William Simpson, one of the Tellers, to go to Glasgow and commune with the two Glasgow Banks concerning their taking a loan of £50,000 at 5 per cent, and empowered him to offer the money at 4 per cent in case they would not agree to give the legal interest".

In January 1777 John Campbell died, and so an old link with romantic Edinburgh vanished. He would doubtless have felt out of his element in the newer Edinburgh now coming into being. The North Bridge was completed before he died; the exodus of grand old lords and ladies, and the capital's *élite* in general, from the ridge where they had dwelt "but-and-ben" with poverty to the fairer land of promise beyond the hollow of the winds, would soon be in full flood.

Mr. George Innes, the second Cashier, succeeded Mr. Campbell as chief, and, as he was of advanced age, his nephew, William Simpson, first teller, was associated with him in the post, though a second Cashier, it was felt, could otherwise have been dispensed with. Mr. Innes's salary was fixed at £120; that of his nephew at £100. As the occupancy of the Bank House and the charge of the offices would be too much of an anxiety for the chief Cashier, Mr. Simpson became the resident, with £80 a year for coal and candle. He became chief Cashier with a salary of £220 in February 1780, his uncle's health by that time having compelled a complete retirement. Salaries were going up; the pay-roll of the establishment was augmented by £240 per annum "in consequence of the expenses of the necessaries of life".

At the end of December 1777 Sir Lawrence Dundas, having transferred his stock, could no longer remain Governor. His place was taken by Henry, third Duke of Buccleuch and fifth Duke of Queensberry, who was a great-nephew of the Bank's first Governor, Lord Ilay, afterwards third Duke of Argyll. In Duke Henry was revived the character which Sir James Melville gave his renowned predecessor in Queen Mary's reign—" Scot of

Henry, Third Duke of Buccleuch
Governor 1777-1812
from an engraving by H. Meyer after a drawing by J. Heath.

## The Royal Bank of Scotland

Buccleugh, wise and true, stout and modest ". Ever since, save for an interregnum between 1820 and 1838—most of which period the fifth Duke was a minor—five successive Dukes of Buccleuch have been Governors.

A counterfeit Royal guinea note turned up in Dumfries at this time; no surprising matter, for the original plates for printing the guinea note were now so worn that they gave but faint and blurred impressions, tempting to a ready draughtsman. A new guinea note was therefore issued, with the words " One Guinea " in blue, and the King's head in red, as calculated to make forgery more difficult.

There arose, at the same time, a problem apparently new to the Royal—what policy should it adopt with regard to its notes if accidentally destroyed while in the possession of customers? The question was raised in a letter of 17th May 1779 from Lord Gardenstone to Lord Elliock, director, which said:

My Lord

You may before this comes to hand have heard of the calamity by fire at Inverness, in which I have had my share, as a sufferer, tho' I have also been fortunate and have great reason to thank God that I have escaped with my life. About twelve at night the 15th. the fire broke out in the house where I lodged. I was alarmed very critically, and escaped by two or three minutes before it reached my apartment. Naked as I came into the world I retired to the public house at some distance.

All I had with me, Cloaths, Gown, Money etc. was consumed in the flames. There is one circumstance in my loss which I must beg leave to mention, particularly for your good advice and direction. When I set out from Edinburgh I drew from the Royal Bank 160 odd pounds upon our quarterly precepts mostly in twenty pound notes. My expense at Perth and on the journey had reduced my large notes to four in number, these together with some gold and silver and small notes perished in the fire. If I was not really a very poor fellow I should not think of troubling the Bank with any proposition of relief however reasonable it might appear in the particular circumstances of my case, independent of any Credit which may be thought due to my own testimony. My draught from the Bank to serve on the Circuit, my necessary expenditure in part and my naked escape from the fire are particular and pointed circumstances of real evidence that the four notes of 20 Pound besides several small ones of which I make no account, are consumed and can never come against the Bank, I trust you will at anyrate forgive this freedom, and I beg you'll be assured that I am with Sincere regards, my dear Lord your most obedient humble servent  FRA: GARDEN:

INVERNESS
17 *May* 1779.

*P.S.*—There is no circumstance in my own part of the misfortune that I feel so sensibly as the loss of poor Caesar—a proof of my narrow escape, for he never was two minutes from my heels in his life.

This letter was brought before the Court of Proprietors, when it was decided that the

William Simpson
Cashier 1780-1808

## The Royal Bank of Scotland

Cashier should pay Lord Gardenstone eighty pounds sterling for the notes burnt as above mentioned, and take his receipt for the same.

By the beginning of 1781 it was surmised that the British Linen Company were applying for a banking charter; and it was decided by the Royal and the Bank of Scotland to lodge a caveat that they should be heard before such a charter should be granted. It remained a bogey for many long years thereafter.

In Glasgow the sugar trade with the West Indies, cotton-spinning, and calico - printing were giving a new animation to the Clyde by the time the American War ended; shipbuilding was rapidly increasing; James Watt's steam engines were taking shape, with the promise and the potency of gigantic changes to come on manufacturing methods. Everywhere hand labour was giving place to machinery. On 25th November 1783 the British troops evacuated New York. America had won her independence, and we had lost half a continent and added 115 millions to our National Debt. On the eve of this historic hour, the Royal Bank decided to increase its capital from £111,347 to £150,000 in order to " add to the credit of the Bank and increase the Security of the Public ". Power to this extent, though not hitherto exercised, was conferred by the Charter of May 1783, and the £38,653 required was to be found in undivided profits without any payment on the part of the proprietors. But this was only a step preliminary to the application for a new Charter, the fourth, authorising a capital of £300,000, which was secured and made effective in the following year, the increase again being provided from profits.

On 3rd September 1783 it was decided to abandon the policy of concentration and open a Glasgow branch, " for discounting bills, and purchasing bills on London or Edinburgh, and circulating their notes in Glasgow and the neighbourhood ". Robert Scott Moncrieff, merchant in Edinburgh, and David Dale, merchant in Glasgow—to be known as the firm of Scott Moncrieff and Dale—were appointed agents and cashiers. They found caution to the amount of £10,000 for their intromissions from eight substantial business men, mainly in the East of Scotland.

This appearance of a chartered bank in Glasgow calls here for some detail, even if it were only to show how comically the possibilities of the intrusion from the east were underestimated. It was little imagined that in less than half a century this Glasgow branch would be doing more business than any other individual office in Scotland, or out of London.

Banking for David Dale, even at this early stage of his wonderful career, must have been a leisure-hour recreation, like the game of golf

David Dale
First Agent of the Bank in Glasgow 1783-1806
from a photogravure by T & R Annan & Sons, Glasgow
from the original Tassie dated 1792

## The Royal Bank of Scotland

which almost certainly he never indulged in. Certainly not wholly upon the affairs of the Royal Bank branch "office" opened in Hopkin's Land, east side of the High Street, five doors from the Glasgow Cross, were his interests concentrated. Its rental to the Bank was £2 : 10s. per annum; "but-and-ben" with it was his own tiny draper's shop.

Dale had, in his youth, been a herdboy in Stewarton, Ayrshire, and an apprentice weaver in Paisley. " At the time the bank employed him he was ", says Doctor John Buchanan in his racy *Banking in Glasgow during the Olden Time*, " a linen draper on his own account." He was much more than that, as might be obvious from the fact that he had just entered into occupancy of a house which Robert Adam had designed for him, and which he had built for himself in Charlotte Street near Glasgow Green at a cost of £6000—conspicuously one of the finest mansion-houses in Glasgow. He was then aged forty-one.

He had " carried a pack " as a pedlar through the country for a time, gone into a more dignified drapery business with a moneyed partner in 1763, developed the importation of linen from Holland, and did so well that he had, in this year 1783, got rid of this partner, and was embarked on great schemes of making up for the wane in the linen trade by exploiting the spinning-jenny.

## The History of

Many portentous things in which Dale had a hand were to start that year in the West of Scotland, besides the branch of the Royal Bank. With the help of Richard Arkwright, his English partner, he acquired from Lord Justice-Clerk Macqueen of Braxfield, a director of the Royal, and known to the reader of fiction as " Weir of Hermiston ", a site for a cotton mill on the Clyde near Corra Linn Falls in the Upper Ward of Lanarkshire. This time Dale was the partner with the money; Arkwright's contribution to the enterprise was his waterframe spinning-machine, which very quickly was to make " New Lanark " the largest mill of its kind in Britain. Dale's brains and capital were behind many other cotton-spinning enterprises in the country, and 1783 was his busy year. It saw the start of his Barrowfield Turkey-red works, first in the kingdom, and himself taking an active part in forming the Glasgow Chamber of Commerce, of which he was one of the first directors; he was also a member of the Glasgow Town Council.

He helped to found the earliest auxiliary of the Bible Society, and acted as its treasurer; took much interest in visiting prisoners, and gave money away (as it was said) " by sho'ls fu' " to help those less well-off than himself, and his time was as liberally devoted to philanthropy as his purse. At his death, £5683 of Royal Bank Stock figured in the inventory

## The Royal Bank of Scotland

of his estate. He was computed to have given away during his lifetime more than £50,000 in charity. Shortly after his appointment as their Glasgow agent, a party of the Royal Bank directors drove to Glasgow and were entertained in his house in Charlotte Street. Unfortunately the Clyde was in spate; the kitchen was flooded, and cooking was impossible. Dale was not to be daunted by a mishap of this kind; he promptly requisitioned the kitchens of some neighbours, and engaged a " sea-faring man " to wade down to the flooded cellar with Miss Caroline Dale (the future Mrs. Robert Owen) on his back to select the best vintages in the bins.

The tiny shop in Hopkin's Land became the source of extraordinary business for the Royal Bank. The merchants of Glasgow crowded to it. The first cash credits it gave were to half-a-dozen flourishing merchants, manufacturers, tobacconists, calico - printers, etc., who in one day got credits between them for £3200. They were modest in their demands to start with; in succeeding years the credits conferred through the Glasgow branch were generally on a much larger scale, and for the accommodation of the biggest businesses in the city. Scott Moncrieff and Dale were resorted to by men whose names are prominent in the commercial history of " the Second City in the Empire "; the business there began to have supremacy in the minutes of the directors in Edinburgh.

In April 1804 Scott Moncrieff and Dale's bond of £10,000 was discharged and delivered to them, the Court in its minutes expressing the " fullest conviction " that in every respect they had conducted the business entrusted to them " with ability as well as the strictest integrity ", although there had been considerable losses which " in such a magnitude of business are unavoidable ".

Whatever they may have lost on the swings they had doubtless made up for on the roundabouts. Their accounts in succeeding years show no evidence of the slightest hesitancy on the part of the Edinburgh Board to give growing Glasgow businesses command of capital to any reasonable extent. When David Dale died in March 1806, he left to his successor, Mr. John More—elected sole agent six months later—an inheritance of incalculable goodwill to the Royal and a host of valuable connections.

How unmistakably the industrial and commercial developments in Scotland were concentrating in the West, and notably on the Clyde, was obvious throughout the 'eighties. " Wheresoever the carcase is, there will the eagles be gathered together." There were four local joint-stock trader-banking companies with their headquarters in the city—the Ship Bank, the Glasgow Arms Bank, the Thistle Bank,

# The Royal Bank of Scotland

and the Merchant Banking Company, and at least half-a-dozen like concerns, originated from Stirling, Greenock, Falkirk, Paisley, Dundee, Leith, and Renfrewshire, were represented there by active agents. All of them issued notes; there was no law to prevent it, and as they took no deposits it was on the circulation of their notes their profits depended; their partnerships were small, their paper issues were looked askance on by the Edinburgh banks, though notes of the Ship and Merchant Banking Companies were exchanged on the most amiable terms. The constitution and management of the four native Glasgow banks, as a matter of fact, gave no occasion for criticism; within the limits of their powers they served the city well, and carried on for periods covering from twenty-four to eighty-six years.

In June 1788 the Royal got a fifth Charter, and doubled its capital, now raised to £600,000. The bonus shares to the value of £38,652, distributed five years before, were far from exhausting the undivided profits at the time, and the residue left was rapidly being augmented. Furthermore, the investments of the Bank in gilt-edged English securities, when they stood at a low war-time level, had continued to prove exceedingly profitable, and the Bank Stock held by the Cashier for behoof of the Bank was still considerably undervalued in the books. There were no doubt many

The History of

proprietors anticipating a bonus distribution equal to that of 1784, but the Board of Directors exercised more caution, and of the £300,000 new capital, took only £100,000 from the undivided profits, and invited the proprietors to subscribe the other £200,000. They could either pay it all at once or by instalments, or by allowing their dividends to accumulate. Very soon after, the Bank was significantly selling its Bank of England Stock in reasonably sized blocks at frequent intervals.

Till 1792, an era of national peace subsequent to the Treaty of Paris gave industry, commerce, and banking in Scotland an enormous impulse; Royal Bank new stock was steady at £240. That halcyon period of nine years closed with the outbreak of the French Revolution, followed by long and sanguinary wars. There was an instant check to mercantile credit all over the kingdom. Over twenty bankers failed in England alone. The first crisis led to the downfall of Murdoch Robertson and Company (the Glasgow Arms Bank) and the Mercantile Bank of Glasgow. In both cases the whole liabilities were ultimately paid in full, without interest. In Edinburgh, the house of Bertram, Gardner and Company also came down—the only casualty in the city; its estates were liquidated at 17s. 6d. in the £. All the country banks of Scotland weathered the storm.

Britain was now launched on a Continental

## The Royal Bank of Scotland

warfare that was to go on for twenty-two years, but her manifest superiority on the high seas, whence she swept the French marine, to the relief of commerce, inspired a certain confidence at home, and trade was never better during a time of war. Few echoes of international tumult appear in the Royal's chronicles. The patriotic spirit of the board was shown by their subscribing £100,000 to the Government scheme for raising one year's victualling supplies by voluntary subscription in 1796.

A second crisis came in 1797, when the alarm of invasion and the scarcity of gold caused another sharp but shorter run on the banks, during which the Bank of England itself seemed on the point of stopping payment. So meagre was its supply of bullion that the Chancellor of the Exchequer procured an order of Privy Council prohibiting it from making any more issue of specie for its notes. A panic ensued, mainly due to the public hoarding of coin; nearly a hundred country banks in England became bankrupt. For the first time the Bank of England conceded the issue of a £5 note, its paper money hitherto having been of larger denominations; but this gave no conspicuous measure of relief.

On 1st March (1797) news of the Bank of England's position came to Edinburgh from Thomas Coutts and Company, London. Sir William Forbes gives us a graphic account of that agitated morning, when, going into his place of business in the Parliament Close, he found it crowded with excited customers demanding gold for his Company's notes. There followed a consultation there and then with the Cashier and Deputy Governor of the Royal Bank, the Treasurer of the Bank of Scotland, and Mr. Hog, the Manager of the British Linen Company. It was agreed to follow the example of the Bank of England and suspend all payments in specie, a decision which created confusion and uproar all over the country. Tradesmen could not pay wages and small purchases could not be made.

"The action of the Scotch bankers in suspending payment in specie was, of course, illegal," cheerfully admits Mr. Andrew Kerr in his *History*; "and any creditor could have prosecuted his claims for payment in legal tender. The authority granted, or rather the order given, to the Bank of England did not extend to other bankers." Fortunately nobody put this to the test in the law courts.

The Bank of England subsequently took another step and issued a £1 and £2 note, which it had been wiser to grant at the very beginning of the trouble. In Scotland even the £1 note was a burden like the grasshopper of Scripture, and the public resumed their old-time habit of tearing it into halves and quarters as required; but later, the Scottish banks were

## The Royal Bank of Scotland

temporarily authorised to issue 5s. notes, which they did.

Very quickly the Scottish public was accepting the notes of its banks in an inconvertible form as readily as if they were specie; they never went under par, whereas the Bank of England's paper lost nearly a third of its purchasing power during the suspension of specie payments, which Parliament prolonged till 1821. Let us not make too much of this difference, however; it was the solid phalanxes of Bank of England notes on the Continent, good anywhere for gold, that always scared Napoleon. With our enormous expenditure on the Army and Navy abroad, and subventions (paid in gold and notes) to Continental Powers, the foreign exchanges were continuously against London. The difference in exchange could not be paid by the Bank of England in specie; it had to pay it in notes, which the Continent would not accept at full gold value. " Thus exchanges fell and continued to fall beyond the limits of the lower bullion point by a sum which generally equalled the difference between the British mint price of gold, £3 : 17 : 10$\frac{1}{2}$ per ounce, and the market price of the day. In 1813 the latter rose to £5 : 10s. per ounce in London."

With commendable prudence the principal banks in Scotland restricted their paper issue to the strict commercial wants of the time.

## CHAPTER XII

#### THE PRIVATE BANKS

WHEN the century ended, there were still in store for Britain fifteen dreary years of Continental war—" the malady of Princes " as Erasmus called it, but we passed that chronological milestone as pioneers of a new industrial age, at the head of the manufacturing world. Our capital resources magically grew with the exploitation of new mechanical developments discovered by ourselves. This continuous warfare closed many avenues of commerce, but we opened others, and somehow the money for this was always forthcoming. So far as Scotland was concerned, bank vaults seemed inexhaustible.

It has been impossible here to recount all the changes in directorate which occurred in the previous century; they will be found in an Appendix. The official personnel of the Bank, though remarkable for the years most of its individuals held tenure of office, suffered, of course, the changes that come upon all human associations in a world of time. Let it suffice

## The Royal Bank of Scotland

that the century opened with the Duke of Buccleuch and Queensberry as Governor, Mr. Gilbert Innes of Stow as Deputy Governor, Mr. William Simpson as Cashier, Mr. John Macintosh as Accountant, Mr. James Innes as Secretary, and Mr. William Mitchell as his assistant. There were four tellers—Alexander Simpson, George Mitchell, James Heggie, and Andrew Bogle. The staff in all comprised thirteen persons. The salary list had been rising for thirty years as the cost of living increased; at Christmas 1805, increases were given that brought it in the aggregate up to £2480. Mr. Innes did not long enjoy his increased emoluments; he died in the following year, and Mr. George Mitchell succeeded to his post and its £220 salary.

In the same year died Mr. David Dale, the Glasgow agent, to be succeeded by Mr. John More. The tiny shop in Hopkin's Land had long since been ludicrously out of keeping with the great business there transacted; Mr. More took up his quarters in the manager's house of new bank premises acquired in St. Andrew's Square, then in its heyday as a resort of Glasgow's gentility and big business. So influential was the Royal Bank's first branch that it was credited with securing the removal of the city's Post Office from Princes Street to its immediate neighbourhood in the Square.

"Liveried Lackeys and gay Equipages lent

life and animation to the Square," says the chronicler McUre; "the Royal Bank had its office and Manager's Dwelling House in the two Tenements in the South-east Corner of the Square; and the two large square Freestones on which were placed the Sentry-Boxes for the Soldiers, who, with loaded Musket and Bayonet, guarded the Treasure within, still remain inserted in the Pavement."

We can hardly imagine the sentries were a normal feature of the Bank; they must have been observed by the historian only on some riotous occasion in the city.

Mr. More, the new agent, was a man of wealth, and, while having an official house " above the shop " in old urban Scottish fashion, he had a country house of much more pretensions at Wellshot, with extensive grounds, gardens, vineries, and a bowling-green, all of which had cost him £17,000. The style of his housekeeping may be estimated from the fact that he possessed 1200 ounces of silver plate. Here Mr. More spent his week-ends; every Saturday a splendid carriage, with a black servant on the rumble, drove up to the Bank to take him to his rural retreat.

In June 1808 Mr. Simpson, in supreme control at Edinburgh, died at Parsons Green, and the directors recorded with regret " the loss of an invaluable officer, who has for thirty years executed the office of Cashier faithfully

# The Royal Bank of Scotland

to the Bank, honourably to himself and in the most satisfactory manner to the Directors and the public at large ". Mr. George Mitchell became his successor as first Cashier, with a salary of £400, the tenancy of the house above the Bank, and £80 per annum for coal and candle. His brother William was made second Cashier, with £350, and Mr. Andrew Bogle became Secretary.

In June 1811 Duncan Macfarlane, by reason of age and infirmity, resigned his post as porter to the Bank, and in consideration of his long and faithful services was given a pension of £40 per annum from " the fund for the behoof of the decayed and superannuated officers of the Bank ".

Mr. John Macintosh resigned the Accountancy in March 1815, after more than fifty years' service. He was given a year's salary of £230 and superannuation of £120 for life, but this was not to be regarded as a precedent. Mr. Charles More declined to accept the post of Accountant, and Mr. John Stirling was appointed.

A final obituary finishes an unusual period of mortality in the Royal Bank. Mr. George Mitchell, first Cashier, died in October 1816, and was succeeded by his brother William.

In the latter years of the eighteenth century, both Old Bank and New Bank had increased their respective capitals to £1,000,000. The

## The History of

Royal's Charter for this augmentation was secured in 1793. New joint-stock companies to the number of sixteen came into being in the early years of the new century, with note issues, nearly all of them with high-sounding names suggesting vaults and reserves unlimited, but with the most trivial of resources behind them and a handful of inconspicuous shareholders. They hoped for rich gleanings from fields fertilised and reaped by Edinburgh, but their careers were brief; the country had not yet forgotten Douglas Heron and Company, and the Edinburgh banks refused to traffic in those new country notes.

Stamp duties were for the first time directly levied on Scottish bank-notes—to begin with, a twopenny stamp had to be impressed on all £1 notes; five years later it was raised to threepence; the climax was reached in 1815, when the costs of the war demanded a stamp duty of fivepence.

There was a second spate of new Scots banks in 1809–10, when the Dundee Union Bank, the Glasgow Banking Company, and the East Lothian Bank started. The latter did considerable business in Haddingtonshire till 1822, when its manager, William Borthwick, absconded with nearly £30,000 of the Company's notes, most of which he put in circulation. The amazing Borthwick, when he suspected some of his directors might find out

## The Royal Bank of Scotland

how things were shaping, had actually devised a scheme for clapping those gentlemen into well-ventilated empty wine-puncheons, and shipping them from Dundee to Dantzig. The creditors of the firm were paid in full.

By far the most important newcomer appeared in 1810—the Commercial Banking Company of Scotland, a bold national designation which at the time seemed unwarrantable in a concern as yet without a Charter, but whose use was speedily vindicated by the really national scope on which it entered into business, and the national support accorded to it. Even a loyal Royal Bank historian like Mr. Kerr admits that the Commercial Banking Company (now the Commercial Bank of Scotland) really " met a long-felt want ".

With this for a summary introduction, explanatory, in a measure, of the situation of Scottish banking in the first two decades of the nineteenth century, it becomes necessary to get closer down to the chronicles of the Royal, and see how contemporary affairs presented themselves to the directors of the great corporation, and what history-making men and events march through the pages of dusty old tomes that are treasured in St. Andrew Square.

It was not, let us repeat, with such a heterogeneous clientele as patronises our banks to-day that the chartered banks of Edinburgh did business at that time. They were fastidious, and chose their customers, who in almost every case were obviously possessed of capital to a more or less degree, of known financial experience, and not to be confounded with the *hoi polloi* having no tangible stake in the country or the community. A certain amount of business was of course done with the general public, but the general public, as a rule, confined its business to petty transactions of deposits and discounts with the private bankers. The private bankers, in their turn, resorted to the chartered banks, which had all the dignity of the present-day Bank of England, being Banks of Banking, the authorised and authentic source from which the country's coffers in the last resort must be replenished.

It admirably suited the private banker to make his profits as a middleman out of the difference between what he paid to his bank for accommodation and what he charged his customers. On the other hand, the chartered bank was glad to be relieved of a bewildering multiplicity of little higgling transactions by entrusting generous supplies of its notes to the private bankers; it not only saved trouble, but it greatly helped the circulation.

In not a few instances, so valuable was the auxiliary service of the private bankers that some of them were represented on the boards of the chartered banks, and, according to Mr. Kerr, " to a large extent controlled the pro-

## The Royal Bank of Scotland

ceedings of the latter ". The charge was made by many of the less influential business firms of Edinburgh that the private banker at board meetings of a chartered bank would often refuse approval of paper which he would gladly discount in his own office. No clause in the constitution of the new Commercial Bank was more popular or contributory to its quick success than that which stipulated that no private banker could sit on its board.

The Commercial started—as yet without a charter—with the large nominal capital of £3,000,000, of which £450,000 was paid up; and it made branches a prominent feature of its policy. In less than ten years it had fourteen country branches as compared with the seventeen of the British Linen Company's, thirteen of the Bank of Scotland, and the Royal's single branch in Glasgow. By 1826 the Commercial had opened thirty-one new offices, and was everywhere diverting business from the private banking firms, whose doom was sealed.

The "New Athens" was well under way in July 1815; the Bank of Scotland, the Royal, the British Linen Company, Messrs. Ramsays, Bonars and Company, and Sir William Forbes and Company between them gave a loan of £37,000 to the Commissioners of the Calton Road and Bridge.

At this period the Royal had £100,000

lying in the Bank of England, and thought first of putting it into Consols, but changed its mind, and acquired £50,000 of 3 per cent reduced Annuities and £50,000 of Exchequer Bills.

The relationship which existed between the chartered banks and the Edinburgh private bankers gets considerable illumination from the minute of a Board meeting of 21st February 1816, and has direct connection with such investments in Government stock as have just been recorded. Two of the partners of Ramsays, Bonars and Company were directors of the Royal and important customers. Mr. James Ferrier, one of the ordinary directors of the Royal, at this meeting stated that he had received information, from a quarter so respectable that he could not entertain any doubt of its correctness, that the house of Ramsays, Bonars and Company had set on foot a canvass among the proprietors, the object of which was to influence the approaching election of directors and in particular to remove from their situations certain gentlemen now on the direction of the Bank and to get others appointed, a step which might very materially affect the interest of the Bank.

On the following day a committee considered this matter, and reported that the attempt of Messrs. Ramsays, Bonars and Company to influence the approaching election of directors took its rise from an incident of the

## The Royal Bank of Scotland

preceding June. At that time some of the directors of the Bank had made inquiry as to a balance of more than £130,000 which stood against the firm in the Bank books. By what authority were such large sums advanced? " It was answered and not contradicted by two of the Partners present (Ramsay and Bonar) that they were taken without any authority whatever." Thereupon had Mr. Ferrier moved to call back monies which individual stockholders in the Bank had been allowed to draw without the authority of the directors and contrary to the rules of the Bank. Mr. Ferrier's motion had been approved of, yet the sums so taken out were never wholly replaced until the 20th November following.

It is desirable to throw some more light upon an incident which, thus briefly recorded in the minutes, suggests a very perfunctory way of doing business. Ramsays, Bonars and Company had, from the previous century, been represented on the Board of the Royal Bank, and in that capacity indulged themselves as a private firm with frequent and large advances. There was never any question as to the sufficiency of their securities, but the casual manner in which they availed themselves of credits was, as Mr. Ferrier's intervention shows, becoming objectionable to their fellow-directors.

Had the private bankers thus accommodated by great and frequent credits been using them exclusively for conventional banking, there would probably have been little criticism, but it was become notorious that the majority of them carried on mercantile and stock-jobbing transactions which, though then considered fair trade, were really outside the sphere of a banker. A great proportion of their credits at this time was used by them in speculating in the Government funds, which were at a very low price, but certain to rise in value with a declaration of peace — a prospect which the chartered banks themselves were making the most of. The advent of the Commercial Bank, and the public light its promoters threw on this too amiable understanding between the old joint-stock banks and the private bankers on their boards, compelled a change of policy, which dated from the Ramsay incident.

The defence of Ramsays, Bonars and Company, when all this came out, has what we would regard to-day as an incredible *naïveté*. "The current account of our house with the Royal Bank", they said grandiloquently, "rests on much stronger grounds than the form of applying for a credit, and obtaining it at any recent date from a board of directors. It rests on the best understanding and usage of near half a century, grounded on the close connection of having been of the greatest national advantage to each other for the last thirty-four years.... Mr. Ramsay, the senior

## The Royal Bank of Scotland

partner of our house . . . devoted his whole attention to the concerns of the Royal Bank, and placed it in a train of management that has produced greater prosperity than, we believe, ever attended any chartered company in the same period (1781–1807)—not excepting even the Bank of England—in proportion to their respective capitals."

Mr. Ferrier was apparently to become a watch-dog of the Board, and obviously had a considerable following among his fellow-directors. Five months after discomfiting Ramsays, Bonars, he protested against a credit of £10,000 being given to the Lord Provost and Magistrates of Edinburgh for their wet docks at Leith on the security of dock dues and the Corporation. So far as the docks were concerned, the directors, fifteen years before, had loaned £10,000 of the Bank's money, which had been thrown " into the sea " with little prospect of its ever being recovered. He was for more satisfactory securities than any yet offered by the Corporation. The loan was granted, however. It was on the strict understanding that it was to be repaid in twelve months. Seven months later the Board seemed to have been infected by Mr. Ferrier's doubts, and wrote to the Lord Provost that " any failure on the part of the city to fulfil its promise would compel them to adopt every legal means for the recovery of the debt and exclude the

Bank on any future occasion from giving the smallest accommodation to the city on any pretence whatever ".

Mr. Innes the Secretary was, in November 1816, sent to London on a delicate mission. Messrs. Pole, Thornton and Company, who were the Bank's agents there, and held for the Bank £210,000 of Exchequer Bonds, were out of favour; it was the Secretary's business to take possession of those bonds.

Although there were grave losses in Glasgow on account of the gentleman with the negro on his rumble, the year wound up well, with a proposed dividend for the preceding six months of $4\frac{3}{4}$ per cent, being an increase of $1\frac{1}{2}$ per cent on the previous half-year. As this was somewhat short of what optimistic proprietors had been expecting, the latter were consulted. The average profits for three years might warrant an increase of 2 per cent on the dividend, but caution suggested 1 per cent with a bonus of £100,000 to be taken from the fund which was set apart for increasing dividends, and now amounted to about £309,000. The proprietors chose 2 per cent without the bonus.

At the same time Mr. John Thomson, who had been the Bank of Scotland's agent in Aberdeen, became agent for the Royal in Glasgow, where he was formally " inducted " on 20th February 1817 by the Deputy Governor and Mr. Bonar, who carried with

## The Royal Bank of Scotland

them in the coach from Edinburgh the sum of £30,000. There was for a long time, it has been stated, a tacit agreement that while the Royal left all the rest of Scotland to the Bank of Scotland as sphere of its branch activities, the Bank of Scotland should not compete with the Royal's Glasgow branch. If such understanding there was, it had been abandoned in 1804, when the Old Bank opened a Glasgow branch.

Not till 1817 (by which time Bonaparte the "ogre" was in St. Helena) was it apparently thought essential to have a periodical inspection of books and cash at the Glasgow branch, as a result, no doubt, of the irregularities discovered the previous year. The proposal to introduce this procedure was made by Sir William Rae, Lord Advocate, one of the Royal's new directors, and two directors in rotation made a surprise visitation every two months. Balances were struck from the books against each individual teller, and his notes and cash were counted. The first inspection disclosed that the cash of two of the tellers was deficient £1 : 18 : 3 and 4s. 4d. respectively, and that of the two other tellers was in excess by £2 : 14 : 4 and £2 : 19s. respectively.

On one of those inspectorial visits, two directors, Messrs. Duncan and Jardine, were approached by Mr. William Stirling, of the firm of William Stirling and Sons, with a suggestion that the Royal might find his house in Queen Street more central and more dignified for its branch business.

At an earlier period Queen Street had been known as the Cow Loan, being the common thoroughfare between the west end of Old Glasgow and the north-west district where the burghers grazed their cows.

When this squalid area of the town was rescued from its primitive rurality and feued and built on, one of the greatest Virginia merchants, William Cunningham of Lainshaw, who had made a huge fortune, took off three plots and, on the ground thus acquired, built, in 1778, one of the most imposing mansions in the West of Scotland at a cost of £10,000. Stirling of Cordale had bought the house and garden from Lainshaw in 1789.

Having examined the premises and got the advice of Bank stockholders in Glasgow, the directors met Mr. Stirling and offered £12,000 for the property, telling him they would give him two hours to consider it. "That gentleman, however, declined to avail himself of the time so allowed, and, in a manner certainly far from courteous, promptly rejected the offer so made." On the evening of the same day, however, he accepted the terms offered, and soon thereafter there was a "flitting" from St. Andrew's Square to what were now the most imposing bank premises in Scotland.

## The Royal Bank of Scotland

There was only a vague idea on the part of the directors in Edinburgh as to the character of the bill-discounting that went on at their Glasgow branch, and a committee was appointed at the end of 1818 to go there and investigate.

"Before this examination of the Bills," they reported, "the Committee must acknowledge that they were in the belief that a very large proportion of the bills discounted at Glasgow were accommodation bills granted by one friend or one neighbour to another without value and to be employed in Speculations, and there is no doubt that a part of the bills now under discount are truly of that description and that such things will often be done in future. The Committee however are now satisfied that it is only a very small proportion of the bills discounted by the Royal Bank that are of that nature, and that the great mass consists of bills granted in the course of trade for value actually received.

"The West India Merchant builds a ship for that trade and purchases goods for that market; he makes insurances in both, he grants bills to the Shipbuilder and to the Manufacturer who endorse them to the wood merchant and the importer of cotton, and they discount them to raise money, and purchase fresh cargoes of Timber and Cotton.

"In this way extensive West India trade

must require a great deal of money to carry it on, and Banks seem to be safe in furnishing it to them. They get the Security in this case of the general Merchant, of the wood Merchant and of the Shipbuilder, in the other case the Security of the General Merchant, of the Manufacturer and of the Cotton Merchant—at least three respectable persons for each advance. The Banks also have the assistance of intelligent agents, themselves interested to a certain extent in the sufficiency of the Security, so that it is difficult to employ money for a short period more profitably, and securely than in such discounts.

"When the Ship returns from the West Indies, the Merchant, to enable him to take up the bills granted for her outfit must sell the Cotton, the Sugar, the Rum, the Coffee, the Mahogany, and other India produce, each of these articles probably to one or more different persons, from each of whom he obtains bills. These bills or part of them are offered for discount, and it is thought that they are entitled to Credit at the Bank if the Situation of the cash there admits of discount at the time.

"When the weekly list of bills discounted at Glasgow is looked at, one is apt to be surprised at the large amount annexed to particular names, but the surprise vanishes when the particulars of the debt are examined and the great number of names of respectable persons

## The Royal Bank of Scotland

seen who are the true debtors, and that the person or Company whose name is on the weekly List is in a manner only guarantee for the true Debtors.

"The bills so discounted, besides the usual profit, must be of great use to the Bank in circulating the small notes of the Company, if care is taken to supply the Glasgow Branch with small notes, as to which there has been some neglect in times past.

"The Committee are aware that this dissertation may be thrown away upon the other Directors, who may have had no opportunities of becoming acquainted with all that has been said and the advantage of being able to act accordingly, but as the Committee must acknowledge that much of it was new to them till the present occasion, they thought it right to speak it out for the benefit of such of the Directors as have like themselves been in the dark, if there be any such."

The warrant of a seventh Charter got in 1804 had authorised an increase of capital to a million and a half. In Christmas 1817 the capital was so increased without any call being made on the proprietors. They had reserve funds of £454,076 in their "Fund Set Apart for an Increase of Dividend"; £125,000 worth of Bank of England Stock standing in their books at £131,438 was brought up to its real current value, which permitted other

## The History of

£118,541 to be added to the said fund, bringing it up to £572,618, from which the £500,000 of increased capital could be taken.

Again the Edinburgh premises of the Royal's headquarters were becoming inadequate for its ever-increasing business, and a change became imperative in 1819. St. Andrew Square in the New Town seemed the most desirable location; negotiations were opened with the owners of two contiguous houses there—one of them an hotel, and the other the domicile of Doctor Monro, the famous anatomist. The properties were bought for £8400 and £6500 respectively, and plans for their adaptation to banking business were prepared by Mr. Archibald Elliot, architect. On 30th May 1821 the new premises were opened.

An unusual note is struck by the record that now gold was too plentiful; the Bank of Scotland and the British Linen were offered the Royal's surplus and refused to have it, so £10,000 of guineas were forwarded by sea to Pole, Thornton and Company in London.

In the West of Scotland began the excursions and alarms of the " Radical Rising "; already the Clyde was notorious for its " red men ". In consequence of reports of mobbing in Glasgow " by seditious persons " in December 1819, the Cashier, Mr. Stirling, the Accountant, and two directors, Messrs. Bruce and Ferrier, proceeded to the western city, and, reaching

## The Royal Bank of Scotland

it on the evening of the 11th, "found all concerned most joyful at their appearance". Mr. Thomson had been that day under the greatest anxiety for the safety of the Bank's moveable property, which he felt must be sent to Edinburgh.

Discounted bills, with the exception of those falling due on or before the 20th current, cash to the amount of £56,100, and all vouchers for current accounts were packed up and sent to Edinburgh in two post-chaises the following morning, a trip which took seven hours.

The authorities had put patrols on all the different roads leading into Glasgow, not only for the protection of travellers, but to procure speedy and accurate intelligence of any seditious concentration of the radicals; as the expense of this was to be defrayed by voluntary subscription, the Royal directors, having the previous day been convoyed by patrols between Airdrie and Glasgow, subscribed £100.

For more than a week a captain's guard of the Glasgow Sharpshooters was quartered in the Bank premises, with triple sentries at the gates, while vedettes moved briskly up and down Queen Street and Ingram Street. In Mackenzie's *Reminiscences of Glasgow* the narrator says: "The Royal Bank,—then in the old beautiful House once the Property of Mr. Cunningham of Lainshaw, and afterwards of John Stirling, Esq., of Cordale, in Queen Street, forming now the Site of The Royal Exchange, was carefully Barricaded all around, including its spacious Gardens, now covered over with handsome Shops and Counting-Houses; and the Bank was thus Barricaded, because the Interior of it contained much of the valuable Plate, and much of the Treasure of the City; in fact, the Royal Bank might then be represented to be as The Mint or The Tower of Glasgow. The whole of Captain Smith's Company of Sharpshooters, with 20 Rounds of Ball-Cartridges in their Cartouches, were drawn up within it; and Ladies and Gentlemen of the City were actually seen Sobbing, and Crying, and Wringing their Hands, and rushing to the Bank to take Farewell, through the Gape of its Iron Pillars, of some of its devoted Inmates, ere they might be finally Slaughtered. We positively saw one of the venerable Magistrates of the City, with the tears trickling down his cheeks, coming and bidding Farewell to his eldest Son, forming one of the front rank of those armed Sharpshooters."

Upon Sir William Rae, one of the Bank directors, fell, as Lord Advocate, the responsibility of dealing with a state of affairs which came within measurable distance of civil war, and he handled the situation with promptitude, courage, and success. Sixty thousand malcontents were reported to be on the move against the city from its surrounding shires on

# The Royal Bank of Scotland

5th April; to meet them 5000 troops were drawn up in the streets, and the incursion was checked by a cavalry charge. The worst that happened was a skirmish between rioters and yeomanry at Bonnybridge, when a few lives were lost. Twenty-four of the rioters were sentenced to death, but only three were executed, to vindicate the law and *décourager les autres*.

In December of this year Mr. Thomson made the startling suggestion to the directors that the Royal was over-capitalised.

The Memorandum of his proposals is preserved, and states that " Mr. Thomson thinks the present Capital too large and too difficult to manage so as to increase the percentage of Profit, and therefore that any measure having the effect to lessen the Capital and the amount of dividends is likely to make the concern more advantageous for the Proprietors.

" He also thinks that were a Bonus of £20 per cent given to the Proprietors, two great ends would be gained, a very handsome profit realised, and an excellent opportunity afforded for reducing the Dividend to six per cent."

Remark by Mr. Charles Selkrig, one of the directors, relative to the afore - mentioned Memorandum—

" It is very true in the present State of the trade, Agriculture, and Manufactures of the country it is not easy to employ so large a

## The History of

Capital as that of the Royal Bank so profitably as might be wished. But to anyone who takes but a short retrospect of the Bank, it must appear obvious that notwithstanding the depression that has formed so general a subject of complaint, the affairs of the Bank for some years past have not by any means been unprosperous.

"About five years ago the Capital of the Bank was a Million, and the annual dividend was at the rate of 8 per cent or £80,000 a year. Since that time half a million has been added to the Capital out of the reserve profits without calling on the Proprietors to advance a shilling. The Capital is now therefore a Million and a half and the Annual Dividend is at the rate of 7 per cent, amounting to the sum of £105,000 a year, hence the annual income of the proprietors is better by £25,000 a year than it was five years ago. This however is no more than the nominal advance of income that has accrued to the Proprietors. The real advance is very considerably greater, as must appear obvious to anyone who compares the State of the Currency now with what it was some years ago, and takes into account its improved value. Mr. Thomson seems to think that it would be an advisable measure that the Bank should give a Bonus of £300,000 to the Proprietors, and then reduce the Dividend from 7 to 6 per cent: the annual sum payable in name of Dividend

## The Royal Bank of Scotland

would thus be reduced from £105,000 to £90,000 a year.

"For my part I have great doubts of the propriety of such a measure. But if the Proprietors choose to submit to such a sacrifice of income, they may, by selling so much of their Stock as brings them in £15,000 a year at the present market price of £175 per cent get the command of a much larger sum than £300,000 —for stock yielding £15,000 a year at 175 per cent would produce £375,000.

"Many of the Proprietors may not have any occasion for a Bonus, or any wish that so much of the Bank's funds be paid away in the manner proposed. There may be some, however, to whom a command of ready money may be very convenient, but if those who are in this predicament will just proceed to sell one-seventh part of the stock they hold they will get the command of a larger sum than their share of the proposed Bonus would amount to, and they will be left with precisely the same income as the adoption of that measure would leave to them."

The Memorandum was ordered to "lie on the table".

Five years after the Glasgow branch had removed to Queen Street, Mr. Thomson, the agent there, apparently had reason to anticipate sooner or later a considerable building development in its immediate propinquity. There was

## The Royal Bank of Scotland

a project for an Exchange and other public buildings which would improve the amenity, but there was also the risk of other edifices of a less desirable character rising in the neighbourhood. On his recommendation it was decided to buy the ground to the west of the Bank, part of which was in line with St. Vincent Street, but this was not done till November 1824, when the price was £7000.

Loans had, for nearly a century, been granted on securities which a banker would hesitate to accept to-day, but only of late had they been given on policies of life insurance. In 1823 the wisdom of this was questioned. "Although there appears little probability of any ultimate loss owing to the respectability of the parties," says a memorandum, "yet your Committee can by no means recommend any encouragement of future loans upon such securities.

"The objections to such securities are various. The Policies are vitiated if they shall have been obtained upon false information at the time they were effected; in the case of suicide, or falling in a duel, or by the hands of justice, and in all cases of parties going out of the limits of Europe, or dying upon the seas, except within certain limited bounds specified in the Policies."

## CHAPTER XIII

### FOUNDATIONS OF PROSPERITY

BEFORE the death of George III. in January 1820, it was obvious that though the war had left a doleful legacy of high prices and low wages for the unfortunate masses of the British people, financiers, merchants, manufacturers, and shippers were laying the foundations of great national prosperity. In 1821 the Bank of England resumed specie payments. Foreign loans for British capital became popular; there was a mania for investment in the funds of Spanish South American Colonies; bubble companies at home awoke a fever of speculation.

In August 1822, interest on deposits with the Royal was reduced from $3\frac{1}{2}$ and 4 per cent to 3 per cent. At the same time both Royal and Bank of Scotland reduced their terms for cash credit loans from 5 to 4 per cent.

On 1st February 1823 the Cashier set out from Edinburgh on the Carlisle mail coach for London to buy and sell Government stock; he was held up by a snowstorm at Selkirk, and reached his destination only on the night of the

## The History of

14th. Messrs. Pole and Company were still the Bank's chief London correspondents (having succeeded George Farquhar, Kinloch and Sons, bankers, in 1790); with Mr. Mitchell they negotiated the sale of £200,000 new 4 per cents at an average of 93 per cent, and, on the other hand, bought £140,000 of 3 per cent Consols at an average of 73 per cent, and £400,000 reduced 3 per cents, plus dividend, at an average of $74\frac{1}{2}$ per cent. While in London, Mr. Mitchell made arrangements with Messrs. Parkins and Heath, steel-plate engravers, for a new plate for the 20s. note.

There was more of its own cash in the Bank's possession than it could employ to advantage. Its reserved profits fund amounted to £285,125, so of this sum it now distributed among the proprietors £187,500 " as a bonus or extraordinary Dividend, affording them at the rate of $12\frac{1}{2}$ per cent on their Capital Stock ". This pleasant windfall accompanied the ordinary half-year's dividend of $2\frac{1}{2}$ per cent at Christmas.

Ten months later, interest on deposits was reduced to 2 per cent, with the idea of helping to relieve the Bank of a superfluous million, whose owners, as the minute considerately put it, might be induced to employ it " in pursuits tending to the National improvement ".

As its own picturesque contribution to national improvements, the Royal, anticipating by a century the age of really grand new bank

## The Royal Bank of Scotland

buildings, decided to expend some of its surplus resources on securing bigger and handsomer offices. Contiguous with the building it had removed to in St. Andrew Square, six years before, there was a much more imposing and commodious edifice known as Dundas House, built in 1772-74 for Sir Lawrence Dundas, Baronet, of Kerse in Stirlingshire, who at that time was Governor of the Royal. Dundas, who was of dignified pedigree, though the family fortunes had sadly declined at the period of his birth, had been Commissary-General to our army in Flanders in 1748–59, and was made a baronet in 1762. He bought from the Earl of Morton the Isles of Orkney and Zetland for 60,000 guineas, and in 1768 became Member of Parliament for Edinburgh, a seat to which he was elected three times. In his latter days he had at least three homes simultaneously—Kerse House, in whose neighbourhood he founded the flourishing port of Grangemouth on the Forth; Aske Hall, Richmond; and the house in St. Andrew Square, upon whose creation he had long deliberated.

There seems to be something about the Royal Bank that inspires in its least conspicuous officials an unappeasable filial curiosity as to its history. Nowhere can the career of Sir Lawrence Dundas and the story of Dundas House be more readily gathered than from an

## The History of

unpublished manuscript record by Mr. John Smith, formerly Head Messenger of the Royal Bank, now retired. One learns there of St. Andrew Square as in 1780 the most ambitious feature of Scotland's first attempt at town-planning, and an ocular demonstration of the elegance henceforth to be aimed at in urban domesticity.

The first building erected in the Square was apparently a house for Mr. Andrew Crosbie, a partner in the Douglas Heron Bank and the original of Counsellor Pleydell in *Guy Mannering*. Its striking Italianate design has been accredited to the famous Robert Adam, but not all reputed Adam houses owe anything to the architect of the Adelphi, and this, however charming, was not in the Adam convention. It was impressive enough, however, in the eyes of the Edinburgh Town Council, for them to decide it should be a standard for the houses henceforth to be put up on the ground which was their property. This was the building acquired by the Royal Bank in 1819; to-day it is the head office of the Scottish Union and National Insurance Company, its Ionic façade as attractive to an artist's eye as it was in the eighteenth century.

Between the Crosbie house and the one next built to the south of it on the same lines in 1781 for Mr. John Young, an architect (it

## The Royal Bank of Scotland

is now the British Linen Bank), was a still vacant area, bought by Sir Lawrence Dundas before Crosbie had come on the scene. It was a site on which, for a long period, had stood a cottage used as a rural refreshment-room by Old Town pedestrians on their summer rambles. Over its doorway was the sign-board " Peace and Plenty "; in its garden visitors sat out on good days to alfresco strawberries and cream. Sir Lawrence had in project the erection here of a mansion-house recessed from the building line of the other houses, which would provide for it sheltering wings, and there is little doubt that in consultation with those who were to be his neighbours, terms were arranged for securing a harmony of style.

When Sir Lawrence died in 1781, he was succeeded in the occupancy of the noble mansion-house he had raised in St. Andrew Square in 1772 by Lord Dundas, his son and heir, the ancestor of the Earl of Zetland. In 1794–95 the house with its grounds was bought by the Government for, it was said, £10,000, and converted into the principal Office of Excise for Scotland.

On 9th September 1824 the *Edinburgh Evening Courant* aroused some agitation in the breasts of the Royal Bank directors by publishing an advertisement that the Excise Office was for sale at an upset price of £28,000. They were alarmed lest it might be bought and used for purposes inimical to the amenity of their own premises. The upset price, however, kept off purchasers for nearly six months; in the following February it was advertised for sale by auction at an upset price of £26,000. There was obviously to be keen competition for it; the Royal Bank decided to bid as high as £35,300 for it, and got it for that figure. Considerable internal changes had to be made on the edifice to adapt it to its new purpose, and it was 24th April 1828 before the old Dundas House, unchanged in its external aspect, opened its doors for the first time as the Royal Bank of Scotland. It still remains the Bank's headquarters, retaining most of its ancient decorative features; the present directors' room was Sir Lawrence Dundas's drawing-room. It was in later years that the dome of the present spacious telling-room was added.

There stands in front of the Royal Bank an equestrian monument to John, Earl of Hopetoun, who served with high distinction in the West Indies, Holland, Egypt, the Walcheren Expedition, and the Peninsula, and died in 1823. The monument, whose inscription is said to be from the pen of Sir Walter Scott, was originally intended to be erected in Charlotte Square, but St. Andrew Square was ultimately preferred, and on the green sward fronting the classic façade of the Royal Bank, it com-

FRONT VIEW OF HEAD OFFICE, EDINBURGH
Formerly the Mansion-house of Sir Lawrence Dundas

## The Royal Bank of Scotland

memorates not only a great Scots soldier, but one who, at the time of his death, was Governor of the Bank.

The year 1825, when Dundas House was bought, saw four new banks of fortunate destiny started in Scotland — the Aberdeen Town and County Bank (now conjoined with the North of Scotland Bank), the Arbroath Banking Company (amalgamated with the Commercial in 1844), the Dundee Commercial Bank (second of the name), and the National Bank of Scotland, most ambitious of all, with a capital of £5,000,000, of which, however, only £500,000 was issued.

The speculative mania of the country reached its crisis at this time; the autumn blighted a host of delicate new joint-stock companies, and a few English country bankers suspended payment. Apprehension seized the nation, and there was panic. Early in December there were rumours in London that Pole, Thornton and Company were in difficulties — a serious matter for the Royal, which, like many other provincial and Scottish banks, was represented in London by that firm. The Bank of England came to the rescue with £300,000, but ten days later Pole, Thornton and Company stopped payment, and the financial and commercial world was staggered till the Bank of England again sent out its lifeboat, so to speak, and, giving assistance right and left to all who could produce fair security, averted complete disaster.

The Edinburgh banks seemed to experience no inconvenience, though Glasgow and the West of Scotland were somewhat shaken; but three Scots county banks succumbed, the most disastrously the Fife Banking Company, fourteen of whose shareholders had paid £5500 per share beyond the original amount by the time its affairs were finally settled in 1850. Mr. Ferrier and Mr. Stirling, the Accountant, went to London to recover from Pole, Thornton and Company all bills and other assets of the Bank in their possession, which they did without difficulty, the bills amounting to £304,234 and the cash to £6580. This terminated a long association. Down, Thornton and Free, bankers, had become the Royal's London agents on 16th August 1790. The name of the firm changed several times, and became Pole, Thornton, Free, Down and Scott in September 1813. Thornton was a shareholder in the Royal Bank. Henceforth the Royal's business affairs in London were to be in the hands of Coutts and Company in the Strand—also an old connection, for the Royal had opened an account with Coutts on 21st March 1785, when the "style" of the London firm was Thomas Coutts and Company, a designation changed about 1820.

Glasgow very quickly got over this panic;

## The Royal Bank of Scotland

by the end of the following year America was buying its wares as never before, and the city business men now definitely decided on opening an Exchange. Its merchants had now found a simple coffee-room at the Cross insufficient for their daily conventions. Three possible sites for a building were in view—one on the ground occupied by the Star Inn, in Ingram Street, one at the Trongate, and one on the property owned by the Royal Bank. The committee of the new Exchange, whose chairman was Mr. James Ewing of Strathleven, ultimately decided to deal with the Royal Bank, and bought the old Cunningham mansion premises in September 1827 for £14,000. The Bank regarded it as somewhat too good a bargain for the buyers, but other prudent considerations decided the sale. By its presence in the area, very soon to be surrounded on three sides by handsome new shops and offices, the Exchange would improve the amenity and value of what remained of the Royal's property to the west.

While Mr. David Hamilton, one of Glasgow's most distinguished architects, was proceeding with the designs for the new Exchange, he and Mr. Archibald Elliot, architect, London, son of the former architect of the Bank—Mr. Archibald Elliot of Edinburgh—were invited to submit plans for the new Royal Bank to be erected a few yards to the west of the Exchange.

Mr. Hamilton refused to compete; Elliot's plans proved thoroughly satisfactory, and in a remarkably short time the Bank staff was in occupation of what still remains the most impressive example of the Greco-Roman style in Glasgow.

Hamilton's treatment of the old Lainshaw house was to incorporate it in a stately new building with a grand classic portico.

As a consequence of the money crisis from which the country had just recovered, an Act was passed in February 1826 reviving the Act of 1777, which forbade the circulation of notes under £5 in England, and the same restriction was contemplated by Lord Liverpool's Government for Scotland and Ireland. Such a menace to the £1 note — the only paper currency familiar to the great masses of the Scottish people — roused the utmost indignation. Sir Walter Scott's influential pen came to the defence of Scottish banking in the " Malachi Malagrowther " letters; our Members of Parliament and our Press and a host of pamphleteers clamoured against uniformity with England in this limitation to our paper money, and a commission was given to committees of both Houses of Parliament to inquire into the utility of small notes in Scotland and Ireland.

Witnesses appeared for the Scottish chartered and private banks. Mr. Thomson of the branch in Glasgow, representing the Royal

PRINCIPAL OFFICE IN GLASGOW

## The Royal Bank of Scotland

Bank, incidentally declared that much more gold was brought to the country on account of Glasgow merchants than all the coin sent from London to Scotland on account of the banks. The committee, after full investigation, were convinced that it was best to leave the note issues of Scotland and Ireland on their old footing. Two years later the circulation in England of Scottish or Irish bank-notes under £5 was prohibited by Act of Parliament, though the gentry, merchants, manufacturers, and tradesmen of Cumberland and Westmoreland memorialised the Lords of the Treasury protesting. They pointed out that the greater part of their money transactions was negotiated in Scotch paper. "An Act of Parliament", they said, "limited the number of partners in our English banks to six at the utmost, while the absence of any such limitation in Scotland gave a degree of strength to the issuers of notes, and of confidence to the receivers of them, which several banks established in our counties have not been able to command.

"The natural consequence has been, that Scotch notes have formed the greater part of our circulating medium, a circumstance in which we have reason to rejoice, since, in the course of the last fifty years, with the solitary exception of the Falkirk bank, we have never sustained the slightest loss from our acceptance of Scotch paper; while in the same period

## The History of

the failures of banks in the north of England have been unfortunately numerous, and have occasioned the most ruinous losses to many who were little able to sustain them."

If the directors of the Royal Bank in 1827 celebrated its first centenary even so modestly as by a thanksgiving luncheon or dinner, the fact has escaped the chroniclers; the occasion seems to have passed wholly unobserved.

Mr. Thomson, the Glasgow agent, had evidently forceful qualities and initiative which impressed the directors almost as soon as he had taken up the appointment, and it was not without significance that he should have been chosen to represent them at the Parliamentary inquiry into small bank-note issues. At the beginning of 1828 it was decided that he should be transferred to the head office in Edinburgh as "joint-cashier" with Mr. Mitchell, and that Mr. Laurence Robertson, Perth, should succeed him in the post vacated. The fact that Mr. Thomson was to have a salary of £1200 a year, while Mr. Mitchell's was £840, created a delicate situation, which was amiably enough relieved by the latter's intimation that he was desirous of retiring on an allowance. He was, accordingly, granted a pension of £800, and Mr. Thomson took up his duties in the new premises in St. Andrew Square on 24th April.

The Earl of Dalhousie, an illustrious member

## The Royal Bank of Scotland

of that Ramsay family who had " not crawled through seven centuries of their country's history ", who had done so much to distinguish the British name in every quarter of the globe, and was an old school companion of Walter Scott's, was at this time Governor of the Royal. In October he wrote to the Governor of the Bank of England suggesting a change in the conditions upon which the Royal had a credit with the former of £170,000 at 4 per cent on whatever part of it might be borrowed. As security for this credit the London bank held £100,000 Bank of England Stock and £23,000 of 3 per cent Reduced Stock. As it happened, however, it had for years been holding, further, bills current for negotiation for a much larger sum than ever happened to be due on the account of the Royal Bank at any period.

Lord Dalhousie's suggestion was that after more than a century of the most agreeable business relations between the two Banks, the credit might well be continued without the necessity for those pledges vested in the name of the Bank of England, provided the Royal never operated on it except when its bills in London were double the amount that might be drawn out of the account.

The change was immediately agreed to by the Governor of the Bank of England.

Again it was decided that the capital should be increased—by half a million, bringing it up to £2,000,000. The new and eighth Charter warranting this augmentation was sealed on 22nd February 1830, and conveyed certain further powers, even more gratifying, perhaps, to the directors. When the Royal came into existence in 1727 there was hardly any commercial intercourse between England and Scotland, and so little was an extension of it regarded as likely, that the power of the Royal to sue and be sued was limited to the Scottish Courts. This new Charter extended the right of suit and defence to any of His Majesty's Courts in any part of his dominions, and further gave power to employ Royal Bank funds in purchasing or acquiring Government stocks or securities of any kind transferable at the Bank of England, and every kind of personal property whatsoever, in as full and ample manner as any body politic or corporate or individual whatever in any part of His Majesty's dominions.

As *douceur* for their zeal in securing those new privileges, the Lord Advocate was granted an honorarium of three hundred guineas, Mr. Thomson the Cashier, two hundred guineas, and Mr. Sym Wilson the Secretary, one hundred guineas. A sum of £100,000 of the new capital was taken from reserves; the remaining £400,000 was got by making a call on the proprietors. It was an old office tradition of the Royal that this increase of capital, though hardly justified on principles

# The Royal Bank of Scotland

of financial expediency, was dictated by an apprehension that the Government contemplated the abolition of bank-note issues and the substitution of a State issue, in which case a large capital might secure special privileges in the conduct of the new system.

## CHAPTER XIV

### EXTENSION OF BRANCHES

PRIOR to 1826 were premonitions in the directors' minutes of the financial straits in which Sir Walter Scott found himself through his unconventional association with his publishers. His prosperity during those years when he was magnificently transforming the cottage of "Clarty Hole" into the stately Abbotsford never had a sound commercial basis, despite the facility with which he could turn his imagination into gold; and he was never free from financial cares. Unhappily a partner in the business of James Ballantyne and Company, his printers, and later in that of the Constables, he was ruined when they crashed commercially in 1826. There is no more heroic incident in the life of any man of letters than Scott's subsequent effort to clear off his debts, which he did, though not in his lifetime. He was involved in Constable's failure to the amount of £117,000. Fifty-four years of age, and in a state of health which gave him no hope of surviving many years longer,

## The Royal Bank of Scotland

he set himself with unimaginable labour and endurance to paying off his creditors. In two years he had earned for them £40,000, and before his death in 1831 had created literary property which was posthumously to satisfy them all.

It is interesting to know that the longest reference to Scott in the archives of the Royal is a recognition of his dauntless sense of honour. To the directors, on 3rd November 1830, was read a letter from Sir William Forbes and Company and Messrs. Ramsays, Bonars and Company dated the 2nd of September, to the trustees for the creditors of Scott and Ballantyne and Company:

"Gentlemen," it said, "we request you to call a meeting of the creditors of Sir Walter Scott and of James Ballantyne and Company for the purpose of considering and determining on the following motion which we shall then propose and recommend to the adoption of the meeting, viz.:

"That Sir Walter Scott be requested to accept of his Furniture, Plate, Linens, Paintings, Library, and curiosities of every description as the best means the Creditors have of expressing their very high sense of his most honourable conduct and in grateful acknowledgment for the unparalleled and most successful exertions he made, and continues to make for them."

The proposal met with the unanimous

approval of the Royal Board. Two years after, its directors subscribed £100 to the fund for raising the Scott Monument, but Edinburgh, never precipitate where the actual erection of monuments was concerned, did not complete the Scott one till fifteen years later, by which time the Royal had added £50 to its original contribution. Not the least wonderful thing about this imposing Gothic cenotaph, the ornament and pride of Princes Street, is that it cost less than £16,000.

There was a panicky feeling in the country at the end of 1830, and the credit of the Royal with the Bank of England was increased to the extent of £500,000, for which £600,000 of new $3\frac{1}{2}$ per cents were lodged as security. A General Election and a new Parliament which assembled in November after the death of George IV. showed an immense accession of strength to the Whig Opposition. For sixty years there had been a demand for the reform of Parliament and its system of representation, which left the election of the House of Commons entirely in the hands of a very limited number of individuals; the agitation now came to its height.

Lord Russell's first Reform Bill, introduced in March 1831, proposed to give fifty Members of Parliament to Scotland instead of forty-five, the franchise to all burgh householders paying £10 and over of rent, and a vote also to all

## The Royal Bank of Scotland

country householders paying £50 or over. It was estimated that 60,000 new voters would thus be added to the register. Petitions poured in from Scotland in favour of the Bill, some of them sponsored by men of weight and high influence, not to be regarded as hot-heads or revolutionaries.

The Government was defeated on a detail of the English Bill, a dissolution followed, and the election that ensued turned solely on the question of Parliamentary Reform. It was attended by riots in many parts of the country. In Edinburgh the mob got out of hand, and when Dundas was elected instead of Jeffrey, who had been persuaded to stand for the constituency, the magistrates ran the danger of being lynched for their presumed preference of the Tory candidate. There was feverish uproar all day and wild rioting at night.

It perturbed the customary serenity of St. Andrew Square. On 6th April the directors minuted that " In consequence of the late mob and confusion in the City of Edinburgh, which may be followed by worse measures than have lately taken place, the following committee is now appointed for taking steps to prevent future mischief, viz.: Baron Clerk, the Lord Provost, Sir John Hope, the Deputy Governor, and Mr. Ferrier, with power to them to apply for an armed force should the same appear necessary."

This committee of defence must have spent a good many agitated evenings thereafter; at all events, it was 20th April when it reported that, anticipating an attack on the Bank the previous evening, it had directed that the whole of the staff should remain in the Bank throughout the night, " or at least till such time as tranquillity should appear to be sufficiently restored to admit of their leaving the premises under the usual protection ". At the same time the directors, however agitated, had a shrewd eye on the usual effect of popular riots on Government securities; they directed the Cashier to order a purchase of £200,000 of 3 per cent Consols, should they fall to 75 per cent.

The Scottish Reform Bill—to cut short an exciting chapter in our political history—passed the House of Lords in July 1832, but by this time an outbreak of cholera in the country had doubtless cooled partisan ardour. The cholera was very bad in Glasgow, whose Board of Health appealed to the Royal for a subscription to its funds, and got £100.

Five months before this died the Deputy Governor, Mr. Innes of Stow, and the Duke of Buccleuch was appointed his successor. There were, at the same time, two vacancies on the direction of the Equivalent Company (still unostentatiously carrying on in London), and as it seemed of great advantage to the Bank to

## The Royal Bank of Scotland

have these vacancies filled by two gentlemen connected with the Bank, the Secretary was instructed to prepare powers of attorney for transferring the requisite Equivalent Stock to Mr. John Ferrier and Mr. Thomson the Cashier, who should take up the vacant seats.

The tranquillity which came to the country after the passing of the Reform Bill, and the absence of any war cloud on the Continent, were obviously likely to stimulate Consols, and in June, Messrs. Coutts were instructed to sell the greater part of the Royal's Exchequer Bills and buy £100,000 in new $3\frac{1}{2}$ per cents and £150,000 in 3 per cents. Four months later Mr. David Marjoribanks was cheerfully writing from London: "Stocks all better; $87\frac{1}{2}$ and no limit, in my humble opinion, to the rise. I am quite prepared to see them 90 and above it.

"Rothschild said to me several times when alone, 'Take my word for it—So long as France and England have a good understanding, and their Governments act and stick together, the peace of Europe is safe, and all others must and will come in in time. . . . The moment you see a prospect of England and France disagreeing, that instant begin to look about you.'"

Though fifty years had elapsed since the Royal had opened its first branch in Glasgow, with results eminently satisfactory, and though

The History of
its younger rivals were setting up branches even in the most remote little towns throughout the country, no further step was taken to repeat the Glasgow experiment elsewhere till 1833. By this time the Old Bank had seventeen country branches, the British Linen Company twenty-eight, the Commercial Bank thirty, and the latest newcomer, the National Bank, eighteen. In June of that year Mr. Roger Aytoun of the Renfrewshire Bank, at Greenock, which was started in 1802, appears to have made overtures for an absorption with the Royal, whose directors seemed disposed to regard the project favourably. In a correspondence which ensued, it emerged that the money lodged with the Greenock bank and its branches on open account and deposit receipt for the previous year had been £339,000, and that its circulation was £49,000. There were, at the time, three banking houses in the sugar town, none of them of great means; Greenock and its neighbour, Port-Glasgow, collected more customs than any other port in Scotland. The Renfrewshire Bank's proposal came to nothing; unfortunately for its proprietors, for it struggled along under great difficulties for forty years and then made a disgraceful failure. But the expediency of establishing a branch at Greenock was too obvious to be postponed much longer, and a branch was opened there two years

## The Royal Bank of Scotland

later, Mr. Thomas Turner being appointed Agent.

In the spring of 1834 the directors were " as much puzzled as ever about the disposal of our money ". £210,000 was, in May, paid into the hands of Coutts and Company by the bill-brokers, and whether to re-lend on bills, invest in British stock, or buy American securities was a problem which St. Andrew Square found ticklish. The Royal hitherto had never dealt in foreign stock, though its Charter gave it the option to do so, but was now much tempted by the opportunities which were afforded of purchasing Pennsylvania 5 per cents at about $103\frac{1}{2}$, a low figure they had reached as the result of a panic during President Jackson's administration. This stock, which was not to be redeemable till 1858, had been standing six months before at 113 and 114. The decision to take this chance of breaking into the foreign money market, and acquiring an American stock confidently expected to rise by at least 10 per cent when the panic subsided, was only made after the directors had consulted Sir William Rae, Coutts and Company, Mr. Capel of the London Exchange, and the always helpful Mr. Marjoribanks of Coutts and Company, who declared Pennsylvanians " about the best security in the world ". A few months later Rothschild secured for Coutts on behalf of the Royal half a million stock in West Indian Loan, the greater part of which was advanced by Coutts at 3½ per cent.

Investments of such a character as the two just mentioned were becoming advisable for the chartered banks in view of the fact that there were many bank failures in England and Ireland, and that joint-stock banking in Scotland was rapidly increasing upon dangerous lines. To have in reserve solid securities— Government stocks or others equally marketable—sufficient to guarantee stability became all at once incumbent on every reputable banking house in Scotland, and they conjointly brought pressure to bear on such as showed no inclination to follow their example. They were particularly dubious of the Western Bank, started in Glasgow in 1832, with a capital placed at £209,170, held by 430 partners.

The Western was managed with great activity, and its business quickly grew to an extent that alarmed its older rivals, who knew better than the public did upon what a gimcrack foundation its reputation for easy cash accommodation was raised, and how recklessly it defied all sound banking principles. In two years its own London correspondents were dishonouring its drafts, and it had to appeal to the Edinburgh banks for assistance. This was given reluctantly on condition that the money was put to reserve in Government funds. There

# The Royal Bank of Scotland

is, in the Royal Bank, a pathetically abject letter in which the Western management—faced with the imminent prospect of having its notes refused by all the other banks—pledged itself to build up a genuine reserve like theirs, and amend its reckless system of discounts.

In September 1835 the Equivalent Company's affairs came momentarily under notice. Its directors wrote to inform the Royal that they had decided to divide the Equivalent Stock held by the Company amongst the proprietors at the rate of $10\frac{1}{2}$ per cent on their respective capitals, and also to realise such a sum of consolidated 3 per cent annuities, also held by the Company, as would provide the proprietors with $12\frac{1}{2}$ per cent of an extraordinary dividend.

February of the following year found Mr. Thomson in somewhat of a petulant mood in a letter he sent to the directors, giving up his house in Register Lane, "the access" being "disagreeable to females", the accommodation not allowing of a spare bedroom, and the state of his health requiring that he should take more exercise. He was manifestly worried otherwise. "You are aware", he proceeded, "that during my agency for the Bank of Scotland at Aberdeen my income, exclusive of free house, averaged £1041. That for the first eight years at Glasgow I had only £1000, and that for the last ten years it has been £1200 per annum. The income at Aberdeen went much further than it has done either in Glasgow or Edinburgh."

On considering this, the directors decided to recognise " the zeal and ability with which both Mr. Thomson and Mr. Wilson have discharged the duties of their respective offices of Cashier and Secretary " by adding £200 to the salary of each of them.

Inquiries discreetly made in Liverpool as to the duties and emoluments of the Bank of England's provincial branch agents and sub-agents find their explanation soon after in the appointment of a sub-agent at the Glasgow office, and the opening of branches in Dalkeith, Dundee, Leith, and Rothesay. The superintendence of a committee of subordinate directors for Glasgow had been considered, but the appointment of a sub-agent was regarded as more likely to ensure satisfaction and harmony.

Municipal corporations could not, at that time, accumulate large public loan funds to finance their schemes; they had to resort directly to the banks, and we find the city of Edinburgh, in August 1836, applying to six of the banking houses, including the Royal, for an advance of £291,661 " to pay off the creditors of the city ". As a guarantee of the repayment of principal and interest, substantial securities were given in lien on the annual revenues of the burgh. They are worth

# The Royal Bank of Scotland

enumerating as evidence of Edinburgh's assets less than a century ago:

| | |
|---|---:|
| Feu Duties | £5,500 |
| Vassal Compositions | 750 |
| Rent and Tack Duties | 1,420 |
| Impost on Wines | 1,200 |
| Multures | 300 |
| Common Good | 4,200 |
| Dues of Union Canal | 420 |
| Produce of Ale Duty | 2,000 |
| | £15,790 |

At the end of 1836, when there was serious apprehension that a panicky feeling in England and Ireland might extend to Scotland, Ramsays, Bonars and Company contemplated retiring from their business and transferring it to the Royal; Mr. William Bonar, writing to the directors in St. Andrew Square, said: " The death of our lamented friend and partner without whose company and co-operation my brother and I did not care to carry on the concern (when we had sufficient fortunes of our own to retire upon), led us to think that when our minds were made up to withdraw, the sooner arrangements were made for us doing so the better ".

It proved impossible to make such terms for an amalgamation as Mr. Bonar would have liked, and in the following February Ramsays, Bonars and Company intimated their retirement from business. In the same month (four months before Queen Victoria's accession to the throne), Mr. James Capel, the London stockbroker, was writing to his Royal Bank clients: " I perceive you have directed a purchase of Bank of England stock. . . . Generally, I may say, it is not thought by London people a good investment. An old friend of ours, to whom we once introduced you, and who, from his advanced age, retired from the Direction, sold his Bank of England stock almost immediately upon quitting it, because he did not think favourably of the prospects of the Bank.

" The Ministers of the Crown can, at the expiration of seven years, bring their Charter again under consideration, and many persons go so far as to aver that should their Charter be renewed it will be upon less favourable terms than the present, and their dividend will be limited to much less than the present, and all profits beyond the limited dividend will have to go to the Consolidated Fund."

Mr. Capel's " old friend " was obviously suffering from the " cold feet " of a money crisis, and the apprehensions created by the start of 102 new English provincial joint-stock banks in ten years—three-fourths of them banks of issue; by the huge amounts of specie and bullion being shipped to America; and by a purely temporary declension of the Bank

## The Royal Bank of Scotland

of England bullion reserves to less than a third of their normal figure.

"The position of banking in Scotland at the close of 1837", says Mr. Kerr, "was as follows:

"There were five chartered banks, with aggregate capitals amounting to £4,600,000 on which dividends averaging 6 per cent were paid. Five other joint-stock banks had capitals amounting to £1,550,000, on which the dividends averaged slightly less than 6 per cent. These ten banks had 213 branches, of which the chartered banks held 158. There were, besides, seven other joint-stock banks, and seven private banks, with 37 branches. This gives a total of twenty-four banks with 274 offices. The average circulation of these banks does not appear to have much exceeded three millions sterling, the small notes forming about two-thirds of the total amount. The amount of the deposits was estimated at twenty-five millions; but little weight can be attached to a circulation which, in the absence of official information, must have been largely founded on imagination. The average price of the stocks of the chartered banks was 178 per cent, and such of the shares of the other banks as were quoted stood at high premiums."

During the following year six new joint-stock banks were established in Scotland, the most notable and happily destined of them all

## The History of

being the Clydesdale Banking Company in Glasgow, with a paid-up capital of £375,000 in £20 shares with £10 paid. The Western Bank was applying for a charter, against which the Royal vigorously protested unless the whole nominal capital of the concern was paid up, and an annual account of its weekly circulation given to the Treasury. "The practice so common of setting agoing Banks of ostensibly large capital and calling up 5, 10, or 15 per cent and dealing in their own stock is certainly introducing a very dangerous system", wrote Mr. Thomson in a letter to the Right Honourable C. P. Thomson of the Board of Trade, London.

By this time an inspector of branches had been appointed. On one of his visitations to the Dalkeith office he was critical of some irregularities in the hours of opening and shutting the premises.

"Banking in the country is very different from what it is in large towns, and rules too strictly adhered to will not do", wrote the Dalkeith agent very bluntly to the Head Cashier in Edinburgh. "Particularly when there is as much opposition as there is in Dalkeith, and this being a business to make, it requires us to be as accómmodating as possible. I have had experience of a landed proprietor in this county calling upon me at 4 A.M. for money, and am almost daily waited

## The Royal Bank of Scotland

upon before and after Bank hours both to give and receive money."

A Sunday delivery of letters has never been countenanced in Scotland, but even as far back as 1839 certain post offices were opened briefly on that day for the handing over the counter of what letters might be called for. Sir Andrew Agnew of Lochnaw, Wigtownshire, who was a zealous Sabbatarian, wrote to the Royal Bank's Cashier to say he had got the Commercial, the Edinburgh and Leith, the Clydesdale, the British Linen Company, the National, the Bank of Scotland, and Sir William Forbes and Company to agree that they should not send for their letters and papers from the post office on the Lord's Day.

The reply of the directors lacked nothing in emphasis. "While deeply impressed with the importance of observing the sanctity of the Sabbath," they wrote, "they have the satisfaction to know that the officers and clerks of their Establishment enjoy on that day an exemption from secular business as full and complete as that which is allowed to any other class of Her Majesty's subjects.

"The Directors are quite disposed to consider favourably any proposition to be submitted to Government for the purpose of shutting the Post Office entirely on the Sabbath. But so long as the Post Office is kept open on that day by lawful authority, the Directors do not

## The Royal Bank of Scotland

feel themselves warranted to renounce on behalf of their constituents the power of sending for their letters, more especially as experience convinces them that while the present rule of the Post Office continues in force such renunciation may in particular emergencies be attended with serious detriment to the Bank."

# CHAPTER XV

### REGULATION OF NOTE ISSUES

On New Year's Day, 1840, the emeritus Cashier, Mr. William Mitchell of Parsons Green, sent to his late directors such a communication as rarely comes from an annuitant, and one which must have gratified them as much by the loyal and independent spirit which inspired it as by the message it conveyed. "Having lately succeeded to a large fortune by the death of my relative Miss Innes of Stow," he wrote, " I beg most respectfully to resign into the hands of the Directors of the Royal Bank the annuity of £800 which they were so kind as to allow me upon my retiring from the active management of the Bank.

"In doing this, I hope they will not think that I am taking too great a liberty when I suggest to the Directors the propriety of their granting an annuity of £200 to the widow of Andrew Bogle, their late Cashier, who was a most zealous and interested servant of the Bank during a very long period of service extending to the whole of his life."

## The History of

The Court instructed the Secretary to offer their best acknowledgments to Mr. Mitchell for the handsome manner in which he had given up his annuity, and to inform him that they had great pleasure in adopting his suggestion with regard to Mrs. Bogle.

A bank manager's continuous daily presence at his post was too vitally important to allow of its abandonment for a few days even upon the most solemn personal engagement without consultation with his superiors. In April, Mr. Robertson of the Glasgow branch was elected by his Presbytery as one of their elders to represent his church at the coming General Assembly. It meant eight days' leave of absence. "I shall be very grateful for the favour", he wrote. "It is a duty which is not likely perhaps to be assigned to me again. I have therefore a desire to comply with the wish of the Presbytery on this occasion. I use the liberty of writing thus early so that in the event of the Directors having objections to my leaving home, I may afford the Presbytery an opportunity of electing another in my room, but as business is now going on very satisfactorily and no people coming about of suspicious credit, I think the interest of the Bank cannot suffer in any way from my absence for the period specified"—a conclusion with which the Board cheerfully agreed.

On his visitation to the Dundee branch in

## The Royal Bank of Scotland

October, the Inspector reported the disquieting fact that only the shipping trade was in a healthy condition. The manufacturers were selling their yarns at lower prices than they could purchase the flax for, and it was " a very general opinion in Dundee that not a single manufacturer, if his estate was wound up at present, would be found solvent, and there appears very little prospect that Dundee will ever recover itself as regards this branch of trade, the number of mills and the quantity of machinery in it being very great. Indeed when the trade of Dundee was at its height, it was a trade carried on, not by means of capital, but by credit entirely, and that credit granted to parties who now appear to have been most undeserving of it."

From other quarters came equally sinister accounts of the situation in Dundee; on 9th October the Inspector was advised for his own private guidance that the directors were determined to shut the branch there " without pressing too hard on parties already indebted to the bank ". The branch, however, was not closed till 1842.

No more rosy were the accounts that came from Lerwick and Paisley. The Shetland Bank, which had been started in 1821 by the firm of Hay and Ogilvie, is stated in the Banking Memoranda of C. W. Boase to have failed in 1830, with debts of £60,000, on which a dividend of 6s. per £ was paid; but it had obviously resumed business after a further composition, for, on 14th December 1840, Mr. William Hay, its manager, was dolefully reporting to the Royal directorate "the unprecedented and total failure of the herring fishery in Shetland this past season", and asking an advance of £5000 or £6000. Lerwick was not soon to recover from this disastrous year, however; the Shetland Bank finally closed its doors in 1842 with liabilities of about £140,000, of which its creditors got 6s. per £.

A few months later Mr. Robertson, the Glasgow Manager, was reporting the failure of at least twenty firms in Paisley where all the banks would suffer severely. "One firm", he wrote, "is on obligations to the extent of £150,000; altogether the town has received a shock it will not recover the effect of for many years. . . . Business generally in Glasgow is very dull, and no prospect of any speedy improvement."

Mr. Robertson was "beginning to find the close confinement in this large town, incessant application to business, and constant inhaling of the impure air of our city" telling on his health. Dr. Rainy, his physician, now informed him that he must remove his residence to the outskirts of Glasgow, a transition approved by his directors, who had established more than one precedent for their Glasgow agent enjoying

## The Royal Bank of Scotland

a suburban domicile, and knew that in any case the efficient sub-agent, Mr. Robert Bell, lived close enough to the counter to meet all requirements.

Mr. Thomas Paterson, Inspector of branches, died early in 1841, and Mr. James Wright of the Accountant's office was appointed to succeed him, the vacancy thus created in the Accountant's office being filled by Mr. T. W. Kilgour, teller, from the Glasgow Union Bank. In August 1842 there were other changes in the personnel of the head office. Mr. Gregory, the teller, in ill-health after more than thirty-five years' service, was retired with an annuity equal to his salary of £330. In his room was appointed Mr. Andrew A. Kerr, second teller, whose place in turn was filled by the appointment of Mr. Ebenezer Kerr.

In a previous chapter it has been recorded how eloquently the North of England protested against Lord Liverpool's proposed restrictions on the circulation of Scottish bank-notes south of the Border, where they were by far the most popular circulating medium, and for fifty years had been as good as gold, while ruinous losses had arisen from the many failures among North of England banks. The English memorialists on this occasion put their finger upon the inherent weakness of the English provincial banks when they pointed out that the Act of Parliament limiting the number of their partners to six put them in a vastly less secure position than were the Scottish banks, whose partnerships were large and unlimited in number. This particular difference in banking legislation originated in the monopoly given to the Bank of England, which had prevented such a natural development of banking as in Scotland.

For a hundred and fifty years after the establishment of the Bank of England, any competition on sound lines, or at all events on lines to secure public confidence, was legislatively made impossible in the English provinces. Though it was manifest that one bank in London could not meet the requirements of all England, the continued monopoly terms of that bank's charter were so interpreted as to render impossible the establishment of any other joint-stock bank with the power and prestige of those chartered houses now flourishing in Edinburgh and Glasgow. Until 1826 not more than six persons could associate themselves for the business of English banking. This restriction, narrowing the responsibility and security of any new English bank to a mere handful of persons, had the inevitable result. Such new banks as came into existence looked too much like family concerns and were based too much upon a family's fidelity and resources to be wholly trusted. Not a few of them were quite sound and made good history, but for a hundred and twenty-

## The Royal Bank of Scotland

six years every financial crisis found an appalling list of unseaworthy craft either crippled or derelict, and their notes as useless as any Teutonic "scrap of paper". A partial remedy was found in 1826 in Lord Liverpool's Act which emancipated all English provincial banks from this hampering partnership restriction, while still maintaining the apparently complete inviolability of the Bank of England's monopoly within a radius of sixty-five miles of London, where, as it happened, strong joint-stock, note-issuing banks were most required.

Metropolitan joint-stock concerns immediately came into existence without any Government sanction, having discovered they could get round the monopoly of Threadneedle Street by dispensing with a note issue. In the provinces most of the existing private banks made no change in their constitution, and what new real joint-stock firms came on the scene were mainly county or town affairs with small capital and no experience, bringing the name of joint-stock banking into disrepute and degrading more than ever the reputation of paper currencies. English provincial banking, in short, was at the stage of Scottish banking half a century before.

Sir Robert Peel took the opportunity, when the Bank of England's Charter came up for renewal in 1844, of passing a Bank Charter Act whose main object was to regulate the

## The History of

issue of notes. The Bank of England itself should not be authorised to issue more than £14,000,000 in notes unless a corresponding amount of specie were retained—a restriction in relative degree applicable, of course, to all other banks in the United Kingdom. Further, no new banks established after the measure became law were to issue their own notes, and the old banks were not to increase their issues. All banks of issue were to be allowed to issue only an amount equal to their average circulation for twelve weeks preceding 27th April 1844.

The Act regulating the circulation in Scotland followed in 1845, when the nineteen banks of issue were authorised to issue notes up to the aggregate amount of £3,087,209, that figure being based upon the average circulation as in the case of England. Only eight Scottish banks of issue now exist, and according to a recent Return the average actual circulation amounted in the aggregate to £21,054,845. Prior to 1914 the excess over the modest amount fixed in 1845 was covered by gold (and silver in a certain proportion) held at the Head Offices of the Banks. This arrangement still holds good so far as such coin is available, but the great bulk of the cover now consists of Currency Note Certificates held at the Bank of England under the provisions of the Currency and Bank Notes Acts of 1914.

If one may judge from the Royal Bank

## The Royal Bank of Scotland

records of that time, the feeling among the directors was one of cheerful acquiescence in Peel's legislation, and Mr. James Simpson Fleming, Cashier of the Royal, could say with assurance over thirty years later, that "never did Scotland make such progress during a single generation as she has done since 1844; I firmly believe that but for these Acts our banking system and our general financial position would more than once have been exposed to shocks which would not have left them in the almost unstained credit in which they stand to-day".

It was while free trade in banking was on its last legs that Scottish banking circles got something to speculate about in the removal of Mr. John Thomson from his office as Cashier of the Royal. On 22nd January the directors, "after full deliberation," were "unanimously and decidedly of opinion that the interests of the establishment absolutely required that there should be a change in the office of Cashier", and three of their number were appointed to communicate this decision to Mr. Thomson, with power to give assurance of a retiring allowance.

Mr. Thomson refused to resign, and the Board formally terminated his engagement, appointing in his stead Mr. Robert Sym Wilson, whose place as Secretary was, on 5th February 1845, filled by Mr. James Wright.

Subsequently Mr. Thomson became Manager of the Edinburgh and Glasgow Bank, and his retiring allowance from the Royal terminated.

For the next two years the country was infected by that railway-projecting mania so amusingly satirised in Professor Aytoun's *Glenmutchkin Railway*; even the land behind the Bank in St. Andrew Square was threatened with the intrusion of the "Edinburgh and Leith Atmospheric Railway", a designation which to our slangy age would not inappropriately suggest "hot air". Only the most tangible railway schemes, however, seem to have interested the Royal directors; the Edinburgh and Glasgow Railway, the Perth and Inverness Railway, the North British Railway, and the Caledonian Railway were granted very considerable and augmented credits despite the reflection suggested by Mr. Robertson, the Glasgow Cashier, that "railway accounts are desirable enough in times when money is of low value and difficult of profitable employment, but when rates of interest rise and money becomes more in demand they are not so advantageous".

Money was certainly not of low value at the moment (1847); the Edinburgh and Glasgow banks were paying $3\frac{1}{2}$ per cent interest on current accounts and 4 per cent on deposit receipts—rates instituted first by the Western Bank, which was desperately in want of funds.

## The Royal Bank of Scotland

As an example of how funds may be realised from unredeemed pledges, the case of the ship *John Ker* of Greenock is worth a note. The Royal Bank fitted her out for a voyage to America in the hope that she might reduce the amount at her debit; she came back with a good cargo, and a profit of from £1300 to £1400. After having her bottom cleaned in Scott's graving dock, Mr. Turner, the Greenock agent of the Bank, was confident she could make a second trip which would wipe out all her indebtedness. The barque, however, was put up by Mr. Turner for auction on the directors' instructions at an upset price of £1900, and sold to a Glasgow firm for £2035.

Sir John Gladstone of Fasque, the father of William Ewart Gladstone, was, in October 1846, the means of discouraging any inclination the Royal Bank staff might have to a private flutter in stock speculation. " I lately bought ", he wrote to Mr. Wilson, " fifty . . . shares . . . and on receiving the transfers to-day I find they are executed by two clerks and a porter in your Bank. It occurs to me that your Directors may possibly think as I do, that such speculations may possibly not produce good fruit. All dubbed ' Esquires ' in the Transfers! "

A notification was accordingly made to all the Bank employees that the directors highly disapproved of such transactions " where the risk of loss incurred may eventually bring the individuals concerned into serious difficulties, and be the means of incapacitating them from performing their respective duties to the Bank ".

Let us hope the young gentlemen in St. Andrew Square got rid immediately of what personal sporting scrip they possessed. In a few months, prospects of easily earned money lost their radiant hue. The Bank of England minimum discount rate rose in ten months from 3 to 8 per cent; "there was a sudden and almost total cessation of commerce, and in mercantile cities it appeared as if men were liquidating debts, winding up concerns, and retiring," according to a contemporary writer who probably only reflected the Gloomy Dean side of the situation. Many joint-stock banks and private banks in England gave a final sigh and succumbed.

Hastily, on 6th October 1847, Mr. Horne, one of the Royal directors, Mr. Wilson the Cashier, and Mr. Turnbull the Inspector, dashed to Glasgow, trembling with apprehensions created by failures in London, Liverpool, and Manchester, as a vast amount of bills usually fell due on the 1st and 4th of every month. No doubt they lunched in a happier mood later in the day. They found that the English crisis, which looked so alarming seen

## The Royal Bank of Scotland

from Edinburgh, had a much less disquieting aspect on Clydeside. All the bills discounted at the Glasgow branch falling due two days before, amounting to £43,294, had been retired with the exception of four bills of the value of £798, which were certain to be paid in a day or two.

By 25th October 1847 the crisis snuffed out as suddenly as it had started; accommodation could be got with ease, and was comparatively little asked for.

"Most extraordinary times have passed," wrote Mr. Capel from London on Hogmanay, "the most difficult the Commercial world ever experienced. The Banking Panic in 1825, for the short time it lasted, was more severe, but then it was over—at least the great pressure of it—in a fortnight, whilst the late panic, both Commercial and Banking, lasted for months." He goes on to speak of the great losses made by the public interested in railway stock at high prices and the doubts expressed of the railways' mode of keeping their accounts, also the fears that they have been paying rates of dividends that could not be maintained.

Sensitive to the faintest commercial zephyrs, Mr. Capel, in February 1848, was concerned about the situation in France. "Should they proclaim a Regency in the name of the Count de Paris," he wrote, "for a time at least our markets would most likely improve, whilst if a Republic should be declared, the general opinion is here that stocks would decline further. It is thought that whatever government is formed it will be acknowledged by ours, and that should France wish to remain on friendly terms with us, our Ministers would do so, let the government assume what shapes it will. The time for crusades in favour of dynasties is over, and too much money had already been spent in favour of the ungrateful Bourbon race."

When the midsummer dividend of the Royal had to be considered in May 1848, the directors wisely " played for safety ", deciding on $2\frac{1}{2}$ per cent for the half-year, free of income tax. It appeared to them, quite seriously, that they were faced by " the ruin of our West Indian trade and Colonies by successive measures of legislation by irresistible operation of which Companies and individuals of the highest respectability and worth, and but lately of undoubted wealth and mercantile stability, have been brought to bankruptcy ".

The outlook was not quite so hopeless as all that, but their prevision of imperial history might well be obscured by the clouds in which, for the time being, Britain was wrapped. Revolution had broken out again in France and a republic had been declared; at home, the Chartist agitation reached its climax; conflicts between labour and capital were wide-

## The Royal Bank of Scotland

spread and bitter, and the spring of the year had found Scotland — Glasgow particularly— under a profound trade depression, with thousands of poor people unemployed and desperate — a time of "famine, pestilence, riots and rebellion", in the words of Dr. Norman Macleod. On 6th March 1848 the tellers of the Royal Bank in Glasgow had only to look out of their windows to see the mob looting the gunsmiths' shops preparatory to conflict with the military. Glasgow became very familiar with the exact phraseology of the Riot Act and the tragic consequences of paying no heed to its imperative terms. No doubt tremulous Royal Bank stockholders for the moment put the snibs on their shutters and took to their prayers; but by summer-time they were going "doon the water" as usual in a jovial holiday spirit.

Glasgow, in truth, was on the eve of another great progressive period; in its Dean of Guild Court, in December 1850, plans were passed for extensive building operations over the whole city. The most important, as affecting the external aspect of Buchanan Street, was a project of the Royal Bank to erect behind its office a great new building confronting that thoroughfare and looking westward along the vista of Gordon Street. The site comprised the area between Royal Bank Place and Exchange Place. Its clearance involved the demolition

The History of

of a dwelling-house which had a sunk area, awkwardly intruding on the pavement of Buchanan Street, and garden ground behind. Already Buchanan Street was gaining some renown as the Regent Street of Glasgow, and its aggrandisement by the Royal's improvement policy was warmly appreciated by the City Fathers.

Less than fifty years before, hares were shot, and a covey of partridges was sometimes flushed at what, in 1850, was to become the most fashionable shopping centre of the city; the dwelling-house now to disappear had been built in 1805 by Mr. Alexander Gordon, known as " Picture Gordon " for his reputation as a connoisseur of art, and was considered the most substantially built private edifice in the city. Mr. Laurence Robertson, the Bank's Agent, occupied it as his private dwelling for some years after the removal from the old Lainshaw mansion, and in 1850 it was the residence of Mr. Edward Fairley, Accountant of the Bank. On the site now to be cleared was erected an imposing block of shops and offices, designed by Mr. Charles H. Wilson, architect.

" The Royal Bank ", said the *Glasgow Herald* of the period regarding the reconstruction, " has in this and other cases set an example to builders in the liberal and comprehensive character of its arrangements, and

## The Royal Bank of Scotland

it should not be forgotten that we are principally indebted to the Company for our noble Exchange; for the Plans were laid down by the Banking Company, and they were chiefly instrumental in promoting the establishment of an Institution which is now the pride of the West of Scotland."

Idyllic, innocent times! — a present was always apt to be coming at Christmas to anyone friendlily disposed to the Royal Bank. Annually, from the start, supernumerary but useful functionaries in the office of its London agents got a *douceur*; later a hundred guineas was sent from Edinburgh for distribution among certain officers of the Bank of England through whose hands passed the business of this old Scottish client. It was an old-world gentlemanly transaction, open and above-board; the allocation and distribution of these vales was left to the management in Threadneedle Street. Not till 1849 was this custom terminated; in December that year Mr. Marsden of the Bank of England wrote to Edinburgh intimating that " as the system of receiving gratuities from the customers of the Bank of England is about to be discontinued, and another arrangement made as regards those clerks among whom they were shared, it would be agreeable to the Governors if you would in future withhold the liberal remittance to which I have referred ".

# CHAPTER XVI

### FALL OF THE WESTERN BANK

A HUNDRED and twenty-seven years after the formation of the Equivalent Company from which the Royal Bank took its origin, that Company was dissolved by Act of Parliament in 1851. The power of redemption had been reserved at the incorporation of the Company in 1724. All the London shareholders were paid off on 8th January, and those of Edinburgh two days later. It then appeared that £1474 in debentures had never been transferred into Equivalent Stock, and that amount remained unclaimed. Altogether, a sum of £26,992 was divided among the proprietors, and a final dividend of 11 per cent was declared. The Equivalent directors, in announcing to the Royal the nature of this impending settlement, wrote: " This probably being the last opportunity we may have of addressing you as colleagues, we beg to assure you of our continued good wishes for your welfare, and of the high esteem with which we have the honour to subscribe ourselves ".

## The Royal Bank of Scotland

All the old books and documents of the Equivalent Company that were in Edinburgh were removed to the Royal Bank for preservation. It appeared to the now disbanded Board that " to no Establishment could the trust be with more propriety confided than to that of its *eminent offspring*, the Royal Bank of Scotland ".

In 1852 Balmoral was acquired as a Highland estate and residence for Queen Victoria. The Keeper of the Privy Purse transferred £31,500, a deposit on the price of the estate, to the Royal Bank through Coutts and Company, an interest of 2 per cent being the terms agreed upon during the period the money should be with the Royal till the estate came into Her Majesty's hands.

A year later was opened the Australian Joint-Stock Bank in Sydney, New South Wales, with a London agency. Its directors had resolved to grant bills upon England, and, as " there were a great many Scotch and Irish in this country who would infinitely prefer remitting drafts on their own Capitals to remitting them to London," the Royal Bank was elected to act as agents in Edinburgh, on a ¼ per cent commission basis. A valuable connection, which continues to the present day, was formed by the opening of an account with the Bank of New South Wales on 16th November 1857.

In 1853 a deputation of Scots bankers had

an interview with the Lords of the Treasury, with proposals that the stamp duties on their bank-notes should be commuted. The Bank of Scotland, the Royal Bank, and the British Linen Company had special privileges to issue small and other notes on unstamped paper, on accounting for the duties to the Commissioners of Stamps and Taxes; all others were put to the inconvenience of sending their notes to London to be stamped. By the Act 16 & 17 Vict. c. 63, all the Scottish banks were now released from the necessity of stamping their notes; furthermore, a commutation was arrived at by which the banks should be taxed 8s. 4d. annually upon each £100, or part thereof, of their notes circulating in the hands of the public.

On Monday, 29th July 1854, was opened a branch at Lanark, under the charge of Messrs. James and John Annan, Writers there. On 17th October one was opened at Hamilton, with Messrs. T. J. and W. A. Dykes, Writers, as agents, and on 5th December one at Stirling, under the management of Mr. Andrew Hutton, Junior, Writer there.

At this time the name of William Paterson of the Darien Scheme comes again before us, after being forgotten for more than a century. Saxe Bannister, M.A., was preparing a three-volume work on *The Writings of William Paterson*, and got the consent of the Royal

## The Royal Bank of Scotland

directors to consult their contemporary records of Paterson's association with the old Equivalent. His main object was to ascertain whether any trace existed in these records of the payment of £18,000 from the original stock to Mr. Paul D'Aranda, a London merchant, whom Paterson on his death, without issue, in 1719, had left his sole executor. Mr. Bannister, like a good many of his contemporaries, misunderstood the exact relationship between the old Equivalent Company and its offspring, the Royal Bank, and shared the popular idea that the two incorporations were identical in the eighteenth century. It was pointed out to him that it was only a part of the stock of the Equivalent Company that was set aside by such of the proprietors as chose to do so for the purpose of banking, and that after the institution of the Royal, the Equivalent remained a distinct and separate corporation. As William Paterson had died in 1719, his name was of course nowhere to be found in the records of the Bank, which did not exist till 1727. But Paul D'Aranda, his executor, was an original proprietor of the Equivalent, and transferred £2000 of its stock to the capital of the Royal.

This was not the last the Royal Bank directors were to hear of William Paterson's affairs, and at a sacrifice of chronological sequence it may be well now to finish for good and all with a mythical Paterson fortune which

## The History of

Paterson's descendants seem to have believed in up till comparatively recent times.

Paterson, not without considerable and prolonged pressure on the Government, had in 1714 been assigned the sum of £18,241 out of the Equivalent money and got it in the form of debentures. He had been in pecuniary embarrassment pending the adjustment of his claims. There were arrestments to a considerable amount against him, and ten years before this he had executed a deed of assignment of all his claims against the Commissioners of the Equivalent to James Campbell of London, who had loaned him £2000 at 6 per cent. When Paterson's claim was settled he discharged the arrestments, paid off Campbell's debt, and was left with £13,500 of debentures in his own name. They were of course transferable by simple endorsement, were readily negotiable in London, where Paterson was living, and were apparently disposed of by him soon after they were issued. When the Equivalent Company was incorporated seven years after his death, all the debentures issued in his name were subscribed into the new Company by various parties resident in London, who thereby became proprietors of stock of the Equivalent Company. He never had a penny in the Equivalent Company, nor, of course, in the Royal Bank. Full details of the intromissions in Paterson's government grant are to be found

## The Royal Bank of Scotland

in an appendix to James Samuel Barbour's *History of William Paterson and the Darien Company*, in the form of a letter written to the *Scotsman* on 5th August 1880, by Mr. James Simpson Fleming, then Cashier of the Royal Bank.

Paterson's will, dated 1st July 1718, gave evidence that his latter years were unclouded by monetary cares, and explained his ability to subscribe so handsomely, as he always did after he had got his Darien indemnity, to the charitable funds of the Royal Scottish Corporation, London.

In his will he bequeathed about £7000 to his relatives, and a special legacy of £1000 to his old friend and executor, Mr. D'Aranda. He had one sister still alive in Kirkcudbrightshire; to her he left £800; to the two daughters of a deceased sister Janet he left £200 each, and to John Mounsey, their brother, he left £400. "I give the surplus of my estate, if, after payment of my debts, any such shall be, to be equally divided among the said persons, legatees, in proportion to every person's sum hereby bequeathed," continued the terms of the disposition. It is manifest that Paterson was under no illusion that he had any interest to bequeath in the fortunes of the Equivalent Company or any other concern.

There was a survivor of the family still in

## The History of

occupation of William Paterson's ancestral farm of Skipmyres as late as 1843—one Alexander Mounsey, who in that year went to Canada, and died there. His grandchildren in 1861, with some romantic belief that ancestral wrongs were still to be righted, for a time, through a firm of Toronto lawyers, badgered the Bank of England and the Royal Bank for explanations and counts and reckonings. The actual position of affairs was explained to them in detail, and for thirteen years no more was heard of Paterson's mythical millions. In 1874 another Toronto legal firm tried to reopen the question, and once more Mr. J. S. Fleming traversed the old story and laid before the representatives of the Mounsey family such a minutely documented account of what had happened to their ancestor's estate as no doubt extinguished for ever hopes based solely on mere rainbow gold.

Coming back from the picturesque search for phantom fortunes to the sequence of more prosaic history, we find that in 1855, 1856, and 1857 the prosperous quietude of Britain was disturbed by the outbreak of war successively in the Crimea and in China, and last of all by the Indian Mutiny. By the latter date the last surviving private banking firm in Edinburgh — Messrs. Alexander Allan and Company—had disappeared.

Of the Crimean Campaign in the winter of

## The Royal Bank of Scotland

1855–56, Mr. Capel was writing to Edinburgh " on good authority " that " the Porter sent out seven months since by Hanbury and Company is still unladen off Scutari upon the ships in which it was sent, and that when some of the packages of warm clothing were opened, a great many excellent drawers for boys of from nine to twelve years were found instead of those adapted for men ".  When the Crimean War closed, and the Turkish Loan guaranteed by Great Britain and France was floated, the instructions telegraphed to its broker in London by the Royal Bank were explicit enough for all their brevity: " Two hundred thousand pounds or three hundred thousand pounds at your discretion ".

Branch banks were springing up all over the country; the Royal, in 1855, on their part opened branches in Ayr, Campbeltown, Dalmellington, Doune, Falkirk, Girvan, Irvine, Maybole, Saltcoats, Kilmarnock, Elgin and Perth.  There were estimated to be over two million pounds on deposit in Ayrshire, whose industries were growing rapidly, and the conviction that no other county in Scotland at the time offered better prospects for expansion in banking business was justified by the immediate success which attended those new branches opened under the superintendence of Mr. Primrose William Kennedy as District Manager.  In the following year the Royal's

## The History of

outposts spread to Cumnock, Drymen, Dumfries, Grangemouth, Hawick, Lossiemouth, and Wishaw. On 12th September was read a letter from Mr. John Brown of Marlie suggesting the establishment of a branch of the Royal in London, but the time for that was not yet come.

In 1833, when Mr. John Learmonth of Dean was Lord Provost of Edinburgh, £613 : 10s. stock of the Royal had been transferred under trustees for the purpose of paying the dividends to a certain Eleanor Reid during her lifetime. Twenty-five years after her death the stock was to be sold, and with other funds which had been left in trust to the Edinburgh Corporation by Mr. Hugh Reid of Cornwall Terrace, London, a memorial to Wallace and Bruce was to be erected, " say an ornamental piece of water in the North Loch of Edinburgh, with a Fountain in the centre and colossal statues in Bronze of each Hero in conference ". This brilliant patriotic scheme fell due for execution in October 1858, when the capital amounted to £810, but no such monument to the Scottish Chiefs has yet come into being. It is interesting to note, however, that now (1927) the scheme, in a greatly modified form, is approaching consummation.

Towards the end of 1856 a district branch of the Glasgow head office was decided upon as desirable " somewhere towards the west end of the city ".

# The Royal Bank of Scotland

By the beginning of 1857 Mr. Sym Wilson, the Cashier, was compelled to resign on account of bad health, after thirty-one years' service with the Bank; he was voted a superannuation, with the first vacancy on the Board which should arise, if his health then permitted his taking up such a duty. Mr. Wright had, for a prolonged period during which Mr. Wilson was unable to attend the office, acted as Cashier. To the vacancy created in Edinburgh by Mr. Wilson's resignation, Mr. Laurence Robertson, the Glasgow Cashier, was appointed, and at the Glasgow office Mr. Archibald Robertson, who in 1853 had been appointed sub-Cashier, was settled as Cashier, with Mr. Hugh Cowan, son of an Ayr banker, as his deputy.

At the same period Mr. Turner, the Greenock agent, had also to resign on account of ill-health, and Mr. Latham took his place.

There had been several years of unexampled prosperity extending over both Europe and America. British exports had been doubled between 1848 and 1857, rising from about 60 millions to fully 122 millions. Overtrading set up reaction first in America, and the trade of the United Kingdom was speedily affected to a disastrous degree. So far as Scotland was concerned, the first alarm was caused by the failure of two or three Glasgow firms with great commitments, and more or less dependent upon credits from the Western

Bank, which, in its turn, was known to have quite inadequate reserves, and to be losing heavily on a discount agency it had set up in New York. In Scottish banking circles there had long been distrust of the Western's banking principles, but it had the confidence of a public whose experience hitherto had been that public loss through bank failures in Scotland was never very serious, and was exceptional. In October 1857 Western Bank £50 shares were standing at £84 : 5s.; it had the largest paid-up capital of any Scots bank except the Royal, deposits amounting to about £6,000,000, and a very large note circulation. In the middle of the month the crisis made plain to the management the rottenness of its foundations; its Cashier, Mr. Taylor, resigned office, and was succeeded by Mr. J. S. Fleming, who was then Law Secretary of the Bank. It was too late for even that safe pilot to avert disaster.

Before a meeting of representatives of the "big six" banks, held in Edinburgh on 26th October 1857, was laid a proposal from the Western for an advance of half a million. They were prepared to give it on condition that the loan should be covered by a deposit of satisfactory commercial bills to the amount of £750,000, and that the Western Bank dissolved and wound up its business. An appeal to the Bank of England was even less successful.

## The Royal Bank of Scotland

The "big six" thereupon prudently advanced £510,000 in Consols on 29th October, but the crash of Dennistoun and Company of Glasgow and London with liabilities of over two millions on 7th November brought the crisis to a focus so far as Glasgow was concerned, and on 9th November the Royal Bank directors got a telegram from Glasgow intimating that the Western had closed its doors. Over a hundred branches throughout the country closed their doors simultaneously, with what effect on Scotland generally may be left to the imagination. The total liability of the Bank at its stoppage was about ten millions exclusive of capital. After some effort at reconstruction it went into voluntary liquidation. The net loss to shareholders exclusive of premiums on purchases of shares, including capital at par value, and reserve fund was £2,816,354. As the other banks agreed to accept Western Bank notes in the ordinary way of business, and grant deposit receipts in exchange for those outstanding at the debit of the Western, the national excitement quickly subsided. On 10th November the City of Glasgow Bank, under the stress of the panic, suspended payment for over a month — *its* tragic termination was not to shake the country till twenty-one years later.

An immediate result of the Western Bank's closure was a hearty competition among the

## The History of

other banks for the business that it had done through its numerous country branches. The Royal opened new branches in Arbroath, Ardrossan, Ayton, Bathgate, Biggar, Brechin, Campsie, Coatbridge, Cupar, Ecclefechan, Forfar, Galashiels, Granton, Jedburgh, Largs, Lesmahagow, Leven, Lockerbie, Meigle, Methven, Montrose, Musselburgh, Portobello, St. Andrews, Stewarton, and Strathaven—twelve of these being taken over from the Western.

In the quieter years which followed this disturbing time, a great new telling - room and other additional accommodation behind the Bank in Edinburgh was designed by Messrs. Peddie and Kinnear, architects. The Banking Hall, as it is called, is now the most imposing feature of the headquarters in St. Andrew Square, crowned by a massive dome, designed after the Pantheon, through which the sunshine radiates in a symmetrical arrangement of stars. At the same time a branch was established in the Old Town of Edinburgh.

What a gold reserve for the Royal meant at this time is indicated by a minute stating that, on 5th November 1858, " the committee opened the chest in which £65,000 in gold was deposited the previous April; and counted and deposited in the same chest £50,000 further, making in all £115,000, which they re-locked with the key on the top and two padlocks in front, and sealed with their seals,

BANKING HALL AT HEAD OFFICE

## The Royal Bank of Scotland

giving a key to each of the Cashier, Secretary, and Accountant ". A few days later this gold deposit was brought up to £250,000. Not long after, much more modern means were adopted for the security of this bullion.

Except for a " Second Chinese War " which, to a later generation that has passed through Armageddon, seems remote and trivial as a Border foray, the last three years of the 'fifties saw Britain at peace, though in a more or less precarious armed neutrality. France and Sardinia fought with Austria; dismayed at the peace terms signed at Villafranca, the Italians, kindled to action by the red-shirt Garibaldi, the Mussolini of his time, found a king in Victor Emmanuel, and the liberation and unification of Italy was begun.

" Far-off unhappy things! "—no echo of them is reflected in the chronicles of the Royal Bank. Those three years, for St. Andrew Square, were a time of exceptional progress and prosperity. In those three years the deposits of the Royal had more than doubled. Its business was on a sound footing, and no discount accounts of any magnitude were to be regarded as in any way precarious. If the next three years were to prove so favourable, it was probable that the Rest (or reserve) would soon approximate to a maximum in keeping with the Bank's desires. In these circumstances—not uninfluenced by the consideration

## The History of

that evidences of unmistakable prosperity in any bank confirm the public confidence in it —a dividend was declared at Christmas 1859 of $6\frac{1}{2}$ per cent under deduction of income tax, which then stood at 1s. 4d.

At the same time prudence dictated the reduction in book valuations of all assets of a fluctuating character. As a matter of fact, none of them—even the oldest—was immoderately valued.

In February 1860 the directors recorded with the deepest regret the death of their venerable colleague, Mr. William Mitchell Innes of Ayton, in his eighty-first year, expressing the debt of gratitude "due to his memory for his valuable services to the bank during the long period of his connection with it, first under his uncle, Mr. Simpson, as Cashier, and finally as a director". Sometime later, on the proposal of the Deputy Governor, Sir William Gibson Craig of Riccarton, a replica was painted of a portrait of Mr. Mitchell Innes by Mr. Colvin Smith, R.S.A., the most accomplished of the Raeburn school and successor to Raeburn's studio. It was hung in the directors' room of the Bank, where it is to be seen to-day.

Of all that happened in the world in 1861, the most far-reaching and permanent consequences rose from the protracted and bloody Civil War in America. How little it affected

BOARD ROOM AT HEAD OFFICE

## The Royal Bank of Scotland

Scotland commercially can be estimated from the fact that in June the Royal raised its dividend to 7 per cent.

It had become a little grotesque to designate the practical controlling head of a great national incorporation the " Cashier ", as if he were a functionary paying out weekly wages through a pigeon-hole and personally at the call of creditors on a monthly cash-day. The modest old term had persisted from 1727, when Mr. Whitefoord was, in the literal sense, a Cashier, and correspondingly remunerated. But by the nineteenth century banks were intricate and highly technical concerns, intersections in the ganglions of the whole nerve-system of a world financially governed. Long before the mid-nineteenth century the so-called Cashier was no more to be recognised in that capacity than the puissant practical head of the Hudson Bay Company is to be identified under the primitive designation of Factor. His position was completely altered from that of the "old unable years", and the actual performance of the practical duties of a cashier had obviously to be deputed so as to leave him free for the far more important charge of superintending the employment of the funds of the Bank and the business of its network of branches.

In February 1860 it was the unanimous opinion of a committee of the Royal directors that " Manager " more correctly described

# The Royal Bank of Scotland

their chief official, and that the charge of the cash should be vested in an officer specially appointed for this purpose. Nevertheless, the antique nomenclature was not changed till after the European War!

# CHAPTER XVII

#### FIRST LONDON BRANCH

CONTENT, so long, to carry on and develop a business of its own creation without seeking to absorb any business elsewhere ready-made, the Royal abandoned this policy in 1864 and annexed the Dundee Banking Company.

Dundee in a hundred years had risen from the status of a derelict small town to a position of great commercial importance. Two attempts of the Bank of Scotland to establish a branch there—in 1696 and in 1731—had failed, which is not surprising, for till after 1745 it was an impoverished and struggling community with a dying trade and a declining population. Only six stone houses were then in its main street, the others being mostly of timber, and all its shopping was done in premises rented at about £3 sterling per annum. "A single horse chaise", wrote Mr. W. G. Leggatt in a handbook for the British Association which met in Dundee in 1912, "supplied the demands of the whole population."

There was, in 1746, little money and less

credit in Dundee, yet a bankrupt was hardly ever heard of north of the Tay, unless it might be an occasional laird whose estate, brought to the hammer, left less than a reversion. There were no banks of any kind, of course; dealers got cash and notes the best way they could from Edinburgh. The money part of farm rents and the like was paid in specie. A few shopkeepers would give cash for bills on London or sell bills on London to parties desirous of making remittances to other parts of the kingdom, but the facilities thus afforded were of a limited and precarious kind.

After the Rebellion was suppressed, a naturally shrewd, clever, and industrious people, geographically situated to exploit to the best advantage trade by land and sea, got into the main stream of Scotland's new progressive era. In half a century its population increased from 6000 to nearly 25,000.

In 1763, as mentioned in Chapter X., a number of local gentlemen started the Dundee Banking Company with a modest capital of £12,600, whereof only £1260 was called up to begin with. The venture succeeded so well that another local bank was started before the end of the century—the Dundee Commercial Bank, whose business was transferred to the Dundee New Bank on its erection in 1802. George, Lord Kinnaird, with a baronial title that went back to 1682, who had an extensive

## The Royal Bank of Scotland

estate in the immediate vicinity of Dundee, who had married the daughter of Mr. Ransom, head partner of the London banking house of Ransom, Morland and Company, and had succeeded his father-in-law in that connection, was, with Mr. John Baxter of Idvies, a Dundee merchant, one of the chief partners in the new bank.

Serious defalcations (never definitely to be fathered on anyone) were discovered in the balances of 1805. Lord Kinnaird summoned the assistance of two experts from London— Mr. Henry Boase, a fellow-partner in Ransom's, and Mr. William Roberts, one of the principal clerks in that house—to investigate the state of affairs, himself assuming all responsibility for the rectification of whatever injury was done. A few months later Lord Kinnaird died, and Mr. Roberts continued the business of the Dundee New Bank in the interest of his executors till the arrival from abroad of the heir, Charles, Lord Kinnaird, in the following year.

A new co-partnery was formed in 1806, composed of the new Lord Kinnaird, Mr. Boase, Mr. Morland of Ransom, Morland and Company, Mr. John Baxter (whose career in banking had started with the Commercial), and Mr. Roberts, who had now married a daughter of Mr. Baxter's, and become sole Manager of the reconstructed business.

## The History of

Mr. Roberts was its Manager till 1829, when he retired, and was succeeded by Mr. Charles William Boase, a son of Henry's. Henry Boase, during his investigations in Dundee, had realised the great potentialities of Scottish banking and the value of the training it provided, and put his son from London into the Dundee New Bank in 1821 to learn a profession to which he was convinced Scotsmen obviously had a peculiar "call", however unfortunate the Dundee New Bank had been to start with.

Charles Boase succeeded Mr. William Roberts as Manager of the Bank in 1829. Nine years later the wholly unprofessional directors of the Dundee Banking Company, finding the technique of modern banking and all its responsibilities too much for them, decided to engage someone who thoroughly understood the business. They invited Mr. C. W. Boase to become their Manager, and, to make such a change practicable and agreeable to all concerned, secured the purchase of the business of the Dundee New Bank, whose name was henceforth to disappear.

Under Mr. Boase's management, the Dundee Banking Company entered upon a career of greatly enhanced prosperity. Its story from the beginning may be found in Boase's *Century of Banking in Dundee*—a work unique of its kind, ranging far beyond the implication

## The Royal Bank of Scotland

of its title, and the quarry from which much of the material of all subsequent Scots bank histories has been taken.

The name Boase was destined to become pre-eminent in the north-east of Scotland, and several of Henry Boase's descendants still figure largely in commercial affairs. His great-grandsons, Mr. W. Norman Boase, C.B.E., and Mr. Philip M. Boase, are principals in the old-established business of the Boase Spinning Company of Dundee.

In 1863 the Dundee Banking Company had a capital of £100,000, a note circulation of £53,943, and £722,219 of deposits, and was dividing £10,000 in dividends. It had on the credit side of its accounts £903,459. The head office was in Castle Street, Dundee, and there were branch offices at Alyth, Broughty Ferry, Forfar, and Lochee.

Mr. John Stirling of Kippendavie, one of the Royal's ordinary directors, was the first to bring before the Board a suggestion that the Dundee bank might be worth acquiring. He spoke not without some knowledge of the feeling entertained by the gentlemen at the head of the concern. Mr. C. W. Boase, its Manager, considering that its centenary provided a good sentimental occasion for his retirement, had simultaneously given in his resignation and the first printer's proofs of his classic history of a business with which he had so long been associated. Mr. William Lowson, one of the Dundee directors, had apparently at this stage broached the idea of absorption to Mr. Stirling. There was, soon after, a meeting in Dundee of Mr. Stirling and Mr. Laurence Robertson, Manager of the Royal, with Mr. Lowson and Mr. Boase; full and satisfactory information was obtained as to the business and position of the Dundee bank. At the subsequent conferences a memorandum of agreement was drawn up, signed by Mr. Robertson on behalf of the Royal Bank, and by Mr. Boase, and Mr. William Lowson and Mr. Francis Mollison, his committee of management, on behalf of the Dundee Banking Company. At the same time, by a separate memorandum of agreement between the Royal and Mr. Boase and his brother George Clement Boase, the two latter came to an arrangement to continue their services to the Royal Bank in Dundee as Manager and Cashier respectively for not less than three years.

The seventy-four partners of the Dundee bank were bought out at 60 per cent premium with a dividend of 10 per cent. As for the Royal, one result of acquiring the business was that its authorised circulation was increased by £33,451, raising it to £216,451.

The Royal Bank, seven years before, had, more successfully than at its first attempt in 1836, established itself in Dundee by taking

## The Royal Bank of Scotland

over the Western Bank's branch and business premises in Murraygate. As a result of the merger, the head office of the Dundee Banking Company in Castle Street became the Dundee Castle Street Branch of the Royal Bank of Scotland, with Mr. C. W. Boase as its Manager and Mr. George C. Boase as its sub-Manager. No time was lost in providing further banking facilities for the manufacturing and trading community of what was becoming a great industrial area. Again with some sacrifice of chronological sequence, it may now be mentioned that on 2nd January 1866 two branches of the Royal were opened—one at King Street and the other at West Port. Later were added branches at Perth Road and Hilltown. In 1899 the business so long carried on at Castle Street was transferred to a new building erected on a corner site in the High Street.

By this time probably the reader has forgotten exactly what is implied by the term " authorised circulation " as briefly indicated on page 224, to which he should now turn back for a moment if he would clearly understand the anomalous position in which the Royal and the other banks were placed as a result of the marvellous increase of banking business in Scotland, due very largely to the extension of branches, of which the Dundee case is typical.

## The History of

Prior to 1845, when the authorised note circulation of the Royal was fixed, apparently for all time, at £183,000, subject to revision only in the event of its absorbing some other Scottish bank with its right of issue, it had very few country branches, and its circulation was almost entirely in the cities and therefore limited. The great increase in the number of country branches which was so marked a feature of the Royal's enterprise in the middle of the nineteenth century, and the annexation of the Dundee territory, had the result of circulating £467,984 Royal Bank notes in Scotland, otherwise £284,984 in excess of its certificate, while the average amount of gold and silver held by the Bank for the same period was £353,706.

When a Scottish bank with an authorised circulation dropped out of existence, it was a controversial point whether or not its authorised circulation was "goodwill" and vendable. At the time the Western Bank failed in 1857, the liquidators endeavoured to sell the Bank's right of issue to the highest bidder, but were stopped by the Government with an intimation that the Bank having failed, the right of issue had lapsed and that consequently there was nothing to sell. "The minister who introduced Free Trade", says Mr. Graham in *The One Pound Note*, "was thus responsible for erecting another vested interest, which, value-

## The Royal Bank of Scotland

less as an asset in bankruptcy before his Act, was only refused recognition as a transferable right after its enactment on, as some thought, narrow grounds. One of the immediate effects of the failures of the Western and City of Glasgow Banks, and the consequent lapse of their notes, was the imprisonment of gold coin of equivalent amounts in the other banks, whose circulation naturally increased to fill up the void. In the absence of the Act, the lapse of paper circulation after the failures could and probably would have been replaced by the establishment of another bank, to secure whose issue proper regulations could have been made short of the total abolition of private issue at which Peel, misled by the experience of England, constantly aimed."

How anomalous was the situation thus created can be guessed from the fact that the Royal Bank, with a capital of £2,000,000, had, up till 1864, an "authorised" or "fiduciary" issue of only £183,000 in notes, while another Scottish bank was allowed to issue £438,000 on a capital of £1,000,000. The explanation of this lay on the surface. In 1845, when the average was taken, the Royal had only six branches, while the other bank had forty-four.

Not the least important consideration for the Royal in acquiring the sound and solvent business of the Dundee Banking Company was that at the same time it acquired its right of

## The History of

"authorised issue" and was henceforth entitled to an authorised circulation of £216,451.

In May 1864 the Duke of Buccleuch, Governor of the Royal, seriously disturbed his colleagues, no doubt, by the information that a Bill was to be brought into the House of Commons by Sir John Hay to authorise the Bank of England to open branches in Scotland—in Edinburgh and Glasgow—and to issue their notes there. It was apparently a false alarm; Sir John Hay's Bill had for its object only the legalisation of Bank of England notes as tender in Scotland; branch establishments were obviously not contemplated. Hay's Bill, as it happened, failed to get the approval of the Chancellor of the Exchequer, and it was withdrawn. Nevertheless, two or three banking companies were formed in England, whose object was manifestly more or less to do business over the Border. For eighteen months the Mercantile and Exchange Bank, Limited, of Liverpool had a branch in Glasgow. The London Bank of Scotland had branches both in Edinburgh and Glasgow. A London and Scottish Bank, Limited, also had its nameplate in Princes Street. They were all short-lived and trivial affairs, but they helped to awaken in Scottish bankers the old foray spirit of their ancestry.

The time had obviously come to "haud sooth". Early in 1864 the Royal directors

## The Royal Bank of Scotland

decided that the Bank should, as soon as arrangements could be made for the purpose, have an agency in London for conducting bank business there. Already they had their eye on certain premises for sale at 47 and 48 Lombard Street, and the Cashier was sent to London to inspect them. He was assisted in his investigation by Mr. Hodgson of Finlay Hodgson and Company, and an immediate decision was come to for a purchase. That an immediate occupation of the premises was contemplated is apparent from one of the conditions of purchase laid down, *i.e.* that there should be no obstacles to the early removal of the existing tenants, a stipulation upon which Mr. Gordon, the Royal's solicitor in London, seemed to have no difficulty in securing agreement. On 23rd November it was reported to the directors that the premises were purchased at the price of £21,000. On 20th January following, a telegram was received from Mr. Thomson in London reporting that he had purchased the property adjoining Nos. 47-48 Lombard Street for £15,500.

Nevertheless, the Royal delayed any actual move to London till nine years later, when it should go there fortified by a special Act of Parliament. As yet it had, as a Corporation, no power to hold real property in England, and the Lombard Street premises seem to have been acquired in the names of some individual

## The History of

members of the Board, or of the Board's London lawyers. The " sitting " tenants were not removed, and, as we shall see later, the location in Lombard Street was never occupied by the Bank.

On 17th January 1865 the Royal published its first Abstract, which is here worth reproducing:

FIRST PUBLISHED ABSTRACT OF THE ROYAL BANK,
17TH JANUARY 1865

*Liabilities*

| | | |
|---|---:|---|
| Capital . . . | £2,000,000 | 0 0 |
| Deposits, Notes in circulation, and all other Liabilities . . . | 8,078,190 | 6 3 |
| Rest, after providing for all bad and doubtful Debts | 340,861 | 1 7 |
| | £10,419,051 | 7 10 |

*Assets*

| | | |
|---|---:|---|
| Bills discounted, Cash Accounts and other advances . . . | £7,210,486 | 17 9 |
| Bank Building, Edinburgh and Branches . . | 109,589 | 18 10 |
| Government Stocks and other available funds in London . . . . | 1,506,458 | 19 5 |

# The Royal Bank of Scotland

| | | | |
|---|---:|---|---|
| Gold and Silver Coin and Notes of other Banks . | 604,064 | 7 | 7 |
| Bank of England and other Stocks, Bonds, and other Securities . . . | 988,451 | 4 | 3 |
| | £10,419,051 | 7 | 10 |

The net profit for the year amounted to £185,090 : 4s. Hitherto the practice had been to have a quarterly profit and loss accounting, which now involved vastly more labour than when the business of the Bank was more limited; it was now decided to lay these accounts half-yearly before the General Courts at which the dividends were declared.

This year two new branches were added to those already existing in Glasgow—the Tradeston branch and the Hutchesontown branch, both situated on the south side of the Clyde, where hitherto the Royal had been unrepresented.

On 7th May died the late Cashier, Mr. Sym Wilson. In July 1869 it was decided to open in Duke Street, Glasgow, near the new suburb of Dennistoun, an office managed from Gallowgate branch.

Gladstone's first "Parliament of Democracy" (1868), inspired with legislative zeal, put the case of Ireland in the forepart of its programme. Agrarian disturbances and political agitation went on unabated in the "distressful country", and Britain generally was disturbed by a recrudescence of the Fenian conspiracies which, at the end of 1867, had familiarised us with the threat of a dynamite policy. In the Edinburgh head office of the Royal from March 1870 it became advisable to have porters always on duty day and night, and on Sundays.

Once again was the silver coinage of the country so much worn down by usage that the Master of the Mint decided, in April 1871, to withdraw it from circulation and replace it with new coin. In this he asked for and secured the co-operation of the Royal. The gold coinage was no less defective; in some instances sovereigns accumulated in the large towns by the Royal were depreciated in weight to the value of £7 : 10s. per £1000. The practice of making a deduction for light gold, although continued by the Bank of England, had been departed from by the Scottish banks, which accordingly lost considerably.

That year the Cashier, Mr. Laurence Robertson, seriously stricken with illness, tendered his resignation, greatly to the regret of the Board, and on 13th September Mr. James Simpson Fleming of Glasgow was appointed Manager in his place.

One of Mr. Fleming's earliest commissions as Cashier was to attend a meeting in Aberdeen

*James Simpson Fleming*
*Cashier & General Manager 1871-1891*
*from a photograph by John Moffat Edinburgh*

## The Royal Bank of Scotland

with the management of the Town and County Bank there, which was contemplating a "merger", but nothing came of it. He was, in 1873, to be more effectively concerned in the preliminaries already referred to for establishing the Royal's London branch. It involved, as was shown, a special Act of Parliament. English banking law made it impossible for any English provincial bank of issue to open an office or do business within sixty-five miles of London without abandoning its note issue. The National Provincial Bank of England had to sacrifice a circulation of £442,000 before it could set up a metropolitan office; and there were other English provincial banks in the same position. On the other hand, the National Bank of Ireland had transferred its head office to London without surrendering its circulation of £850,000, and the Bank of Scotland and the National Bank of Scotland had got into London on equally agreeable terms. Naturally English provincial bankers had a sense of grievance.

The Royal Bank in 1873 was, after years of quiet agitation, fortunate in getting Mr. Goschen to interest himself in a private Bill which would put that Bank on an unequivocal footing when it started business in London. There was a likelihood that the Government would oppose it. The Duke of Buccleuch, Lord Colonsay, and Mr. Graham, M.P., with

Mr. Fleming, had a conference with the Chancellor of the Exchequer in May, and in July the Lords Commissioners to Her Majesty's Treasury intimated that no opposition would be offered to the Bill, which on 5th August became the Royal Bank of Scotland Act, 1873 (36 & 37 Vict. c. 215): "To extend the Powers of the Royal Bank of Scotland, and to alter and enlarge the provisions of the Charters relating thereto ".

Its main provisions were that " it shall be lawful for the Royal Bank to establish a branch for the purpose of carrying on the business of banking in London, and to take, hold, and dispose of lands and houses and other real property and estate for the purpose of such branch. Provided that nothing in this Act contained shall authorise the Royal Bank to issue its own bank notes elsewhere than in Scotland."

At a subsequent meeting of the directors, they placed on record their deep sense of the obligation under which they lay, for aid rendered in getting the Bill through Parliament, to His Grace the Duke of Buccleuch, the Right Honourable Lord Colonsay, and Mr. William Graham, M.P. " Further, having in view the indefatigable exertions of the Deputy Governor the Right Honourable Sir William Gibson Craig, Baronet of Riccarton, a portrait of that gentleman should be painted and placed in the Bank."

# The Royal Bank of Scotland

The Deputy Governor and Sir George Warrender of Lochend, one of the ordinary directors, went to London in May 1874 to arrange about premises for the new branch. By this time the conception of what a London branch should be had considerably changed since 1864. The Lombard Street premises owned by the Bank or its nominees were let on long leases and therefore not immediately available; in any case, though situated in the richest street in the world, their frontage had not the dignity consonant with the first appearance in London of a great Scottish Corporation.

Premises of a more imposing character were found and purchased at 123 Bishopsgate Street Within, next door to the famous old " London Tavern ". On 17th June 1874 Mr. John Theodore Horley, who had been Principal of the Branch Banks office of the Bank of England, was appointed London Manager, and Mr. A. S. Michie, who had previously been in the London office of the National Bank of Scotland, was made Accountant. Mr. Robert John Moffat, Senior Cashier with Messrs. Barnett Hoares and Company, was appointed " Counter Clerk ", otherwise teller; three clerks—Mr. William Shaw, Mr. Archibald Dennistoun, and Mr. Patrick Don—were transferred from certain of the Scottish offices of the Bank.

" When we started on Monday, 10th

## The History of

August 1874", writes Mr. Michie, who afterwards became Deputy Manager, "we had the advantage of the friendship and goodwill of the principal officers of the Bank of England, not only because of Mr. Horley's connection with them, but also because of the fact that the Royal Bank's account was absolutely the oldest in the books of the Bank of England. Baring Brothers also were very friendly.

"We had a satisfactory nucleus of business to begin with, arising out of the bank's connections in Edinburgh and Glasgow and elsewhere. Very fittingly, our first account was, I think, that of James Finlay and Company, which firm had had an account with the Glasgow office for almost a hundred years."

Under the advice of his medical advisers, Mr. Wright, the Secretary in Edinburgh, resigned his post in July 1874, having given thirty-six years of faithful and valuable service to the Bank, and he retired with a superannuation, Mr. John Baillie Bishop, Superintendent of Branches, being appointed his successor, with Mr. Huie as Joint-Secretary. Mr. G. L. Rorie of the Commercial Bank took Mr. Bishop's place as Superintendent of Branches. At the same time the Court, recognising the long and zealous service of Mr. Turnbull the Accountant, who had entered the Bank fifty-six years before, presented him with a

LONDON (CITY) OFFICE, 3 BISHOPSGATE, E.C.

## The Royal Bank of Scotland

thousand pounds and a suitably inscribed silver salver.

By 1875, when the Scottish invasion of London preserves was so obviously successful, the irony of the situation not unnaturally came bitterly home to English private bankers who dared not set up shop within sixty-five miles of the capital without forgoing their right of issuing notes.

They argued that while the Scottish banks were not free to issue notes in London, they were issuing notes at home, and so literally infringing the monopoly of the Bank of England. When one of the Scottish Banks — the Clydesdale — suddenly planted three branches in Cumberland, nominally for the convenience of their customers in the south of Scotland, it began to look, to those English bankers, as if soon " all the blue bonnets " would be " over the Border "; London bankers and English provincial bankers rallied to the protection of their common interest and sought to drive all Scottish banks without exception back to their own country.

Mr. Goschen, who had so kindly helped to get the Royal Bank into London, had now apparently changed his mind and become non-intrusionist. With Sir John Lubbock, he brought into Parliament a " Bill to Amend the Bankers Acts "—a measure exclusively dealing with the Scottish banks, though the

## The Royal Bank of Scotland

banks of issue in Ireland, in India, and the Colonies were exactly in the same position and had flourishing London offices.

Mr. J. S. Fleming, the Royal's Manager, promptly mustered the Scottish forces to repel the English attack on their London outposts. They sent a memorial—plainly of Mr. Fleming's drafting—to the Chancellor of the Exchequer traversing the fallacious reasoning of a Bill that bristled with anomalies and missed entirely the obvious cure for the woes of the English bankers—free trade and equal opportunity in the capital for reputable and stable banks of all kinds. Before a Parliamentary Committee of Enquiry evidence was taken at great length; the leading Scottish bankers — Mr. Fleming most conspicuously—came brilliantly through a drastic heckling by Goschen and Lubbock, and the right of the Scottish banks to trade in London or in England anywhere so long as they did not issue notes south of the Border was substantiated; the English assault was routed.

# CHAPTER XVIII

### THE CITY OF GLASGOW BANK

LITTLE more than a year had elapsed after opening the new London office when Mr. Ellis, who was acting solicitor for the owners of the London Tavern property adjoining, informed the Royal's management that it was for sale. It came up for auction, with a reserve bid of £80,000, and was withdrawn after an offer of only £3000 less than this figure. Thereupon the Bank, after a careful survey, acquired the freehold property for the original upset price, and set about demolishing the tavern, whose humble name may create some misapprehension on the part of a Scottish reader. It was, in reality,—though not actually the original " London Tavern ",—an establishment of considerable importance and dignity, its accommodation greatly in demand for the annual dinners of charitable and philanthropic institutions and other public bodies. In February 1876 the Bank came into possession, calculated on spending £30,000, and employed Mr. Thomas Chatfield Clarke, a distinguished architect, for the reconstruction.

# The History of

The foundation stone was laid on 5th March 1877 by Mr. William Thomas Thomson, one of the Royal directors, under it being deposited a metal plate engraved as following:

This plate is deposited in the Foundation Stone of the Banking House in the City of London (Bishopsgate Street, Within) erected for the Royal Bank of Scotland, a Corporation established in 1727 by Royal Charter granted by His Majesty King George the First and empowered by Act of Parliament in 1873 to carry on the Business of Banking in London.

The Stone is laid on the fifth day of March in the year of our Lord 1877 and the fortieth of the reign of Her Majesty Queen Victoria by William Thomas Thomson Esquire a member, and at the request of the Court of Directors of the Royal Bank, the Governing body of which consists of the following Noblemen and Gentlemen:

Governor, HIS GRACE THE DUKE OF BUCCLEUCH AND QUEENSBERRY, K.G.

Deputy Governor, Honourable Sir WILLIAM GIBSON CRAIG of Riccarton, Lord Clerk Register, and Directors.

Head Office, Edinburgh, JAMES SIMPSON FLEMING, Cashier and General Manager.

London Office, JOHN THEODORE HORLEY, Manager.

THOMAS CHATFIELD CLARKE, Architect.

MERRILL AND ASHBY, Builders.

JAMES WILKINSON, Clerk of Works.

## The Royal Bank of Scotland

It is odd to find the directors of the Royal, as recently as October 1876, in some dubiety, apparently, regarding their right to invest in United States Government securities, in view of the wide powers understood to be possessed by them. Whatever the reason for this uncertainty, they sought the counsel of Mr. Watson, the Lord Advocate, on the point. He was, happily, able to reassure them. " I am of opinion ", he wrote, " that the Directors of the Royal Bank have power to purchase and sell American Government securities according to the ordinary course of banking business, and that there is nothing contained in their Charters and Act of Parliament which disables them from making such investments." Fortified by this assurance, an investment was immediately made in £122,338 of United States Funded Loan, 1871.

In the following month died Mr. Laurence Robertson, emeritus Manager and Cashier, who had been living in Edinburgh since his retirement.

There must be something exceptionally salubrious in the air of the New Town of Edinburgh, or a constant tonic influence in intimate dealings with great finance prolongs the active lives of those engaged in it; a lusty old age was generally reached by the Bank's officials before they contemplated retirement. It was so throughout the eighteenth and nineteenth centuries. A good example of longevity in St. Andrew Square was to be found in Mr. William Turnbull the Accountant, who, on 6th February 1878, tendered his resignation at the age of eighty-one, having been connected with the Bank for more than fifty-nine years. Mr. Mackay was appointed to be his successor, with Mr. Kilgour as "Joint Cash Keeper".

In April of the same year died Sir William Gibson Craig, Baronet of Riccarton, who had been Deputy Governor for twenty years, and previously an ordinary director for four years. In his place was unanimously elected the Right Honourable the Earl of Strathmore and Kinghorne.

Two of the Scottish banks now in business in London had applied, some years earlier than the Royal, for representation in the Clearing House, without success. The Royal had been content to make an arrangement with the Bank of England and the Union Bank of London to clear its " charges " on the Clearing Bankers, thus having some of the advantages of the Clearing House. In April 1878 the London Clearing House, apparently relaxing its contention that it existed solely for the benefit of banks having their head offices in the metropolis, expressed its willingness to take in a Wiltshire bank " as soon as its business became important enough "; whereupon the Royal also applied

## The Royal Bank of Scotland

to Sir John Lubbock for admission, with the assurance that there would be no difficulty in satisfying the committee that its London business was of sufficient magnitude to make it for the interest and convenience alike of the public and of the banks that it should be included. The application, however, was not complied with.

This year was to write the blackest page in the history of Scottish banking, and probably the first to sense volcanic rumblings was the staff of the Royal's London office. They had noticed that the City of Glasgow Bank's acceptances coming on the London Discount Market seemed suspiciously large, and that consequently the brokers demanded and obtained much higher rates of interest to cover the supposed extra risk. It was ostensibly from London that a Glasgow newspaper towards the end of September got a report which it guardedly published hinting at grave metropolitan concern regarding a Scottish bank, unspecified, but immediately identified by all readers. No great alarm was created, and for a few days the sinister rumour of the *Glasgow News* was looked on as a Stock Exchange *canard*.

Not improbably — for journalists have a strategy of their own—the newspaper's bombshell was compounded from hints that leaked out from Glasgow banking circles, where the precarious situation of the City Bank was now

## The History of

causing great concern. It had put out an S.O.S. signal to the other Scottish banks, with urgent appeals for assistance to the extent of £500,000, and on their examination of its books it was found to be involved for some millions with a few firms. No relief, in consequence, was forthcoming, and on 1st October the City of Glasgow Bank for the second and last time suspended payment. Five days later, experts, called in to examine the state of its affairs, found them in such a dreadful condition that they advised the immediate winding up of the business, and a meeting of the proprietors was called for the 22nd of the same month.

The actual loss was found to reach the staggering figure of £6,190,983, which, deducting the capital of £1,000,000, left £5,190,983 of a deficiency to be made good by the shareholders. Immediately on the publication of the investigators' report, six directors, the Manager and the Secretary of the bank (the latter subsequently released), were arrested on a charge of fraud, to be tried over three months later before the High Court of Justiciary in Edinburgh, convicted, and sentenced to imprisonment. This was no case of misfortune due to inflation and overtrading, but to unsound and dishonest business methods and the deliberate hoodwinking of the shareholders and the public.

## The Royal Bank of Scotland

The other Scottish banks helped to maintain public self-control by negotiating all City Bank notes in circulation, and a relief fund for the distressed was started, to which Scotland contributed £380,000 (the Royal gave £20,000) and England and elsewhere £20,000. By far the greater number of the unhappy shareholders were absolutely ruined in paying up calls made upon them to the full extent of the bank's liability, for the City Bank, like all but three of its national competitors, and like most of the larger English banks, had not adopted the provisions of the Companies Act. The Bank of Scotland, the Royal Bank, and the British Linen Bank, specially incorporated under Royal Charters and Acts of Parliament, were *de facto* limited companies.

On liquidation, successive calls of £500 and £2250 per share were made on the shareholders; fifteen months later an advance from the other banks made it possible for the liquidators to offer full payment at 20s. in the £ without interest.

So far as the other Scottish banks were concerned there was never any panic; only in a few instances did the timid imagine banknotes might be of questionable value, and there was a singular example of this in one of the Shetland islands, where the natives turned all their notes and deposits at a Lerwick branch bank into gold, which they hoarded for some months, no doubt in sleepless anxiety, and were very glad to return to the bank when they better understood the situation.

An immediate result of the City Bank disaster was that, following the passing of the Companies Act of 1879, all the banks adopted the practice of having their accounts and balance-sheets audited by professional, independent accountants.

As after the failure of the Western Bank, there were now the derelict branch offices of the City Bank to supplant by others; the Royal during the winter opened new branches at Cumbernauld, Douglas (Lanarkshire), Port Ellen (Islay), Kilsyth, Tighnabruaich, and Tranent, retaining as agents there the gentlemen thrown out of commission by the disaster. Positions as joint agents were found for a number of others at the Royal's branches in Edinburgh and Glasgow.

Some of the Glasgow proprietors of the Royal, with a curiosity sharpened by recent events, and not wholly to be satisfied by the now annually published Abstract State of Affairs, applied to the Board asking if the gold at headquarters was counted regularly, if all the Bank's stock was in the hands of outside holders, and if not, the amount held by the Bank. In this *questionnaire* was an implication that the Bank should henceforth not buy its own stock, but sell within a reasonable time

## The Royal Bank of Scotland

any that came into its possession as security for advances, and was forfeited for debt through the operation of the Bank's lien upon such stock.

At a meeting of proprietors on 26th November 1878 the questions were answered. The cash, it was intimated, was counted regularly every week by the superior officers, and the reserve gold, held under the requirements of the Act of 1845, was, and had been for many years, placed in vaults under the seal of the directors. At the annual balance in September 1877, as had been reported in the following year, the Bank had held of its own stock, as it had held for nearly half a century, through the operation of the lien on stock belonging to its debtors, the sum of £195,339. Thereafter it was decided to deal with this holding, and of the stock allotted to proprietors in December 1878—in all £180,449—there was taken up at 220 per cent £169,672, and there was subsequently given off to applicants at the market price of the day, £9562, leaving in the hands of the Bank £16,105.

It was further explained that where a shareholder realising his stock in the open market was left with a fractional part of £100, not easily to be disposed of, the Bank was accustomed to take over such fraction at the market price of the day, and on the other hand, when a shareholder wished to make his holding even,

The History of

the Bank was in the habit of selling such fractions of stock at the market value. There had been twenty-eight transactions of these natures in the past five years, and the total sum involved came to a little over £1000.

"The Directors", said the statement in conclusion, "have neither bought nor sold a single pound of the Bank's stock except in the way explained."

The failures of the City of Glasgow and West of England banks, and innumerable businesses involved in their collapse, were succeeded by a long period of dull trade, to which the Russo-Turkish war further contributed. Money lay idle for lack of national opportunity of using it to advantage, and a great many people took advantage of the higher deposit rates of interest offered by Australian banks.

There is no reflection of all this in the annual report which was presented to the Royal's proprietors at its November meeting in 1880. During the year ended, its deposits had increased by close on £850,000, and the increase since 8th October 1878, when the City of Glasgow Bank closed its doors, amounted to £2,500,000. "This increase", said the report, "has gone on yearly and with scarcely an exception continuously for a quarter of a century." Of the present capital of the bank (£2,000,000) the proprietors had contributed

## The Royal Bank of Scotland

£1,111,348, the balance of £888,652 having been derived from surplus profits or " savings ".

Mr. William Wilson, Law Agent for the Bank, died in July 1880, and Mr. William John Dundas, Clerk to the Signet, was appointed in his place, with some modification of the duties involved.

In June 1881 the Treasury revived an old project for the State issue of bank-notes, and invited the banks of issue in Scotland to join the Government in considering the terms upon which such a State issue, having the quality of legal tender elsewhere than at the place and office of issue in Scotland, might be substituted for the present issues. To this proposal the response of the Royal Bank was explicit.

" We regret ", it wrote back, " that we are unable to enter into any negotiations based upon an immediate surrender of our rights of issue to make way for a State legal tender issue. It would be misleading Your Lordships were we to allow you to suppose that any issue having the quality of legal tender would in our opinion, even if satisfactory to the Banks, be acceptable to the people of Scotland.

" Moreover, we are thoroughly satisfied that such a change would be more prejudicial to the interests of the public than it would be to the banks, for it would involve a great inroad on the resources of the Banks, now available for the wants of the country, and would lead to a serious change in the banking facilities afforded to the public and to the suppression of Branch Banks in many places where they can be kept up only under the present system."

No more was heard of the project; the voice of Scotland on the subject of banking was not to be lightly regarded even by the Treasury; had not Professor Jevons given his testimonial that " Englishmen and Americans, and natives of all countries, may well admire the wonderful skill and caution with which Scotch bankers have developed and conducted their system. There is no doubt that Scotch bankers are guiding the course of development of the banking system in England, India, and the Australian colonies, and elsewhere, with conspicuous success. If we were all Scotchmen, I believe the unlimited issue of one pound notes would be an excellent measure."

Perhaps as a gesture to indicate St. Andrew Square's opinion of the proposed innovation, it issued at this time a pound note of a new design, as close on forgery-proof as chemical experiments by the Professor of Chemistry in Edinburgh University could make it. Even in the early years of the Royal, when its notes were simple script affairs which any competent caligraphist could easily copy, forgeries had been exceedingly rare, and after more complicated designs had been introduced by the engravers, its notes rarely tempted the counter-

## The Royal Bank of Scotland

feiter. But several times between 1860 and 1871 a false £1 note was uttered—apparently printed from an obsolete plate stolen from the premises of the Bank's engraver. The culprits could never be traced, and when, in 1883, a forged note from the same plate turned up, the Bank offered £200 for the discovery of the forger, without avail. It was his final exploit.

In December 1883 the staff in the head office and its branches numbered as follows:

*Head Office*

| | |
|---|---:|
| Officers, Inspectors, and Tellers | 16 |
| Clerks | 66 |
| Messengers, etc. | 6 |
| | 88 |

*Branches*

| | |
|---|---:|
| Agents, Accountants, Clerks, and Apprentices | 573 |
| | 661 |

It was about this time that the controlling administrative head of the Royal—Mr. J. S. Fleming, whose responsibilities were increasing with every fresh extension of the Bank's field of operations—was the recipient of a tangible recognition of the value attached to his personal zeal and influence in furthering its best interests.

On 1st August 1883 the directors' minutes record that " The Board being deeply sensible

## The History of

of the many and great services rendered to the Bank by Mr. Fleming from the time he was appointed Cashier and General Manager in 1871; and, being desirous of recording their high appreciation of his skill and foresight to which they are in great measure indebted for the Act of Parliament empowering the Bank to transact business in London, and his ability and prudence which enabled the Bank to maintain its dividend throughout the critical period of 1878–80, and to develop its business and resources to an extent which has justified the recent increase of dividend, resolve to vote to Mr. Fleming as a special acknowledgment of his invaluable services the sum of £5000, and request the Senior Director to hand to Mr. Fleming a cheque for that amount to be charged to Profit and Loss. They further resolve that this Minute be communicated to the Proprietors at their next Meeting."

At the next meeting of the General Court of Proprietors, held on 27th November following, this testimonial to Mr. Fleming was unanimously approved.

By the death of the Duke of Buccleuch and Queensberry in April 1884, the Bank lost one who had been its Governor for forty-six years. The official connection between the family of Buccleuch and the Royal had been a remarkably long one—the late Duke's father and grandfather having been successive Governors from

## The Royal Bank of Scotland

1777 to 1819, while he himself was elected Deputy Governor in 1832 and Governor in 1838. The Court put on record an expression of its "respect for the memory of one so distinguished throughout a long and honourable life", and unanimously elected his son, the new Duke, as his successor in the Governorship.

Stagnation of trade and the consequent difficulty of employing money materially affected the profits of the Bank during the latter half of 1884—a very exceptional state of things which did not, however, necessitate any reduction of the dividend at Christmas.

Since 1878, £53,000 of undivided profits had been carried to the credit of the Rest, which now stood at three-quarters of a million, and only £4894 was required to be appropriated from this reserve to keep the dividend up to its normal 10 per cent free of income tax.

The continued depression in trade and in the state of the money market became intensified in 1885, however, and though the gross earnings for the first six months exceeded those of the corresponding period in the previous year, the interest payable on deposits had been £42,000 more; consequently, dividend for the period was reduced to 9 per cent.

A further reduction in the Bank of England rate having been made at the end of May, the

## The History of

Scottish banks decided to revise their rates of interest and discount, and accordingly reduced their deposit receipt rate to $1\frac{1}{2}$ per cent. The alteration was recognised as reasonable by depositors in view of the altered condition of the money market, and after a few months' experience of its operation the directors were quite satisfied with the result.

There had inevitably accumulated at the Bank during the first century of its existence a vast deal of *paperasse*—subsidiary account-books and documents never again to serve a useful purpose, even for the historian. Neither worm nor mildew had corrupted them; paper was paper then, and tough as sheep-skin almost; hand-made and water-marked in the mill of Richard Watkins, the surviving books of 1727, with their hand-ruled money columns, seemed assured of lasting still for hundreds of years. And what wonderful penmanship!—legible as modern print, with artistic character in it, as if the writer loved his job and cherished the opportunity to put a little decoration into it.

In 1884 some of this obsolete stuff had been cleaned out and pulped, but a more comprehensive sweeping took place at the beginning of 1888, when all old books and documents of a now useless character were sent in sealed bags to Dartford, where, in presence of a clerk from the London office, they were converted into pulp to make paper for the *Daily Tele-*

## The Royal Bank of Scotland

*graph*. So perished without doubt a good many blank pages, such as the most notable etchers of to-day are now seeking through every part of Europe for the printing of their plates.

# CHAPTER XIX

#### CLOSE OF THE VICTORIAN ERA

FROM 1885 to the end of the century the history of banking in Scotland has been epitomised in a paraphrase—" Happy is the banking system that hath no annals". The previous eighteen years had been a period of excursions and alarms, but also of unexampled prosperity, during which the population had increased more than three-quarters of a million, and bank deposits had gone up 45 per cent despite the intensified competition of investment companies of all kinds. Now we were come to an unsensational chapter, recording steadily continued progress, it is true, but so far as banking is concerned, not quite so wonderful an expansion of business.

The stagnation of trade, and the consequent difficulty of employing money, had materially affected the profits of all the Scottish banks during the latter half of 1884, for funds had been used at rates which left but the scantiest margin for the lenders. A further reduction in the Bank of England rate, on 28th May

## The Royal Bank of Scotland

1885, was followed by a conference of the Scottish bank managers on 1st June, when it was decided that the 2 per cent rate of interest then allowed on deposit receipts should be reduced to 1½ per cent.

In November 1888 the Honourable Henry James Moncrieff resigned his ordinary directorship on his elevation to the Bench as Lord Wellwood. "Nothing short of a sense of duty", he wrote to Mr. Fleming, "would induce me to abandon an office which has given me so much pleasure and information. To yourself in particular I feel peculiarly indebted for your unwearying kindness and the instruction which those who listen cannot fail to derive from you."

Sir George Warrender, Baronet, of Lochend, was unanimously elected to the seat thus vacated, and Lord Wellwood continued his connection with the Board in the less exacting rôle of extraordinary director.

There was a sharp crisis in November 1890, associated mainly with the embarrassment, under exceptional circumstances, of the firm of Baring Brothers, London. A long continuance of unfavourable conditions in business, and a revolution in the Argentine, with whose bonds the Barings had been doing a great business in Britain, found that old, famous, and stainless house for the moment unable to meet its engagements, though the liabilities of £20,000,000 were more than covered by the assets. To prevent the serious consequences which would follow on the suspension of so great a concern, the Bank of England, conjointly with the great banks of the country, undertook to meet all the Baring engagements. The Royal Bank subscribed £350,000 to the guarantee fund. Messrs. Baring soon resumed business, and their liabilities were eventually discharged in full, without any call on the guarantors, but the public lost heavily in discredited securities.

In this year, 1890, Mr. Archibald Robertson, who had succeeded his clansman Laurence Robertson as the head of the Glasgow office in 1857, resigned, and was succeeded by Mr. A. S. Michie from the London office, who had for a brief period been associated with him as sub-Cashier. This was one of the occasions in which a Scotsman, however agreeable he may have found the road to London, is not reluctant to return despite all the allurements of the capital. Mr. Michie, during nearly twenty years of life in London, had never forgotten his nationality; in his hours of leisure from Bishopsgate Street-Within he had two good Scottish hobbies, literature and arms. While he was editing and enlarging Gilbart's classic work on Banking, he found time also to become one of the best rifle shots in the kingdom, a member of the " Scottish Eight ", and a winner in 1884 of the Middlesex Bronze Medal, with

# The Royal Bank of Scotland

what was said to be the record score for the Snider rifle.

On 19th January 1892 Mr. J. S. Fleming the Cashier, on the imperative advice of his doctor, reluctantly gave in his resignation to the directors. In their minutes they record that to his foresight and discretion was due the obtaining, at the most opportune moment and in the manner most conducive to the interests of the Bank, the Act which empowered it to open its London branch, and to his calm and resolute judgement the creation of public confidence during the City of Glasgow Bank disaster.

Mr. David Robertson Williamson Huie, Secretary, became Mr. Fleming's successor. During his secretarial period he had given great assistance in the formation and development of the Institute of Bankers in Scotland, of which Mr. A. W. Kerr, Agent of the Royal Bank in Hope Street, and author of the *History of Banking in Scotland*, was the first Secretary. Mr. Adam Tait, trained to law, appointed the Law Officer of the Bank in 1875, and Superintendent of Branches in 1886, now succeeded Mr. Huie as Secretary. Owing to the continuance of low profit rates, the banks again had to make important alterations in their deposit interest arrangements this year (1892). The old-established system of allowing interest on current account creditor balances was entirely abolished, and the deposit receipt interest was reduced to 1 per cent. On the other hand, the overdraft rate was reduced by ½ per cent.

In January 1894, the Earl of Elgin and Kincardine resigned his ordinary directorship on being appointed Viceroy of India; to the vacancy thus created Mr. Andrew Hugh Turnbull, Actuary, Edinburgh, was appointed. Lord Elgin retained office as an extraordinary director, and on his return to this country rejoined the ordinary Board, becoming Deputy Governor in 1904. On the eve of 1900 the directors' report to the General Court of Proprietors intimated the net profits for the year at £200,666, and the Rest at £803,554. There had been a midsummer dividend at the rate of 8 per cent free of income tax, and this was repeated for Christmas with a bonus of 1 per cent.

It was to be rather an exciting Christmas for Great Britain; the Jameson Raid of 1895 on the Transvaal, and the Boers' apprehension of interference in their rule, had brought about a state of matters which culminated now in a declaration of war by the South African Republic and the Orange Free State, and the British Colonies were invaded. General Sir George White and 12,000 men were besieged in Ladysmith by the Boers' main army; Kimberley was invested; Baden Powell and his handful

## The Royal Bank of Scotland

of irregulars were beleaguered in Mafeking. On 9th November 1899 the first instalments of the greatest army which up till then had ever been sent across the seas by any nation in the world were beginning to arrive in South Africa. We had a "black week" in December; volunteers and yeomen were rushing to recruiting offices, and among the first of them were clerks of the Royal Bank, who sought leave of absence to join the colours for active service as volunteers.

Stopped immediately was an amusing controversy which had been waging in the newspapers as to whether 1900 would be the close of the nineteenth century or the first year of the twentieth, a ticklish problem upon which even savants like Lord Kelvin held unorthodox views. There were more serious things for the country to think about when New Year's Day came, and the war in South Africa was realised as of graver import than a mere Indian frontier squabble.

Neither the Cabinet nor the people had, to begin with, grasped the magnitude of the task that lay before the nation till after the reverses at Colenso, Magersfontein, and Stormberg. Lord Roberts and Lord Kitchener were chosen to conduct a campaign which, it was now obvious, would be bitter and long-protracted. Canadians and Australians fought side by side with English, Scots, and Irish. In the autumn of

## The History of

1900, when, with Ladysmith and Mafeking relieved ; Johannesburg and Pretoria, the Transvaal capital, occupied; the Orange Free State annexed; President Kruger flown to Europe, and Lord Roberts back in England satisfied the war was over, Lord Salisbury dissolved Parliament. He was, in the "khaki election", returned to power with a scarcely diminished majority, so satisfied was the nation that triumph was complete.

That year saw some notable changes on the Board of the Royal Bank. Mr. George Auldjo Jamieson, who had been an ordinary director for ten years, died in July, and Sir George Warrender, who had become an extraordinary director, was appointed to fill the vacancy. In September died Mr. James Walker of Dalry, who had completed a period on the Board which began in 1879, and Sir Thomas Gibson Carmichael was elected in his stead. Mr. Hugh Veitch Haig of Ramornie and Mr. James Haldane, C.A., Edinburgh, were added to the list of extraordinary directors in November. Mr. Haldane became an ordinary director in 1901 and continued in office until his death five years later. In 1901 the Dundee association with the Bank was strengthened by the addition of Mr. William Lindsay Boase, merchant there, to the list of extraordinary directors.

The most important building development

## The Royal Bank of Scotland

of the Bank during this year was the erection of the branch in St. Vincent Street, Glasgow.

By the result of the Election of 1900, the nation had signified its satisfaction at what it regarded as a triumph of our arms in South Africa, but two years more were to elapse before the stubborn resistance of the Boers was ended. Till June 1902 they kept up a fierce and crafty guerilla warfare, stamped out ultimately by the strategy and persistence of Kitchener.

Queen Victoria died in January 1901, her life — long though it was — shortened undoubtedly by the grievous strain of the war, and King Edward came to the throne.

After the distortions of the past few years, national life began to shape itself again. Trade was showing signs of recovery, especially in iron, steel, and textiles, but the war had resulted in the serious and persistent depreciation of British Government securities, and Consols which had stood at 114 per cent in 1896 had fallen to 79. A lower abyss was to be reached by August 1907, when they stood at $60\frac{3}{4}$.

At the start of the war the absorption of private banks into large joint-stock concerns had grown to an enormous system. The big concerns rather extended than contracted the number of local banks, opening branches in places where smaller firms in the old days would not have found business worth their while. Thus it came about that though the actual number of banking concerns in England was now 303 as against 458 a hundred years before, there was a branch to every 6900 persons as against a bank to every 19,200 in 1800. A continued expansion of branches was equally manifest in Scotland, where there was now one branch office to every 4155 of the population.

We approach so closely now on a decade of national history so charged with world upheavals, the fall of dynasties, and threatening even civilisation itself, that the domestic affairs of any bank, in their interest, will seem to shrink to small proportions. But while yet the looming shadow of 1914 is unsuspected, there is an opportunity to note rapidly the main changes in the personnel of the Royal, and the emergence of men who were to keep the flag flying in our years of greatest national stress.

The Earl of Strathmore, Deputy Governor, who had been on the Board since 1868, died in February 1904, and was succeeded in that office by the Earl of Elgin and Kincardine. In January 1905 Mr. Horley, the London Manager, retired, and Mr. William Wallace, Joint-Superintendent of Branches at Head Office, took his place. The vacancy created by Mr. Wallace's promotion was, in turn, filled by the appointment of Mr. Alexander Kemp Wright.

# The Royal Bank of Scotland

In May of this year (1905) Mr. Henry Johnston, Sheriff of Forfarshire, resigned his ordinary directorship on his elevation to the Bench as Lord Johnston, and was succeeded by Sheriff Charles C. Maconochie, K.C., of Avontoun, Linlithgow.

December 13 saw the completion of fifty years' service with the Bank by Mr. Templeton, its Accountant, and the directors presented him with silver-plate. In January 1907 Mr. Huie, the Cashier, retired; Mr. Tait, who was the Secretary, became his successor. Mr. A. K. Wright took up the post of Secretary, and Mr. J. B. Adshead was appointed Joint-Superintendent of Branches. In June of the same year Mr. Frank Martin, Deputy Manager in London, retired, to be succeeded by Mr. Dick. Mr. Templeton retired in April 1908, and his post was taken by Mr. D. S. Lunan as Accountant. In the following June Sir Thomas Gibson Carmichael of Skirling, Baronet, left the Board on his appointment as Governor of Victoria, Australia, and the vacancy was filled by the election of Mr. Ernest A. Davidson.

An unusual episode in British banking is minuted in July 1908—the directorate's recognition of the courage with which two officials of the Motherwell branch had repelled an attempt at a "hold-up" by robbers.

On Friday, 10th April, about midday, three men walked into the Bank in Brandon Street, the leading thoroughfare of the town, and advanced to the counter with every appearance of having some business purpose. There were no customers in the office, where the Agent, Mr. William King, and Mr. John Kay Ferguson, the Accountant, were usually alone at the luncheon hour of the town. As it happened on this occasion, the Agent was in his private room at the moment.

The Accountant, who was the only person visible to the intruders, was startled to see one of them suddenly make for the opening at the end of the counter which led to the safes and the rear part of the office, where a considerable quantity of money was always kept for the day's business. Stepping forward to intercept him, he found himself menaced by a pistol, for whose possession he immediately got into grips with the owner, shouting at the same time for the assistance of his Agent. In the struggle the pistol was discharged, its bullet finding an innocuous target in the planking of the floor. There followed a violent struggle for the retention of the assailant, in which Mr. Ferguson, though his hands were badly bruised and lacerated in the struggle, displayed better wrestling form than his taller and heavier opponent.

Mr. King, the Agent, throwing himself into the mêlée without hesitation, got himself badly injured about the face; in the end the intruder

## The Royal Bank of Scotland

succeeded in wrenching himself free and escaped into the street, to which his confederates, realising the seriousness of the defence, had earlier bolted.

Shortly afterwards the men, under hot pursuit by the police, turned upon them in desperation and fired at them with an automatic pistol, but were eventually captured and brought to trial. They were Lettish Poles, named Ludwig Bruno and Carl Smith, associates of the Polish gang which later on, under " Peter the Painter ", figured tragically at the " Sidney Street Siege " in London, when Mr. Winston Churchill called out military aid for the police. Three men were really implicated in the attempt on the Motherwell bank, but only the two named were caught and convicted. One was sentenced to ten years' imprisonment and died in Peterhead before his term expired. The other completed a sentence of seven years and was then deported.

Lord Johnston and Mr. Hugh A. Allan, shipowner, Glasgow, became extraordinary directors in 1909, and in November of that year Mr. Michie resigned the post of Cashier at Glasgow, to which, in the following May, Mr. Dennistoun was appointed, with Mr. Thomas Lillie, formerly an Inspector at the head office, as sub-Agent. In November Mr. Boase died, and Mr. James A. Reid, LL.D., Writer, Glasgow, was added to the list of extraordinary directors.

# The History of

The retirement into private life of Dr. John Ross (now Sir John Ross), the Agent at Dunfermline, an old and valued friend of the Royal, was minuted on 3rd May 1911. He had come to Dunfermline in 1867 to become partner in the law firm of Bardner, Macfarlane and Ross; was, for some years after, Agent for the City of Glasgow Bank; and following on its failure, became Dunfermline Agent of the Royal. For forty years he was an active force on the Dunfermline School Board. In June 1901, on the institution of the Carnegie Trust for the Universities of Scotland, he was appointed secretary and treasurer, and when the Carnegie Dunfermline Trust of 1903, the Carnegie Hero Fund Trust of 1908, and the Carnegie United Kingdom Trust of 1913 were formed, he was appointed chairman of each of them.

Dr. Ross, who had had the honorary degree of LL.D. conferred on him by St. Andrews University in 1903, was knighted in 1921, and on account of failing eyesight resigned all his official posts in 1923.

After thirty years on the Board, Mr. Ralph Dundas resigned in July 1911, to be succeeded by Sheriff James Alexander Fleming, K.C., son of Mr. J. S. Fleming, the former Cashier; and in 1912 Sir George Paul was appointed Law Agent in consequence of the retirement from practice of Mr. W. J. Dundas.

The only case of Royal Bank note forgery

# The Royal Bank of Scotland

for a very long period of years came up for trial at Edinburgh High Court in November 1912. Eight months before, there had turned up remarkably clever counterfeits of the £1 note, dated 5th May 1908, hand-done on paper somewhat thicker and softer than the genuine article. Nothing was publicly said about it at the time, but all the branch offices were put on the qui vive, and the source from which thirty-one such notes originated was made certain by October. A resident of Kirkcaldy, who at one time had been in the employment of large engraving and publishing firms, was arrested, tried, and found guilty, and sentenced to six years' penal servitude.

# CHAPTER XX

### YEARS OF WAR

In a retrospect of the history of a great banking corporation of old establishment—a retrospect confined so far as possible to its own written records—there is fortunately no call to summarise, even briefly, the history of the world during those years in which nations agonised and fought for life, in which millions died, and empires fell, and the European civilisation built up in a thousand years seemed almost whelmed in a universal disaster.

Naturally, no shadow of presage of the coming terror was cast on a banker's books till the summer of 1914. Nothing is to be found there regarding those political apprehensions and distrusts which were wakening at the growth of armaments in Europe. The first significant hint of danger, not only possible but imminent, came with the raising of the Bank of England rate on 30th July, with its obvious bearing on the strained relations between Austria and Serbia. When two days later it was raised again to 10 per cent, bankers

## The Royal Bank of Scotland

went home that Saturday sick at heart from a knowledge not shared by everyone of what that might presage. Germany had declared war against Russia.

By Royal Proclamation the Bank Holiday of Monday was extended to the following Thursday inclusive. A moratorium was proclaimed, under which the obligation of the banks to pay their depositors was temporarily suspended, and Scottish bank-notes were declared legal tender throughout the branches in Scotland.

Before the prolonged Bank Holiday, in such sinister fashion extended to four days, had terminated, Germany had proclaimed war against France and Britain had declared war on Germany.

On the windows of all bank establishments was a poster:

### NOTICE

1. Customers of the Bank are reminded that only small sums of cash are actually required for ordinary purposes. Cheques should therefore be used for making payments to the utmost extent possible.
2. This is a

### GREAT NATIONAL EMERGENCY.

The banks are not in any way responsible for the financial situation which has arisen, but they have made arrangements which will be amply sufficient for meeting all reasonable needs.

3. Depositors are assured that their interests are absolutely protected. Under the Moratorium the obligation of the Banks to pay Deposits ceases for the time, but they are anxious that their customers should be put in a position to meet all payments for necessary requirements.

4. The notes of the Scotch Banks are now legal tender throughout their branches in Scotland, the wish of the Government as expressed by the Chancellor of the Exchequer being that gold should not be parted with merely to be hoarded. Patriotism, therefore, demands that all should join in strengthening the hands of the Banks at this time of national trial.

The Royal directors were now meeting daily at two o'clock; in St. Andrew Square and in the Glasgow chief office the reopening on Friday, 7th, was looked forward to with some anxiety. This was not from any apprehension that a "run" was imminent, for the people's attitude unmistakably indicated a national cohesion, a sense of consecration to a common cause, a spirit of determination and confidence, and in any case, five feverish days had been occupied in mobilising currency resources. Yet Friday, it was felt, was likely to put unusual strain on bank staffs everywhere.

It was not unamusing to study the psychological reactions of the people of such cities as Edinburgh and Glasgow to a situation absolutely new to them, in which for a week

## The Royal Bank of Scotland

they had to live from hand to mouth on their pocket-money, so to speak, because of the inaccessibility of their bank deposits. As the moratorium relieved them of any anxiety about the immediate settlement of big bills falling due, they were able to make the most of what elements of humour were in the position. An enforced economy is never wholly disagreeable to a Scotsman; it brings out in him reserves of endurance, and stimulates to fresh exertions. During August 1914 the Scotsman's trust in his country's banks was as strong as his confidence in the British Army and Navy. His bank was his citadel; if his money was safe anywhere, it was safe there, as the Royal Bank directors and John Campbell felt about Edinburgh Castle in 1745.

Never was the utility of the £1 note more brilliantly vindicated. With £1 notes and a sufficiency of sixpences, a people who, as a rule, would rather have their money in paper than in sovereigns (so easily mistaken for shillings in the dark!) could contentedly carry on while the English with their dependence upon gold and " fivers " were at a disadvantage.

When the banks reopened on 7th August at the customary hour, it was to find no single embarrassing demand on their resources. Their customers had unabated confidence in cheques and bank-notes, and all they asked in the way of advances for legitimate trade purposes was cheerfully granted. At the close of a busy day, many bank offices were able to report lodgements largely in excess of withdrawals, and cases were not infrequent where gold was patriotically exchanged for notes.

The circulation of the Royal Bank for the four weeks ending 15th August was £1,111,587, and it steadily increased. One of the first steps taken by the Government was to avail itself of the obvious benefits of an extensive £1 note circulation. Here in Scotland was such a circulation ready-made and capable of expansion. The Treasury by a special Act of Parliament (the Currency and Bank Notes Act, 1914) not only gave England a £1 note, but a 10s. one also, and these were placed at the disposal of the joint-stock banks throughout the kingdom to the extent of 20 per cent of their deposits. Although anticipating matters a little, it may here be noted that the highest point reached by the circulation was for the week ending 3rd July 1920, the figure being £3,883,349.

At the outbreak of War the staff of the Royal numbered 901, and practically two-thirds of them saw active service in the Army and Navy and the Air Force. Women were called in to fill their places. There was, from the outset, naturally a continuous strain upon the direction and administrative personnel of the establishment, but during the four years of War,

# The Royal Bank of Scotland

few fell out of the ranks from physical breakdown.

On 11th November 1914 the Board had to record with sorrow the death of William Henry Walter, Duke of Buccleuch, who had been Governor for thirty years. The official association of the Dukes of Buccleuch with the Bank had, as has been mentioned before, been almost continuous since 1777, having only been interrupted for a few years during the minority of the sixth Duke's father. The vacancy now caused in the Governorship was filled by the election of the late Duke's son, John Charles, now seventh Duke.

A world conflict of some years' duration being now in prospect, the closing days of November 1914 saw the flotation of the first War Loan of £350,000,000 at $3\frac{1}{2}$ per cent offered at 95, and over-applied for in a few days. The banks of the United Kingdom made themselves responsible for something like £100,000,000 of this loan—the Royal up to the extent of 10 per cent of its deposits. Thereafter, till the end of the War, frequent subscriptions were authorised by St. Andrew Square to British Government War Loans of an immensely greater magnitude, and to aid in the advances to the Allies. Mr. Adam Tait, at a meeting of the Institute of Bankers of Scotland in June 1916, was able to estimate that Scottish banking had already contributed something like £60,000,000 sterling to the finances of war. That summer the Government guaranteed the banks in respect of credits for meat and sugar. The Royal's participation in the Meat Credit amounted to £190,000, and in the Sugar Credit to £95,000, but this latter sum was subsequently raised to £126,000. In July following the Royal's participation in the American Credit was £350,000, and for the regulation of the American Exchange the directors authorised a loan of securities to the Government of the value of £280,000.

The third War Loan, the "Victory Loan" as it was expectantly called, was floated in January 1917, and exceeded the most sanguine anticipations, over £1,000,000,000 being subscribed, of which £105,000,000 came through the Scottish banks on behalf of their clients. The banks themselves, by arrangement, made no direct contribution; £10,000,000 additional was estimated to have been subscribed by their clients directly through the Bank of England. Viewed in relation to gross deposits of, roughly speaking, £166,000,000 in the Scottish banks, this response from the north showed, as Mr. A. W. Kerr put it, " how Scottish patriotism still burned with its old unquenchable flame ".

In 1915 the Earl of Aberdeen, who had been an extraordinary director for forty-two years, was raised to the Marquisate and resigned from the Board, to be succeeded by Lord Inch-

## The Royal Bank of Scotland

cape on 28th June 1916. The following year found many changes at St. Andrew Square. Mr. Tait, the Cashier, retired after forty-two years' service with the Bank, and Mr. Alexander Kemp Wright was elected his successor. Mr. J. B. Adshead became Secretary in Mr. Wright's place.

The Earl of Elgin, Deputy Governor since 1904, died this year (1917), and was succeeded in the office by the Earl of Strathmore and Kinghorne. Mr. J. P. Wright, W.S., and Mr. A. H. Turnbull, ordinary directors, died; the vacancies thus created were filled by Sir Thomas Dunlop, Baronet, Lord Provost of Glasgow, and Mr. Herbert William Haldane, C.A. Lord Johnston and Lord Dundas, extraordinary directors, resigned, their places being filled by Sir William Robertson of Dunfermline and Mr. William D. Graham Menzies of Hallyburton.

Though the world was still in upheaval, 1918 was a year whose minute books in the Royal Bank contribute little or nothing to the material of the gossiping diarist. The Armistice of 1918, the sudden suspension of hostilities all over Europe, except in unhappy Russia, and the instant need for licking our wounds and starting afresh to build up civilisation, dominated all else.

Of the 582 young men of the Royal Bank who had gone to the War, 84 had died and many were sadly " broken ", as the old term had it. It had been arranged that all members of the staff absent on active service should receive remuneration till the end of the War or their return to their situations, which were kept open for them. The increase in the cost of living was recognised by bonuses to the general staff. Of the Royal Bank's Memorial to its fallen employees we shall read later.

The briefest of comparisons will suffice to show that even Armageddon had in no way weakened the vitality of Scottish banking. In 1901–2 the deposits in the Scottish banks amounted to $107\frac{1}{2}$ millions. In 1916–17 they reached the total of $166\frac{1}{2}$ millions, an increase of 59 millions. In 1917–18 they made a new record at £208,656,000. Bank holdings in British Government Securities and Treasury Bills were equivalent to 58 per cent of the deposits in this latter year.

Amalgamations among English banks had of recent years become of frequent occurrence; such fusions were not regarded by everyone with satisfaction, and Mr. Bonar Law, when Chancellor of the Exchequer, appointed a Committee to investigate and report on the subject. In May 1918 this Committee, under the chairmanship of Lord Colwyn, recommended that in future such amalgamations should be subject to inquiry and sanction by the Treasury before being carried into effect. Before the year was

Robert William Dundas, M.C.H.S.
Chairman of Directors 1926–
from a Photograph by C. & E. Drummond Young, Edinburgh

## The Royal Bank of Scotland

over, an affiliation arrangement was entered into between Lloyds Bank and the National Bank of Scotland, and in 1919 two other Scottish banks came under the control of units of the "Big Five" in London—the British Linen Bank, which affiliated with Barclay's Bank, and the Clydesdale Bank, which was acquired by the London Joint City and Midland Bank.

In that year the young Earl of Elgin, who had served in the War, followed the paternal example and became an extraordinary director. Two ordinary directors died — Mr. E. A. Davidson, after eleven years on the Board, and Mr. Leonard W. Dickson, C.A., who had sat on it since 1906. Mr. Dickson's death was tragic — the result of injuries sustained in a gallant attempt to stop a runaway horse in George Street, Edinburgh. The vacancies thus occasioned were filled by the election of Mr. Robert William Dundas, M.C., W.S., Edinburgh, and Mr. G. J. Lidstone, F.I.A., F.F.A. At the end of the year died Mr. Huie, former Cashier. On 12th May 1920 Mr. David Speed was appointed Accountant to the Bank. Early in June its stock of gold coin, amounting to £800,000, was transferred to the Bank of England in exchange for Currency Notes and Currency Note Certificates.

Mr. Dennistoun, the Agent in Glasgow, retired on 16th June, and died seven months later, and Mr. Thomas Lillie, sub-Agent there, was appointed his successor, with Mr. William Donald as sub-Agent.

There had been a great development in the foreign business of the Royal; it was considered desirable to have its powers more fully defined and extended. In May 1920 a new Provisional Order was drafted and approved, and on 16th August the " Royal Bank of Scotland Act, 1920," received the Royal Assent. Its main provisions were that the Royal should now have power to carry on the business of banking in all or any of its departments in any part of the world, provided that the issue of its bank-notes was confined to Scotland; and should be free " to purchase acquire whether for cash stock or otherwise undertake and continue the whole or any part of or interest in the business property assets and liabilities of any person or company carrying on any banking discount or similar business ". The clauses which followed the last quoted conferred, more specifically, power " to enter into partnership or into any arrangement for sharing profits union of interest co-operation joint adventure reciprocal concession or otherwise with any person or company carrying on or engaged in any business or transaction which the bank is authorised to carry on or engage in ", and " to make arrangements for securing such reciprocity of interests by the issue or sale to such other company or person of any of the

## The Royal Bank of Scotland

stock of the Bank or by purchase of all or any of the shares or stock or debentures or other interest in the business of any such other company or person or by an arrangement of the nature of partnership or by an exchange of such stock shares debentures or interest or by the sale of the whole or any part of the assets of the Bank for the time being or by the purchase or acquisition of the whole or any part of the assets of such other company or person and to exchange any of the assets of the Bank for the time being for any other assets which the Bank is entitled to hold ".

The directors were further empowered to increase from time to time as they deemed necessary, the capital of the bank through the creation of new stock, and the principal officer of the Bank, hitherto known by the title of Cashier, might now be described as "Cashier and General Manager" or as "General Manager", and be eligible for office as a director of the Bank.

The continued increase of business at the London office compelled extensions of the premises early in 1921. In November Mr. William Wallace, the London Manager, retired, after holding that office for sixteen years. During this year died two extraordinary directors—Mr. W. J. Dundas and Sir William Bilsland, ex-Lord Provost of Glasgow. From the Bank's beginning, Lord Provosts of Edinburgh and Glasgow have been well represented on the Board; from first to last there must have been nearly twenty. At the end of the year the Earl of Airlie and Sir George M. Paul became extraordinary directors.

In January 1922 died two retired officers of the Bank—Mr. Horley of London and Mr. Dennistoun, who had been Agent in Glasgow.

The *Journal* of the Institute of Bankers in Scotland in its April number congratulated the President of the Institute, Mr. A. K. Wright, General Manager of the Royal, on having the C.B.E. conferred on him by His Majesty in the New Year awards. " In addition to his distinguished position as a banker ", said the *Journal*, " our President has a long period of public service to his credit. He was for many years Honorary Secretary, and latterly Chairman, of the Edinburgh Chamber of Commerce; and the Scottish Savings Movement, on the Committee of which he has served since the outset, and of which he is now Deputy Chairman, owes much to his personal enthusiasm. Some time ago Mr. Wright was made a Deputy Lieutenant of the City and County of the City of Edinburgh, a local recognition which was very cordially approved. His appointment as a Commander of the Order of the British Empire takes cognisance of important services rendered in wider spheres."

A sensational robbery of the Granton branch

Sir Alexander Kemp Wright, K.B.E., D.L.
General Manager 1917–
from a photograph by A. Swan Watson, F.R.P.S., Edinburgh

## The Royal Bank of Scotland

of the Royal on the afternoon of 20th January 1923 is worth recording in some detail for its transatlantic or cinema features. The staff of the Bank were "held up" by three masked men with revolvers, who were successful in getting away with a sum of £1779 : 19 : 9. As the result of the shock, Mr. James Dick Main, the Bank Agent, subsequently died.

The Bank is situated in a square which on that afternoon was exceptionally quiet, and the only witness who could contribute any useful information to the police was a Corporation labourer who had been digging a trench in the neighbourhood when the crime took place. He had seen the robbers make their escape on a motor bicycle, the number of which he had noted, and was confident he could identify at least one of the men. Every police force in the country being immediately set to work to discover where a motor cycle of this number was registered, it was found by the Glasgow Police to be the property of a man called William Stewart, resident in that city.

Stewart, however, denied all knowledge of the robbery, stating that he had met with an accident while touring with his cycle in the country, and sold his damaged machine for £30 to the driver of a passing motor lorry. Though the Glasgow Police were inclined to accept Stewart's story, Detective-Lieutenant

## The History of

Sangster of the Edinburgh Police sent Kelly, the man who had noted the number on the cycle and was confident of his ability to recognise one of its riders, through to Glasgow, where an identification parade, including Stewart, was arranged.

Kelly had no hesitation in picking out Stewart (still at liberty), from among six men paraded, as the man he had seen in Granton. Incriminating evidence was then found in Stewart's house; and the actual motor cycle, recovered from the Clyde, where he had thrown it, was one of the productions at his trial. Associated with him in the "hold-up" were four other men, and all of them were convicted.

Practically all the money stolen was accounted for, and the major portion was restored to the Royal Bank, which had offered a reward of £500—or *pro rata* according to the sum restored—to those civilians who might assist the police in bringing the bandits to justice.

There had now been erected on the south wall of the Bank vestibule in St. Andrew Square a beautiful Memorial to those eighty-four members of the staff who had fallen in the War. A large panel of green slate, on which the roll of honour was inscribed in gilt lettering, surrounded by a bronze frame, was placed in a recess, with a background of Hoptonwood stone designed to harmonise with the general

## The Royal Bank of Scotland

architecture of the vestibule. In the lunette of the arched head of the recess a circular bronze plaque displayed a three-quarter-length figure, symbolising Sacrifice, standing before a trenched and shell-shattered section of battle-field on which a cross marked a soldier's grave. A wreath of laurel leaves and poppies enriched the moulding of the lunette, which was the work of Mr. Pilkington Jackson, sculptor; the architectural features were the design of Messrs. Dick Peddie & Walker Todd.

On Saturday afternoon, 10th February, this Memorial was formally unveiled by Field-Marshal Earl Haig in presence of a large and representative company, over which the Duke of Buccleuch, the Governor of the Bank, presided—including the Duchess of Buccleuch, Countess Haig, Lord Provost Hutchison of Edinburgh and Mrs. Hutchison, with many of the directors, officials of the Bank, and ex-service men who had been comrades of those now commemorated. The absence of one who had taken a deep personal interest in the Memorial and had looked forward with eagerness to the day of its unveiling was alluded to in the opening words of the Duke of Buccleuch's brief introductory speech. This was Mr. Charles Carlow, Managing Director of the Fife Coal Company, who had been a director of the Bank since 1898, and was Chairman of the Board. He had died twelve days before this

# The History of

consummation of a project close to his heart and owing much to his sound judgement.

Two-thirds of the whole Bank staff had been on active service. They had gone, as Mr. Wright detailed, from the head office and its branches all over Scotland from Thurso in the north to Stranraer in the south, and from the Western Isles to the towns of the East Coast. Included among them were a contingent who went from the London office.

Before unveiling the Memorial (the names on which are given in an Appendix), Earl Haig, in the course of a speech in eloquent and moving terms, spoke of it as standing for something even more than the perpetuation of the memory of the gallant men, members of the Royal Bank of Scotland who, in far-scattered fields of battle, gave their lives to Scotland and the Empire. In that historic house, so long associated with the development and well-being of Scotland, the Memorial further recalled that no small part of the greatness of our country was due to the world-wide reputation for financial integrity of institutions such as this, and the type of men who made them possible.

After dedication of the Memorial by the Reverend George Christie, Minister of St. Andrew's Parish, Edinburgh, wreaths were placed at its foot by Sir Henry Cook on behalf of the directors, by Mr. J. B. Adshead on behalf of the Edinburgh staff, Mr. Thomas

WEST END OFFICE, EDINBURGH

## The History of

consummation of a project close to his heart and owing much to his sound judgement.

Two-thirds of the whole Bank staff had been on active service. They had gone, as Mr. Wright detailed, from the head office and its branches all over Scotland from Thurso in the north to Stranraer in the south, and from the Western Isles to the towns of the East Coast. Included among them were a contingent who went from the London office.

Before unveiling the Memorial (the names on which are given in an Appendix), Earl Haig, in the course of a speech in eloquent and moving terms, spoke of it as standing for something even more than the perpetuation of the memory of the gallant men, members of the Royal Bank of Scotland who, in far-scattered fields of battle, gave their lives to Scotland and the Empire. In that historic house, so long associated with the development and well-being of Scotland, the Memorial further recalled that no small part of the greatness of our country was due to the world-wide reputation for financial integrity of institutions such as this, and the type of men who made them possible.

After dedication of the Memorial by the Reverend George Christie, Minister of St. Andrew's Parish, Edinburgh, wreaths were placed at its foot by Sir Henry Cook on behalf of the directors, by Mr. J. B. Adshead on behalf of the Edinburgh staff, Mr. Thomas

## The Royal Bank of Scotland

Lillie on behalf of the Glasgow staff, Mr. Q. B. Grant on behalf of the Dundee staff, and Mr. Wright on behalf of the staff in London. The Last Post and Réveillé having been sounded by buglers, the ceremony concluded with the National Anthem and the Benediction.

Before the month had closed, the Board lost another valued member — Sir William Robertson of Dunfermline, Lord-Lieutenant of the County of Fife, who had been an extraordinary director for six years, and died on 28th February. In April Field-Marshal Earl Haig was appointed an ordinary director. September saw the plans approved for a new branch office in Hope Street, Edinburgh. A portrait by Raeburn of William Simpson of Parsons Green, Cashier of the Bank for the period from 1780 till 1808, was purchased for the head office.

On Friday, 27th April, a Memorial to those men of the London staff who had died in the war was unveiled in the office in Bishopsgate Street. It took the form of a bronze tablet, designed in the classic Renaissance style by Sir Edwyn Cooper, on which the names of the fallen were engraved.

His Grace the Duke of Buccleuch presided. Mr. A. K. Wright, in a few introductory remarks regarding the war service of the men commemorated, stated that of the London office staff thirty-five had joined the Colours.

The History of

Of these, seven had died, and nine had been wounded. As was to be expected, many of those enlisted had joined the Highland and other Scottish regiments. Three were awarded the Military Cross; one of these, Lieut. Wilson of the London Scottish, did not survive the action on the Somme in which his decoration was earned. Those thirty-five men had fought in one or other of practically all the theatres of war—France, Egypt, Gallipoli, Salonika, and Palestine. Of their survivors, able to resume their old places in the Bank after those years of campaigning, he was happy to say twenty-five were now assembled before him taking part in this commemoration ceremony.

General Sir Ian Hamilton, having unveiled the Memorial, made a short but eloquent and moving speech, in the course of which he said it was good to have such names as those engraved on the tablet before him in our records and in our minds. As of the young Spartans who fought under Leonidas, we might say of these boys that their life was heroic and their end was glorious. They had, doubtless, gone to war from various motives, but even the most diffident must have felt themselves adventurers in a tremendous cause whose greatest triumph ought to be the putting of an end to all wars.

After the dedication, and a dedicatory prayer by the Rev. Archibald Fleming, D.D., of

## The Royal Bank of Scotland

St. Columba's Church, Pont Street, wreaths were placed before the Memorial on behalf of the directors, and the staffs at the London, Glasgow, and Head Offices. The hymn " Our God, our help in ages past " was sung; the buglers of the Scots Guards played the Last Post and the Réveillé, and the proceedings closed with the National Anthem and the Benediction.

When 1923 had opened, an imminent boom in trade was confidently anticipated in many quarters. The efficacy of auto-suggestion as a cure for blushing and low spirits had just been demonstrated by the Nancy school of psychologists, and M. Coué had almost guaranteed that if we whispered firmly to ourselves every night and morning that " every day and every way, trade grows better and better ", the whole wide world would come clamouring to our doors for goods to buy. This pleasing illusion, eagerly adopted by advertising agents, was thereafter to be brought out and polished afresh by newspapers after each Christmas season for the next three years.

As a matter of fact, though 1923, on the whole, found Britain reassured that the painful slump which followed the inflation boom of 1919–20 had passed its worst, there was no great evidence of increasing prosperity, save in a few trades — particularly coal and iron. These had been stimulated by the stoppage of

## The Royal Bank of Scotland

production in Germany and the resultant effect on other Continental countries which had formerly depended on the German mines.

Over all the Scottish banks there was, for that year, a substantial decline in deposits, amounting to over £26,000,000, mainly as the result of the low rate of interest prevailing, though their balance-sheets revealed a strong and liquid position. Country branches were extending wonderfully; the Royal, which had 167 branches in 1918 and 175 in 1921, now had 188. The closing weeks of a somewhat uneventful banking year were enlivened in the North by the announcement of another combination—that of the Midland Bank and the North of Scotland Bank, a corporation whose shares were nearly all held locally.

The more sensational announcement of a step which had been for some time in contemplation, and was now decided on, was postponed by St. Andrew Square till after New Year's Day. Few people, either in London or Edinburgh, could have anticipated the absorption of Drummonds', one of the oldest banks in the West End of London, by the Royal Bank of Scotland.

## CHAPTER XXI

#### DRUMMONDS' BANK

POPULAR sentiment in Scotland was highly gratified by an alliance which by its nature differed from any of those mentioned in the previous chapter. This was no case of a Scottish bank being merged in a London one; the situation was reversed when the Royal—older than any joint-stock bank in England except the mother of all British banking—acquired the business founded in 1717 by Andrew Drummond. To the romantic spirit it seemed something like a clan reunion. The names of Drummond and Coutts in London banking had always had peculiarly national associations for Scotsmen; they were regarded in a sense as bold eighteenth-century pioneers who, for two centuries, had kept the saltire of St. Andrew flying over their outposts in the very centre of the English capital.

There was another reason why, in the North, an amalgamation of the Royal and Drummonds' should appear the most natural thing in the world; the Royal itself owed not a little to the

## The History of

remarkable personality, zeal, and influence of a Drummond who sat on its Board from 1727 till 1745.

The Drummonds are a very old Scottish clan. Tradition has always had it that the first to adopt the name was Maurice, a Hungarian, who came to Scotland in the retinue of Margaret, later queen of Malcolm Canmore, and finally Saint, and established himself in territorial permanence on a ridge of land in Stirlingshire. He so created for himself and his posterity a surname originating, in the Scottish fashion, from the land he owned; " Drymen " or " Drummond " derives from the Gaelic *druim*, which describes a backbone or ridge of landscape.

If there were really Hungarian blood in the Drummonds (and it is always to be remembered that the sennachies were extraordinarily imaginative functionaries), they were truly Scots when they fought at Bannockburn, at Chevy Chase, and for the Stuarts always, up till the day when the Stuart cause went down for ever on Culloden Moor.

Of the Drummond family in the late seventeenth and early eighteenth century were two " Highland cousins ", apparently far-sundered in political sentiment. One of them was Andrew Drummond, born in 1688, son of Sir John Drummond of Machany; the other was George Drummond, Lord Provost of Edinburgh. Let us not imagine they made much of the relation-

## The Royal Bank of Scotland

ship suggested by coincidence of name; it was enough that "all Drummonds were sib to the Duke of Perth", as all Campbells are sib to MacCailein Mor, the Duke of Argyll.

When grand old John Campbell, Cashier of the Royal Bank, Edinburgh, in 1745, had his day's routine of business in the Ship Close spoiled by the invasion of Bonnie Prince Charlie and his *sans culottes*, the attitude of Clan Drummond must have a little puzzled him. John Campbell was a sportsman, willing to make every reasonable allowance for individual idiosyncracies in political affairs. The Drummond nearest to him was "Geordie" the ex-Lord Provost, one of his own directors—unmistakably, and even fanatically, a Whig—a Hanoverian. Ex-Provost Drummond was all right (so far as a bank Cashier, not quite certain how the cat would jump, could decide), but there was this London Drummond, Andrew, a reputed Tory and Jacobite with a bank of his own and the ear of George III. John Campbell and Lord Breadalbane must have often thrashed out this perplexing clan anomaly over mulled port in the Abbey.

The Edinburgh Drummond of 1745—George, ex-Lord Provost of the city, born in 1687, in Newton Castle, near Blairgowrie—had been, at the Union of 1707, appointed Accountant General of Excise, and eight years later was a Commissioner of Customs with a salary of £1000 a year. At the battle of Sheriffmuir, in 1715, he led a company of Edinburgh volunteers, and the first report which the Edinburgh magistrates got of the victory of Argyll was written by Drummond on the field. In 1725 he became Provost of Edinburgh, a position to which he had the remarkable distinction of being elected seven times. To him was largely due the creation of the new town of Edinburgh and the Royal Infirmary. He was a man of great business capacity, but also of a pious and somewhat mystical character — a combination that had some difficulty in adjusting itself at times to the convivial moods of the Board's dinner-parties, as we have seen in an earlier chapter.

Though ex-Provost Drummond was fifty-eight years of age when the Highland army approached to the attack of Edinburgh, he took upon himself the best part of the organisation of the citizens for the city's defence, having little confidence in either the integrity or ability of its Jacobite Provost Stewart. As captain of one of the companies of volunteers hastily mobilised by his direction, he suffered the chagrin of finding the majority of his men, when marching to the West Port to repel the tartan invasion, ingloriously scuttle down the " closes " at the first skirl of the bagpipes. Bagpipes, it must be admitted, are rather unsettling.

## The Royal Bank of Scotland

No doubt Captain Drummond for the moment heartily wished himself back in the Ship Close discussing credits for decent Whigs, but with his gallant remnant he carried on and fought for his King and Sir John Cope at Prestonpans. With Cope he joined in the retreat on Berwick, and he remained out of Edinburgh till Prince Charlie was well on the road to Derby. A subsequent visit to London brought him the acquaintance of a charming Quaker widow with a fortune of £20,000, whom he married in 1755, at the age of sixty-eight; she was his fourth wife! Let us hope there was "nothing disagreeable either in her manners or appearance", as in his Diary he testified of his third wife, who had also brought substantial relief to his domestic exchequer.

At the moment when his remote clansman in Edinburgh was fighting for the King in Scotland, Mr. Drummond of London was providing at least some of the sinews of war for the same good cause—an anomalous position for a gentleman with the reputation of being a sturdy old Jacobite by heredity. How came Andrew Drummond to be in the good grace of George III.?

Doubtless the King had never heard the Gaelic proverb that heredity goes down to the rock, and that sooner or later every Drummond astray comes back to the clan!

Andrew Drummond as a youth had walked

from Edinburgh to London with his heart in his mouth at every change-house, for he had in his knapsack Scottish money to stimulate flagging Jacobite zeal in infidel uncovenanted quarters. There is still in Drummonds' Bank the identical walking-stick he used on the occasion, a malacca cane with a gold crutch handle.

It is significant, too, that the oldest book of accounts in Drummonds' should be a record of moneys collected in Amsterdam on behalf of the Stuart cause—" Journaal Generaal van alle mijne Koopzandel inde Name Godes begonn; Pmo Jannuary des Iaars 1697 "— though it must be observed that Andrew Drummond, when the ledger opened, was less than ten years old.

His father, Sir John Drummond, like many other Highland gentlemen, had shared in the exile of the Chevalier St. George, and joined one Van der Heyden as a private banker in Holland in 1697. Less than two years later the name of the original firm, " Goris and Jan Van der Heyden ", was changed to " Van der Heyden en Drummont ". Of that Dutch banking business two ledgers written in Dutch survive, and the entries show that a good many of its customers were Scotsmen either on the Continent or at home—Drummonds, Hamiltons, Fergusons, Hays, Gordons, Kers, and, more conspicuously, " My Lord Tullibardine ".

Andrew Drummond
Founder of Drummonds Bank in 1717
from the print in Drummonds Bank

# The Royal Bank of Scotland.

The second of these Dutch ledgers closed with two entries in 1690; Sir John had died two years before. His son Andrew opened a new ledger in English in London on 17th March 1716, as a goldsmith " mending, graving, etc., gold and silver ". This ledger, which was in use till 1724, is exclusively concerned with authentic goldsmith business for many distinguished customers, including Lord Belhaven, the Earl of Dundonald, the Countess of Dalhousie, Lord Eglinton, the Duke of Hamilton, Earl of Hyndford, Earl of Sutherland, Marquess of Tweeddale, Marquess of Lothian, Lord Lansdowne, Earl of Rothes, and Robert Walpole.

On 26th September 1717, however, was opened a second English ledger, devoted entirely to banking accounts. Andrew Drummond, as private banker, was well supported by the clan; he had on his books at least eleven customers of his own name, including Lord John Drummond, one of the most active participants in the Rising of 1715. Scottish Jacobites were well represented by such insurgent notabilities as the Duchess of Perth, Lady Margaret Nairne, the Earls of Lauderdale and Kinnoul, Lord Lovat and Viscount Strathallan, Lord Charles Murray, and Lord James Murray.

The young Scots gentleman with the ambiguous knapsack is said to have had his first business premises on the exact site where

## The History of

Drummonds' Branch of the Royal Bank of Scotland now stands. The "till-money" was not considerable to start with. A sailor with an order for £20 prize money, realising this, handsomely offered to take £5 down, and the remainder in instalments—a pleasing example of the come-and-go spirit which has always animated the British tar. The incident is immortalised in an old engraving which hangs till this day in Drummonds' bank parlour.

Till 1741 Andrew Drummond was sole controller of the business, and then, or shortly afterwards, the firm became "Drummond and Company". We might naturally think that a London bank with Simon Fraser, Lord Lovat, as a customer, in 1740, was in a curiously invidious position, but about that very time even ex-Provost Drummond, the Whig of Edinburgh, was a great friend of Simon, who had not definitely made up his mind what his politics were. It was through Drummonds' Bank that the Government paid the Highland Chief his Civil List allowance of £400 a year. When Lovat, condemned to death in Westminster, was being driven to the Tower, it is said that Robert and Henry Drummond went to a window of the bank to see him pass, and that Andrew Drummond (who lived till the age of eighty-one), with Highland instinct, averted his gaze from the humiliation of a once puissant chief whom he had known in happier

## The Royal Bank of Scotland

circumstances, and whose illusions he had one time shared.

Drummonds', by that time—indeed, long before—had many loyalist Scottish clients in spite of its vaguely reputed passion for the Stuart cause — the Earl of Sutherland, for instance, the Earl of Kinnoul, the Duke of Montrose, the Marquess of Lothian, and the Duchess of Hamilton. George III. himself was on its ledgers, and his spendthrift Prince of Wales, whose overdrafts were grimly cut down on the advice of his father.

The truth seems to be that in the far-seeing financial world, particularly among Scotsmen in London, real passion for the Jacobite cause was tepid after the Union. There remained by and by only sentimental memories of days gone by for ever, and the tartan waistcoats put on by Scots *convives* for dinner-parties were mere *panache*—a romantic flourish, as the kilt remains to-day. Bankers did not put on tartan waistcoats to business, and Andrew Drummond doubtless considered the private politics of his customers were no concern of his.

His reputed Jacobitism has had a curious light thrown on it by a discovery made only since this book has been in preparation. *He was one of the original proprietors of the Royal Bank of Scotland, financially as much interested in its welfare as his kinsman George of Edinburgh.*

In 1727 Mr. Drummond, who had held

## The History of

stock in the Equivalent Company, exchanged it for £500 of stock in the Royal Bank, the offspring of the Equivalent, and thus became one of the first proprietors of the new bank, from which he continued to draw dividends till after the Forty-five. In 1742 he added £1000 stock to his Royal Bank holding, having bought the additional shares from a John Drummond of London at a premium of 42 per cent, and his name disappeared from the list of Royal Bank proprietors only in 1746, when he sold out his holding to an Abraham Craiestey.

This old bank, so steeped in Scottish historical traditions though flourishing in London, and continuously owned and administered by successive generations of the same Drummond family, had, when the absorption with the Royal took place, and still has, its headquarters at 49 Charing Cross, near the Admiralty Arch, which opens on the glorious vista of the Mall and Buckingham Palace.

It was on 2nd January 1924 that the agreement to purchase Drummonds' Bank was signed and sealed, with the approval of the Treasury, and the following official announcement was issued by the Royal Bank:

The Royal Bank of Scotland, subject to the sanction of the Treasury, have arranged to acquire the business of the private banking firm of Messrs. Drummond, 49 Charing Cross, London, and will

VIEW SHOWING DRUMMONDS' BRANCH AT CHARING CROSS
(On left of Admiralty Arch)

## The Royal Bank of Scotland

take over their assets and liabilities from January 12, 1924. The assets will include the bank and adjoining freehold buildings.

The business will be carried on as a branch of the Royal Bank of Scotland in the well-known premises adjoining Admiralty Arch, which will be known as Drummonds' Branch. The partners of Drummonds' Bank, Messrs. George, Maldwin, Charles, and Frederick Drummond, will continue to give the same personal attention to their customers' affairs as hitherto, and will, with the addition of certain representatives of the Royal Bank, act as a local board of directors for the administration of this branch, of which Mr. George Drummond will be chairman. Mr. W. H. Smith will continue to act as manager.

Customers of Drummonds' will find that the business is conducted on the same lines as hitherto, and they will have the added advantage of being associated with an important Scottish bank.

The acquisition of a West End branch will also be a convenience to many customers of the Royal Bank, whose City office in Bishopsgate has hitherto been their only place of business in London.

On the same evening Messrs. Drummonds issued a circular, as follows, to their clients:

49 CHARING CROSS, LONDON, S.W.1,
*January 2, 1924.*

We beg leave to inform you that after mature consideration we have accepted an offer by the Royal Bank of Scotland for the acquisition of our business as from January 12, 1924. Thereafter we shall be known as Drummonds' Branch of the Royal Bank of Scotland.

## The History of

There will be no alteration in our Management or Staff, as this will remain as hitherto, the present Partners continuing to give the same personal attention to their customers' affairs.

We have pleasure in enclosing a copy of the last report of the Royal Bank of Scotland.

We feel convinced that this fusion of two of the oldest Scottish Banking Institutions cannot but prove to be to the advantage of our Customers.

We remain,
Your most obedient Servants,
DRUMMONDS.

How the absorption was regarded in Scotland could be gathered easily from the demand which immediately arose for Royal Bank Stock, as shown in the substantial rise which immediately followed those announcements. The Royal increased its capital stock from £2,000,000 to £2,500,000. Of this new stock £60,000 was allotted to Messrs. Drummond in part payment of the business acquired, while the balance was allotted to the existing shareholders of the Royal at the rate of £22 of new stock for each full £100 stock formerly held. The price was payable in full on 26th April 1924, and, in the case of stockholders abroad, on 15th May. The allotment price of the new stock was fixed at £250 per cent, and what part of this stock was not claimed by proprietors was allocated ultimately among members of the staff at the same price.

During those exciting weeks in January

# The Royal Bank of Scotland

1924, while Drummonds' Branch was naturally in the limelight, attention was suddenly brought back to the City Office in Bishopsgate Street by the sudden death of Mr. Alexander Dick, its Joint-Manager. On 11th January he was at his post as usual; on the same evening he died as the result of a heart attack. All his working years had been spent in the service of the Royal, into one of whose branches he had entered as a youth. He had gone to the London office in 1879, and after passing through various grades of the service, and occupying for some years the post of chief of the Securities Department, he was appointed Assistant Manager to Mr. William Wallace. He had, on the occasion of Mr. Wallace's retirement from business in 1921, been made Joint London Manager with Mr. William Whyte, and though his time for retirement was approaching, his colleagues and friends had anticipated for him many years of happy leisure.

In virtue of the powers conferred on the directors by the Royal Bank of Scotland Act, 1873, Mr. George H. Drummond of "Drummonds'" was, in June, elected an extraordinary director. Sir John Hatt Noble Graham of Larbert had, for health reasons, retired in May; he had joined the Extraordinary Board in 1894.

In July 1924 Mr. William Davidson, who had held the appointment of Joint-Superintendent of Branches for many years and who

## The History of

was well known throughout the Bank and its connections, having done much during his long period of service to foster the growth of the Branch system, retired under the Superannuation Scheme of the Bank. On his retirement Mr. James Fife Ferguson, Joint-Superintendent of Branches along with Mr. Davidson since 1917, had associated with him under the same official designation Mr. George F. B. Hunter, senior Inspector.

Throughout the year, trade and commerce still languished, but there were many indications that the country was really tracing its troubles to their source, and British credit stood as high as at any period since the War. Progress had been made in other and more apparent directions; such as it was it was attributable mainly to the improvement which took place in the value of sterling. We were having our first experience of a Labour Government (returned in the election of January and destined for an early dissolution), and the novelty of the situation inevitably was attended with some anxiety. Unemployment continued to give grave concern, and the conflict over the difference between wages and cost of living threatened to develop into class warfare.

For the third year in succession there was a shrinkage in Scottish bank deposits, the result of the process of deflation now in progress, accompanied by a surprising stability

## The Royal Bank of Scotland

in the figures representing advances to customers.

At the beginning of January 1925 the official designation of the chief official of the Glasgow office was changed from "Agent" to "Manager". In July Sir Arthur Worley, C.B.E., General Manager of the North British and Mercantile Insurance Company, London, was made an extraordinary director of the Royal Bank.

The restoration of the Gold Standard eliminated many risks in commercial transactions by confining the exchange to the narrow limits of gold points, but banking figures continued to reflect the dullness of trade, most marked in the case of the heavy industries. There were unprecedented losses in the coal trade; the wages and hours agreement conceded by the coal owners in May 1924 to avert a complete suspension of work had long before its year of trial proved ruinous. A revision of the agreement proposed by the Mining Association was strenuously resisted by the Miners' Federation, and a disastrous strike was averted only by Mr. Baldwin's government granting a heavy subvention in aid of wages from 1st August 1925 to 1st May 1926, pending a report by a Royal Commission on the conditions of the industry. It was merely a palliative, a postponement of the *mauvais quart d'heure* of serious count and reckoning, and though the outlook

The History of

for Scottish banking on the threshold of 1926 appeared to be distinctly favourable, the discerning were not carried off their feet by the usual New Year spirit of sanguine auto-suggestion.

Two members of the Royal's Board died within three weeks of each other in the spring of 1926 — Sheriff Fleming, one of the most popular men in Parliament House, who had clerked in St. Andrew Square under his father; and Sir George M. Paul, who had joined the Extraordinary Board in 1921 and for many years had been Law Agent of the Bank. The vacancies thus created were filled by the election of the Earl of Elgin as an ordinary director and Mr. James Finlay Muir of Glasgow as an extraordinary director.

The name of Mr. Alexander Kemp Wright, the General Manager, figured in the Birthday Honours list of 3rd July 1926 as a Knight Commander of the Most Excellent Order of the British Empire. Before beginning the business on the agenda at the directors' meeting on 21st July, the Chairman said that although no doubt all the members of the Board had already congratulated Sir Alexander on the honour recently conferred on him by His Majesty the King, he thought it was only fitting that the Board should formally express their congratulations and good wishes — " Apart from the invaluable

## The Royal Bank of Scotland

services which he rendered to the Bank, to which reference need not then be made ", the minute records, " the high qualities which Sir Alexander possessed and the great amount of public service he had performed, particularly in connection with the Scottish National Savings Committee, were not only well known to the Board but throughout the country, and it was extremely gratifying that those services should be so fittingly recognised by the honour which had been bestowed on him. In the name of the Board the Chairman therefore congratulated Sir Alexander very heartily, and proposed that this expression of appreciation and congratulation should be recorded in the Minutes. The Secretary asked on behalf of the Officers and Staff of the Bank that they might be associated with what had been said, and this was cordially agreed to."

This penultimate year of the Royal's two-centuries-old history was not without " the promise and the potency " of bright years soon to come, but it witnessed one of the most disastrous labour disputes ever known, not only a bitter and long-protracted stoppage in the mines of the country as a whole, but, for a briefer period, a General Strike which paralysed nearly every industry. It left its mark in the diminished figures of all banks as revealed in the statistics relating to the balance-sheet position at the end of the year.

Nevertheless, the Duke of Buccleuch in submitting the report at the end of the year to the Court of Proprietors was justified in hazarding the opinion that the position of the Bank, as shown in the balance-sheet, would be found eminently satisfactory. The profits, after providing for all bad and doubtful debts, and making allowances for contingencies, amounted to £476,545, just a little above the figure for the previous year. And for the first time in the history of the Bank the Rest exceeded the paid-up capital as recently increased to £2,500,000, the two together now having reached the impressive total of £5,071,249.

The bicentenary year of the Royal dawned upon a nation more cheerfully expectant of better times in prospect than at any period since the depression following the delusive brief prosperity which succeeded the Peace.

The first six months of 1927, which conclude the period of this history, confirmed the spirit of optimism where not too extravagantly entertained. Undoubtedly the clouds were slowly lifting, and patches of blue sky were intermittently showing over most of Europe, though it was still obvious that it might be long before we should see again a clear horizon and a settled calm.

Timid capital became a little more courageous, as the increasing loan business of the banks disclosed. On every hand they proved

## The Royal Bank of Scotland

ready and willing to foster all legitimate trade enterprises, and in several of them the general advances amounted to 50 per cent of their deposits. Yet it should be noted that no inconsiderable part of the credits given were for poor relief, directly or indirectly; though slowly declining, the list of unemployed in Britain was still the largest in Europe.

The annual General Meeting of the contributors to the Officers' Widows' Fund of the Royal, held on 12th April 1927, should not pass unnoticed, for the Fund is an important feature of the Bank's domestic activities, and has a history of more than a century. In 1820 a fund was constituted for the benefit of the widows and children of the staffs in the head office in Edinburgh and in the branch office in Glasgow. In 1870 annuities of £80 were paid to each of the widows of deceased officers and clerks, and annuities of £20 to widows of deceased porters. In that year it was deemed expedient to extend the operations of the Fund, as many new branches had come into existence, and many officers had not become contributors to the Fund within the time limited by the contract. To extend the scope of the Fund so as to include all the officers, agents, and clerks everywhere as contributors, the authority of Parliament was necessary, and accordingly "an Act for better raising and securing a Fund for the Widows and Children of the Officers, Agents,

## The Royal Bank of Scotland

Clerks and Porters of the Royal Bank of Scotland " was passed on 20th June 1870, and in 1878 and 1892 amending Acts of Parliament were obtained.

There were, in 1870, only thirty-nine contributors to the Fund, which had £20,536 invested, and the annuities paid in 1871 came to £539. At Candlemas 1927 there were 388 contributors and 90 annuitants. The annual income was £11,248, and the market value of funds invested was £208,567. Annuities came to £4300. By this time only three of the contributors under the original scheme survived. The annuities payable at present to widows and orphans under the 1870 Act are: First Class, £75; Second, £50; and Third, £25. Since midsummer 1925 the Bank has supplemented each of the annuities under the 1870 scheme (with certain exceptions) by £25.

This domestic note may, appropriately enough, conclude our extracts from the official records of two hundred years of the Royal's history. All that remains to complete a story that may have a sequent volume in long-distant future years—the account of the Bicentenary Celebration in Edinburgh on 3rd June 1927—was given in practically all the newspapers of the United Kingdom for that week, and is here to be found *in extenso* in an Appendix.

# APPENDIX

## THE BICENTENARY CELEBRATION

On the evening of Friday, 3rd June 1927, the Royal Bank celebrated its second Centenary by a dinner at which every department and branch of the establishment in Scotland and England was represented, and leading figures in the world of British banking and finance generally took part. A company of three hundred guests (whose names follow this report of the proceedings) assembled in the Banqueting Hall of the North British Hotel in Edinburgh, with His Grace the Duke of Buccleuch and Queensberry, K.T., Governor of the Bank, presiding.

Apologies for absence were intimated from the Right Hon. Winston S. Churchill, Chancellor of the Exchequer; the Rt. Hon. Viscount Inchcape; the Rt. Hon. the Earl of Airlie; the Rt. Hon. Lord Glendyne; the Rt. Hon. the Lord Justice-General; the Rt. Hon. the Lord Advocate for Scotland; the Lord Provosts of Glasgow, Dundee, and Aberdeen;

# The History of

Sir Hugh Shaw Stewart, Baronet; Sir James Alfred Ewing; Sir John R. Findlay, Baronet; Mr. George H. Drummond; Mr. Charles Drummond; Mr. John Rae; Mr. Lawrence Currie; Mr. J. Finlay Muir; Mr. R. G. Thomas, General Manager, British Linen Bank; Mr. Ryti, President of Finlands Bank, Helsingfors; Mr. J. Maxtone Graham, C.A.; Mr. A. S. Michie, and others.

It was also announced that numerous letters, cablegrams, and telegrams of congratulation had been received from banking correspondents and other friends, not only in the United Kingdom and Ireland, but in many parts abroad.

The loyal toasts having been duly pledged,

The Rt. Hon. the EARL OF STRATHMORE AND KINGHORNE, G.C.V.O., Deputy Governor of the Bank, proposed the toast of " The City of Edinburgh ". He said:

" My Lord Duke, my Lord Provost, my Lords and Gentlemen—There are a good many Scotsmen from different parts of Scotland here to-night, but we all look to Edinburgh as the capital of our kingdom of Scotland, and though I speak more or less as a provincial Scot, I am pleased I have some connection with Edinburgh. In the first place, there is my association with the Royal Bank of Scotland; I greatly appreciate

## The Royal Bank of Scotland

the honour of being its Deputy Governor, and that appreciation is increased if possible by the fact that my name is thus associated with that of my friend, the Duke of Buccleuch. (Applause.)

"All of us in Scotland have a great deal to be proud of in Edinburgh. It was a trite phrase to call it Modern Athens, but to the æsthetic ear it was really more pleasing than 'Auld Reekie'. Edinburgh has been one of the greatest centres of education in the country. From one of its schools, five former pupils formed part of one of the Coalition Governments—they were Watsonians, I think—which shows that some of these schools turn out very good material. Then we know that some of the very greatest lawyers have come from Edinburgh. It has been said that men belong to two types. The first type have more brains than audacity; the other more audacity than brains. I think we may congratulate ourselves that in the former category we can count practically all those men who come from Edinburgh. When in London I have been greatly struck by the fact that it is men from Edinburgh who dominate the medical and surgical world. Then Edinburgh is the headquarters of many great institutions which are a pattern for institutions of the kind throughout the world—great insurance companies, great firms of chartered accountants, great publishing firms, most suc-

## The History of

cessful investment companies, and last, but not least, great banks, foremost among which is the Royal Bank of Scotland.

"It may be interesting—I hope it will be particularly interesting to the Lord Provost—if I venture to ask you to glance back two hundred years to the transactions which took place between the Town Council and the Royal Bank. I am indebted to Sir Alexander Wright for furnishing me with the facts. From the very establishment of the Bank the Town Council showed a friendly inclination. One of the first things they did to show their trust in the Bank was to facilitate the circulation of its notes. Less than a year after the Bank was established the Town Council came to the Bank and borrowed £1500. (Laughter.) It was only from February to Whitsunday, at a rate of 4½ per cent. In 1729 a request came from the Town Council, and in consequence of that the Bank ordered from the Mint £2000 worth of new copper coins. I have reason to think that this was owing to the fact that the passing of counterfeit copper coins was very prevalent over the country. In the early 'forties the Council again approached the Bank, and asked the directors for an advance of £2500. That was a time of great distress. The money was wanted to buy corn and meal for the poor, and, of course, that was granted. Some years later, about the

## The Royal Bank of Scotland

time, I suppose, when Georgian architecture came to its most classical period, the Town Council came to the Bank for a loan to extend and improve the city. They wanted £5000. I hope the Lord Provost will take note that not only did the directors at once grant the loan, but also rebated £250 of whatever interest might accrue. (Applause.) These few instances show the good relations that existed between the Royal Bank and the Town Council during the infancy and youth of the Bank. We are now in the Bank's prime of life, and when we see the head of the Town Council at our festive board, I think it proves that the relations are still of the same happy character. (Applause.) I would only like to add that the Bank started with the enormous capital of £111,000. Now the capital including the Rest is over £5,000,000.

"It must be a satisfaction to the citizens, and, I am sure, to the Lord Provost that the ancient glories of the Palace of Holyrood have of late years been revived, and that their Majesties the King and Queen are soon coming again to Edinburgh. We are all looking forward to their visit to the venerable Scottish capital. Edinburgh has been an extremely well-governed city, and that, no doubt, is in a great measure due to the personalities of the Provosts who have held office. I think it must be a further satisfaction to the citizens to realise that the present Provost is a most worthy successor to those who have gone before. (Applause.) It is a tribute to the public spirit and to the sense of public duty of the Lord Provost that with his many other activities he should accept and undertake the highly onerous duties of Lord Provost and Lord Lieutenant of the city of Edinburgh. My Lord Duke and Gentlemen, coupled with the name of Lord Provost Stevenson, I give you ' The City of Edinburgh '." (Applause.)

Lord Provost STEVENSON replied:
" My Lord Duke, my Lords and Gentlemen —I should like at the very outset to congratulate you, my Lord Duke, and your fellow-directors, on the celebration of the two hundredth anniversary of the institution of the Royal Bank. These two hundred years have been years of progress to you, and I cannot help reflecting that the progress has been equally marked in every sphere of activity in the city, civic, social, and commercial. Two hundred years ago the population of the city of Edinburgh, which included Leith, was 50,000. To-day the population of Greater Edinburgh is 450,000. What appeals to me, however, more than that, is that to-day I have seventy colleagues in the Town Council. The Lord Provost of that day had only twenty-four. Two hundred years ago, when this Bank was started, there was no New

## The Royal Bank of Scotland

Town. Forty years later the North Bridge was erected, and if you try to visualise what Edinburgh of two hundred years ago was like without this magnificent New Town of ours, you have a bird's-eye view of the progress that has been made.

"I am not going to say whether the rise and progress of the Royal Bank are due to the city, or the progress and rise of the city are due to the Bank, but it is true to say that the relations between the Royal Bank and the Corporation of Edinburgh have always been of the most friendly character. I can even go further than you have gone, Lord Strathmore, and I hope it will not be considered bad taste for me to refer to the fact. You have told us that in 1740, when there was great distress in this city, and when the Corporation of that day had to go and buy corn, they went to the Royal Bank of Scotland and asked for money. They got it free of interest ! (Applause.)

"My Lord Duke, if the Royal Bank of 1927 were just to take up the same patriotic attitude and give the city of Edinburgh the money that we need just now, and need badly, for the housing of the people, what a name you would make! (Laughter and applause.) I am very glad indeed that Lord Strathmore has reminded us all that Edinburgh is the capital of Scotland. It does not belong to the citizens of Edinburgh. It does not matter where you find a Scotsman, whether at home or abroad, he remains a Scotsman, proud of his native country, and equally proud of the capital. (Applause.) I do not think I am putting it too high when I say that one of the reasons of that pride is just that for a very long time, including the early years of the Royal Bank of Scotland, the history of Edinburgh was in brief the history of Scotland. (Applause.) I had a gentleman calling on me to-day from Australia. He said, ' I was born sixty-seven years ago in Largo, and, although I have made my home in Australia, my heart remains in Auld Reekie'. Whether we like that term or not, there is something endearing about the homely phrase you and I have known all our lives, and you may take it from me, sir, that the men who comprise the Town Council of the City of Edinburgh, proud as we are of our New Town, are equally proud of our Old Town, with her traditions, with her great history, and of the part that we play in her government to-day." (Applause.)

Sir OTTO NIEMEYER, K.C.B., Controller of H.M. Treasury, submitted the toast of " The Royal Bank of Scotland ". He said:
" My Lord Duke, my Lords and Gentlemen — It is a great privilege, and a great responsibility, to be allowed to propose on so historic an occasion the toast of the Royal Bank of Scotland. I have been wondering why this

## The Royal Bank of Scotland

privilege was conferred on me. I see here among your visitors many persons whom I would much rather listen to than myself. But some, I understand, are under various Trappist vows, including that of silence; others, perhaps, like Sir Gordon Nairne, know too much. (Laughter.) I suppose, sir, an inscrutable Providence seated on my left has chosen me to propose the health of the Royal Bank of Scotland first, because I am not a banker—at any rate not yet—and second, because I am not a Scotsman. He probably, therefore, felt sure that I should have few painful secrets to reveal, either about your past or your present, and that I might feel the well-known optimism of the Englishman about your future.

"I observe, however, from the testimonials which have been paid to you in the Press, certain dark facts. I observe that the Royal Bank arose out of certain transactions with the southern half of Great Britain from which Scotland—on grounds which certainly seem to my Treasury mind extremely inadequate—received nearly £400,000. I observe also that the Royal Bank early discovered the virtues of interlocking directorships. It was a stern and unbending Whig Bank—but one of its original proprietors was the founder of Drummonds, the main opposition Jacobite bank—a secret which you appear to have preserved inviolate until a public amalgamation in 1924. I observe further that

## The History of

you had a total salary list of £476 : 13 : 4 per annum, in spite of which—I quote from my authority—you basked 'from the first in the good graces of the Government'. Who will wonder that your Bank has had a successful career nurtured in such excellent business principles?

" Now, sir, the Chancellor of the Exchequer would wish me to tell you how greatly he regrets that, owing to engagements in another place, he was unable to accept your invitation to be present to-night. Since I have entered the room I have received the following telegram from Mr. Churchill, which I should like to read to you:

> "' Please convey to Royal Bank of Scotland my congratulations on its 200 years of success and my good wishes for the future.
> WINSTON CHURCHILL.'

" Sir, the history of the Royal Bank is indeed the epitome of the history of Scottish banking. Two hundred years ago, when the Bank was founded, conditions were incredibly different from those prevailing to-day. Edinburgh, I believe, had under 50,000 inhabitants. It took twelve hours to go from Edinburgh to Glasgow, and something more like twelve days to go from Edinburgh to Inverness. I believe that the rent of your Glasgow Branch, when it first started,

## The Royal Bank of Scotland

was £2 : 10s. per annum. We have made great advances since then. Scottish banking has made great advances since those days; and it is difficult to overestimate what Scotland has contributed to banking all over the world. If we go to the most distant countries, to China, to India, to Australia, to Canada, everywhere we find among the bankers men of Scottish descent and Scottish name, and, in many cases, brought up in the traditions of Scottish banking, occupying leading positions in the banking world. I am told there are even some in London. (Laughter.) In all this great development at home in Scotland and in imitation of home tradition by Scotsmen abroad, the Royal Bank has played a worthy part. You may well be proud of your past history and your present position, and you may well feel that your achievements justify you in confidently facing the problems of the future.

"I take it as a special compliment, as a member of another ancient institution, the Treasury—possibly even more ancient than the Bank—to be invited to propose this toast. The Public Service, and the Treasury in particular, have had to face many difficult problems in the last fifteen years. We are very conscious of the great and continuous assistance which we have received in innumerable ways, from many people, and especially from the banking world; and we are particularly cognisant of the assistance we have always received from the Scottish banks, and the Royal Bank of Scotland has been a worthy type of Scottish banking. I should like to refer to only one instance in particular. It has touched me personally because I was also interested in the same subject. That is the great interest which the Scottish banks, and, in particular, Sir Alexander Wright, have always shown in the progress and development of the Savings Certificate movement.

"It is therefore with the greatest pleasure and confidence that I ask you to drink to the success and prosperity of the Royal Bank of Scotland." (Applause.)

In responding to the toast His Grace THE DUKE OF BUCCLEUCH, K.T., Governor of the Bank, said:

"My Lords and Gentlemen—I would like to thank Sir Otto Niemeyer very warmly for the kind terms in which he has proposed this toast, and you for the very cordial way in which you have received it. We regard it as an honour that the toast should have been submitted by one who has rendered eminent services to the State, and who at present holds the important office of Controller of Finance in His Majesty's Treasury. Since we approached Sir Otto with the request that he should do us this service, it has been announced that he is leaving his high office in the Treasury to be-

## The Royal Bank of Scotland

come a banker like the rest of us! We appreciate the compliment, but I, as a considerable tax-payer, regret the change. We wish Sir Otto every success in his new appointment, and feel sure his experience and ability will prove of great value to the country and its finance. (Applause.)

"A well-known authority on banking and currency, writing more than fifty years ago, said that the banking system of Scotland is probably the greatest and most original work which the practical genius of the Scottish people has produced in the sphere of political and social economics, and in dealing with the same subject Lord Macaulay was responsible for the statement that 'her schools and banks had transformed Scotland'. It has sometimes been said that it was because the teaching of arithmetic in particular in the Scottish schools was extremely efficient that the Scotsman's knowledge of figures is so largely responsible for what we so often hear of his 'natural bent' towards banking! Indeed, in the old copies of the 'Shorter Catechism' which were used in the schools there was usually printed on the back cover the Multiplication Table, showing how our practical race has always managed to make something of both worlds. (Laughter.) In any case there is, I think, no question that her system of banking has been one of Scotland's greatest assets. The Royal Bank of Scotland,

The History of

whose Bicentenary we are celebrating to-night, is a part of that system, and the two hundred years of its existence embrace practically the commercial history of the country. In the peaceful development of the country after the risings of the '15 and the '45, the banks, although then in the earliest stage of development, played an important part in encouraging trade and commerce, and thus acted as a civilising and moderating influence upon a people who had previously been noted for their somewhat turbulent and warlike instincts.

"The Cash Credit System which, as all students of the subject know, was introduced by the Royal Bank so far back as 1728, in itself was an evidence of Scotland's more settled outlook, because the principle behind it was faith and trust between man and man and the belief that the granter of the bond would be in a position to honour his obligation if and when called upon to do so. There is no doubt whatever that the Cash Credit was a leading factor in the commercial development of the country. (Applause.)

"The Paper Currency System of Scotland is another example of the same principle. We can only feel proud that in the great work which the banks have done for Scotland the Royal Bank has taken its proper share and place, and it is to the directors no small gratification that at the beginning of its third

## The Royal Bank of Scotland

century it is in a position to render continued services and, owing to its greatly increased resources, on a more extended scale than ever before.

"To-night the directors have as their primary object the entertainment of their managers and agents from all parts of the country, also their officials and some of the heads of departments at the Head Office, London and Glasgow. It was obviously impossible to have the whole staff of the Bank here.

"In the same way it was quite impracticable to seek to entertain our customers, who number many thousands, however indispensable the custom of all those friends is to the success of the concern.

"Equally, we could not invite our Stockholders notwithstanding their proprietorial interest in the institution, for the simple reason that they number over five thousand.

"We are honoured by the presence of many important guests connected with banking and other interests—about whom Lord Haig will have something to say at a later stage.

"It is interesting to recall that hospitality is no new thing in the records of the Bank, as we find from a perusal of the early minutes, but in those days the business of entertaining could not be carried out on such a scale as we have adopted this evening, or in such surroundings.

The History of

According to the custom of the times, it was done in the famous old taverns which were situated in the closes of the Old Town of Edinburgh—at 'Fortune's', or 'Mrs. Clerk, Vintner's', or 'Cleland's'. In those days the Bank directors had what was called a 'Tavern Fund', and it was their custom to entertain convivially their business friends from London, such as Mr.Mathias of the Equivalent Company, or Messrs. Coutts, the Bankers, in those old hostelries which were patronised by the best people in Edinburgh.

"We find that the directors and their Cashier let few occasions pass that might give an excuse for a simple but savoury meal, not unaccompanied by the flowing bowl: they adjourned for this purpose *nem. con.* after the General Meetings of the Proprietors, or after a day of destroying cancelled notes. Provost George Drummond, whose name bulks so largely in the civic history of Edinburgh, and whose remarkable Diary is in the Edinburgh Advocates' Library, was at one of those directors' *noctes ambrosianae* on the 6th of January 1738. 'This evening', he wrote in his Diary, 'the directors of the Royal Bank had their anniversary entertainment. My cold got me the privilege of drinking sack and water only —got home early. May the Lord pardon me the guilt of others. Closed the day with God.' He was a modest gentleman. (Laughter.)

## The Royal Bank of Scotland

" It is interesting to read in another Diary—that of the Cashier of the Bank, the well-known John Campbell, generally described as 'John Campbell of the Bank'—kept during the occupation of Edinburgh by Prince Charlie in 1745, that when the cash and other effects of the Bank had been packed up and transported to the Castle for safety (the Castle remaining in the hands of the Government), Mr. Campbell, on the evening of 1st October, finding himself confronted by a demand for change in current coin of the realm for £857 Royal Bank notes presented by Murray of Broughton, an old customer of the Bank who was the Young Chevalier's secretary, desired to consult with the only two directors accessible. These he found at 'Mrs. Clerk, Vintner's'. A meeting of ordinary and extraordinary directors was called for the following day at noon: five turned up, and it was agreed to cash the Prince's notes if access could be got to the Castle. Meanwhile there had been got from Lochiel a convoy with a white flag, and access was obtained to the Castle, where they took advantage of the opportunity, before taking away the gold and silver required to meet the demands which had been made upon them, to burn £60,000 of Royal Bank notes and tear into small pieces a large number more—no doubt to prevent them from falling into Jacobite hands. We read that the white flag was hoisted again and they retired in good order, and inevitably proceeded to dine in Mrs. Clerk's. (Laughter.)

"All that happened in the romantic mid-eighteenth-century period of our country's history. Nowadays the directors carry out their duties under quite sober and prosaic conditions—always excepting to-night. (Laughter.)

"We are honoured to-night with the presence of the Lord Provost of Edinburgh, and it was interesting to know from the Deputy Governor something of the modest borrowings of the Town Council in those far-off days. I feel, my Lord Provost, that you would be a happier man if you could make the rate-payers' cash go as far as it did then.

"I trust I have not wearied you with these antiquarian references, but when I turn to my left and find there Mr. Norman, the Governor of the Bank of England, whose name is a synonym for sound finance and stability, not only in Europe, but all over the world, and who has added such lustre to the high office he occupies, I am tempted to refer to the connection of the Royal Bank with the Bank of England, which commenced within a few weeks of the opening of the Bank and has continued without interruption for the long period of two hundred years. We regard it as a very signal honour that we should have the Governor and other well-known representatives of the Bank of England with us this evening.

# The Royal Bank of Scotland

"I shall make only one other historic reference—of much later date—namely, in the year 1826—when in the minutes of the Bank the name of Sir Walter Scott appears on more than one occasion. It is of special interest to me to bring in that great name because of his intimate associations with my own family. As you all know, Scott had set himself, when in a state of failing health, with indescribable labour and courageous resolution to pay off his creditors. A meeting of the creditors was called to pass the following resolution: 'That Sir Walter Scott be requested to accept of his furniture, plate, linens, paintings, library, and curiosities of every description as the best means the creditors have of expressing their very high sense of his most honourable conduct and in grateful acknowledgement for the unparalleled and most successful exertions he made and continues to make for them'. It was a little thing to do after all, and the Bank is honoured by its name being mentioned in such an association, but it is a profound satisfaction to be able to record to-night that the proposal met with the unanimous approval of the Board of the Royal Bank who, afterwards, subscribed £150 to the fund for raising the Scott Monument.

"I must not be tempted to dip further into our story. That will all appear in due time, with many picturesque and interesting happenings, in the History of the Bank which is

## The History of

being written by that distinguished Scottish author, Dr. Neil Munro, who is with us this evening. You will be pleased to know that the volume is now nearing completion.

"Well, we are here to celebrate our Bicentenary. From the small beginnings in the little office in the close off the High Street of Edinburgh the Bank has continued through all the vicissitudes of our country's history to grow and prosper. It did not extend its operations to Glasgow till 1783, where it has now some twenty-six offices. In 1864 it acquired the Dundee Banking Company — thus extending its influence considerably in the East of Scotland. In 1874 it went to London, where it has a large and growing business. Its branches now cover most of Scotland. It has formed many important foreign connections. In 1924 it acquired the business of the old Banking House of Drummonds, two of whose partners, now members of our Local Board at Charing Cross, we are glad to have with us to-night. (Applause.) The Drummonds had early connections with the Royal Bank, although in different political camps, because a kinsman of the Founder of Drummonds' Bank (Lord Provost George Drummond of Edinburgh), was one of our original directors, and as it now turns out, Andrew Drummond, the Founder, was himself interested in the Royal Bank through having been a stockholder in

## The Royal Bank of Scotland

the Equivalent Company. It is pleasant in these matter-of-fact days to trace an element of romance such as this union supplies.

"We have now existed for the long period of two centuries, during which the Bank has grown and developed into the institution which you now know it to be, and our wish is that in the future as in the past its resources may continue to be available for the increased promotion of the trade and commerce of the country.

"We are glad, on this historic occasion, to have with us so many of our staff and so many distinguished friends who are rejoicing with us at the achievement represented by the operations of these two hundred years, and on behalf of the directors and the Deputy Governor and myself, I would wish to return our most hearty thanks to you all." (Applause.)

Mr. HERBERT W. HALDANE, in proposing the toast of the Officials and Staff of the Royal Bank of Scotland, said:

"My Lord Duke, my Lords and Gentlemen—I am sure that you will all regret the absence of Mr. Dundas, the chairman of directors, and no one will do so more than I do. Mr. Dundas is laid up with a feverish chill and, obeying doctor's orders, he cannot be present to-night. It has therefore fallen upon me, at short notice, to take Mr. Dundas's place. I may, however, tell you in confidence—if there can be any confidential communications in the presence of a ' loud speaker '—that Mr. Dundas was so good as to hand me his notes, and therefore what will follow will be the views of not only one director but of two.

" It is the greatest possible pleasure to the directors of the Bank to see gathered here to-night so many of our agents and representatives from all over the country. From the nature of things the opportunity of meeting in this way is a rare one, and we appreciate it highly. Indeed it is a notable gathering. From Orkney we welcome the commander of our farthest northern outpost, the agent at Kirkwall. From London we welcome those who manage with overwhelming success the two great branches of our business in the south—Bishopsgate and Drummonds. Glasgow is here, Dundee is here. From every town and every region of Scotland we have our representatives; men unequalled in their ability, their energy, and their devotion to the great institution we are all so proud to serve. May I say one word to our agents? Sometimes they must be tempted to regard the directors as a hardhearted and unimaginative band of obstructionists, when we turn down a proposal which, it may be, they have been working for weeks to bring forward. I should like to assure them that we never turn down a proposal without

## The Royal Bank of Scotland

giving full weight to the feelings of the agent. I hope I am not giving away any secrets out of school if I admit that sometimes we have been known to pass a proposal out of sympathy for the agent who has laboured to bring it forward, which on its cold commercial merits we should be inclined to refuse. We know that the branches really are the Bank: they are the limbs and living organs, without which the head office would be a maimed and meaningless trunk. We owe a debt of gratitude accordingly to all those who throughout the country not only maintain the Bank's interests but are constantly pushing them forward, and we are glad of the opportunity to express that gratitude to-night.

"We wish that all the members of our staffs could be here to-night. But for one thing that would mean closing several of our branches to-morrow morning—(laughter)—an opportunity which our very good friends and rivals might be quick to seize upon. For another thing, we could not get a room to hold something over 1270 people. Though they are not all here, they are much in our thoughts to-night. For a moment, too, we cannot help thinking with pride of those others who should have been members of our community still, had not Fate led them, through their own self-sacrifice, to a nobler end. It is remarkable that, out of a staff, which, in 1914, numbered just 900, no less than 582 actively served the country, and of these 84 gave up their lives.

"To all the 1270 of our present staff, as well as to those who are no longer on the active list, a deep debt of gratitude is due from customers and shareholders alike. I would ask you to assure them one and all that their loyal and zealous services are highly appreciated. Without them the Bank would not stand where it does to-day. (Applause.)

"When speaking of the staff I do not forget the high officials; but, where all are so admirable, I cannot single out individuals. Before anyone can aspire to hold one of these high positions in a bank, he must be endowed with a singular combination of ability, industry, and tact. Amongst men so qualified, it seems to me the officials of the Royal Bank—each and every one—stand out as exceptional. But the value of their service is proved far more eloquently by the results they achieve than by anything I could say.

"The directors of an institution like the Bank are regarded, I believe, in some quarters as a necessary, but more or less harmless, incubus. (Laughter.) Sometimes, however, they have their moments of usefulness. (Renewed laughter.) I claim that the directors of the Royal Bank, on one occasion—needless to say I was not of their number at the time—(laughter)—did an act of real greatness when,

## The Royal Bank of Scotland

in 1917, they appointed as their chief executive officer Mr. Alexander Kemp Wright. (Loud applause.) It is a significant fact, too, which Mr. Mill pointed out in *The Times* of last Tuesday, that the resources of the Bank have trebled in the last fifteen years. For all this the causes are no doubt many and varied. The foundations of success have been well and truly built in the past by the prudence and the vision of such men as Mr. Tait and Mr. Wallace, both of whom we rejoice to see to-night. (Applause.) But I am sure that no official of the Bank, either past or present, will grudge me saying that Sir Alexander Wright, guiding its fortunes through the most perilous years that ever a banker had to face, by his brains and by his character, has placed the Bank, on its two hundredth anniversary, in a higher position than it ever held before. (Loud applause.) I will add that none of the eminent bankers here to-night will, I think, much differ from me if I describe Sir Alexander as pre-eminent in the Scottish banking world to-day. I am not going to try and describe the charm of his personal qualities which make it a peculiar pleasure to be associated with him. That must be known to every customer who has been fortunate enough to meet him—indeed I believe that he can even say ' No ' in such a way as to give pleasure. (Laughter.) What I wish that every customer and every shareholder could know is the passion for the interests of the Bank which possesses and dominates every hour of his life. I do not think it possible to say how much we all owe him.

"To all those, then, who serve the Bank so splendidly, I ask you to accord your heartfelt thanks for their efforts and your warmest congratulations on their achievements. I give you the toast of the Agents, the Staff, and the Officials of the Royal Bank of Scotland, coupled with the name of Sir Alexander Wright." (Applause.)

Sir ALEXANDER K. WRIGHT, replying to the toast of " The Officials and Staff ", said:

"My Lord Duke, my Lords and Gentlemen—I regard it as a high honour indeed that I should have been asked to reply to this toast on behalf of the officials and whole staff of the Bank, and I would desire to thank you—I was going to say Mr. Dundas; I say Mr. Dundas and Mr. Haldane, our valued directors, and our present and our immediate past Chairman—for the very kind terms in which this toast has been proposed, and certainly for the far too favourable references to myself—and you all, my Lords and Gentlemen, for the way in which you have received these remarks.

"It is a remarkable fact that Mr. Dundas, our present chairman, represents the fourth generation of his family in the direct line of succession who have held the office of director

## The Royal Bank of Scotland

of this Bank. His great-grandfather, James Dundas, became a director in 1796, and his grandfather and his respected father (whose memory remains warm with many of us, and from whom I received much personal kindness) have all been members of the Court of Directors. (Applause.)

"My Lord Duke, the hereditary principle seems to cling to the Royal Bank of Scotland, and I think it will be conceded, even in these days, that the Bank has done extraordinarily well under it. Since the year 1777, with one brief interval of a few years (owing, I believe, to a minority), five successive Dukes of Buccleuch have honoured us by holding the office of Governor; but the connection is much older than that, because Henry, Duke of Buccleuch, who became Governor in 1777, was a great-nephew of Lord Ilay, afterwards third Duke of Argyll, who was the first Governor of the Bank at its start in 1727. There are other illustrations of direct succession in the Deputy Governorship, which office was held by Lord Strathmore's father for a quarter of a century, and also in the case of Lord Elgin, one of our ordinary directors, whose father also held the position of Deputy Governor. Mr. Haldane himself, one of our directors and our former chairman, is another example of the hereditary principle.

"Whilst that is so as regards what might be

The History of

termed the 'Upper' or 'Directorial Chamber', there is, however, if I may presume to say so, no lack of the democratic element when we come to the officials and staff.

"I am replying for everyone in the service down to the 'youngest apprentice'. I suggested that some other official or senior agent, or one of our quite youthful agents, might be associated with me in this reply, but I was overruled. I have really no difficulty, however, because, as a matter of fact, I was once the youngest apprentice myself, and it is interesting to note that all the principal officials at the head office, at London and Glasgow, and, indeed, all those holding positions of importance in the Bank (apart, of course, from our new friends, the Drummonds of Charing Cross), commenced at the lowest rung of the ladder, receiving for their first year's remuneration not the—shall I say—relatively princely income of the modern apprentice, but what our English friends will, I am afraid, regard as the frugal figure of £10. (Laughter.)

"My Lords and Gentlemen, the growth and development of a great concern like the Royal Bank is never at any time the work of any one man or indeed of any ten men. It is the joint product of the whole staff. It is indeed the result of what is called 'team work' on a large scale and in an intense degree. Those at the top may have done something by their keen-

## The Royal Bank of Scotland

ness and their hospitality to new ideas to inspire that work, but without the co-operation of all such success could not have been attained. I should like to take this opportunity of recording my indebtedness to the principal officials at the head office; to our managers and sub-managers in London, Glasgow, and Dundee; to all our agents not only at the large offices but at the small branches, who have often to carry on amidst a good deal of discouragement; and I desire to testify in a very grateful way to the splendid loyalty with which I have been supported at all times. One of the earliest things which I learned as a Law student was that the Bank as an ancient corporation has a distinct legal *persona*. Well, as the years pass and one's life becomes inextricably knit with the Bank and its concerns, one begins to think that it is not only a legal *persona* but an actual personality, which becomes a dominating influence in everything one does. I am sure many of our older officers have experienced this feeling, and it is because so many have given of their very best and have identified themselves personally with the Bank that it stands in such a proud position to-day. There is room in a service like ours for young men of first-class ability, and the developments of more recent years have opened up avenues for promotion which did not exist before. In these days of industrial problems our guests will be interested to know that well on for 600 members of our staff are stockholders of the Bank, and this, I think, is all to the good. (Applause.)

"I should like also, on behalf of the other principal officials and myself, to express grateful thanks to the Governor, the chairman of directors, and every member of the Court for much consideration, kindness, and help. It is a privilege and a daily pleasure to serve such a body of men.

"In starting on our third century, I think, if I may say so, the directors can look forward with confidence. We have an excellent staff who are all devoted to the Bank's interests. Our resources have grown with the years, and with our large capital and reserves we occupy a strong position.

"I read recently of an old lady who had just attained her hundredth year. Her minister, who was also old, came to congratulate her, and by way of humour said, ' I am afraid you can scarcely hope to reach a second century,' to which she replied, ' Well, I don't know about that, but I can say this, " I feel much stronger to-day than I did when I started my first one " '. (Laughter.) My Lords and Gentlemen, the Royal Bank is in that position. Notwithstanding all that we hear at present of the threats to capital and the proposals of nationalisation and other more sinister schemes, I have a great belief in this country's future, and

## The Royal Bank of Scotland

although it is always foolish to prophesy—and I am not going to do it—I venture to express the hope that when our successors meet together to celebrate the Bank's tercentenary, the institution will still be occupying a high position in the economic life of the country, and that on the evening of the dinner there will be a Duke of Buccleuch in the chair and several familiar names in the directorate.

"My Lords and Gentlemen, on behalf of the whole staff of the Bank and myself, I thank you all very much." (Loud applause.)

Field-Marshal the Right Hon. EARL HAIG, K.T., G.C.B., O.M., G.C.V.O., K.C.I.E., in proposing the toast of " The Guests ", said:

"My Lords and Gentlemen — It is my pleasant duty this evening to propose to you the health of our Guests, coupled with the names of Lord Alness and Mr. James Morton, in which latter combination our Master of Ceremonies has happily allied Commerce (as typified by the President of the Glasgow Chamber of Commerce) with a no less worthy representative of Law and Justice, without which Commerce can never flourish.

"Neither the Lord Justice-Clerk nor Mr. Morton needs any introduction to a Scottish gathering such as this. They are both well known to us, and we hold them both in high respect and esteem as leaders in the respective walks of life to which they have devoted their labours and their uncommon abilities. We are very glad to welcome them here. (Applause.)

"We have also with us to-night other guests, no less distinguished, from the other side of the Border, and it seems that our Scottish sense of hospitality is such that we are content to be honoured by their presence without seeking to impose upon them the penalty of making a speech. It is a concession which (if my own feelings are any indication of the point of view of others on such a matter) they will very heartily appreciate.

"It is, however, in truth a very great honour to have with us the Governor of the Bank of England, the Rt. Hon. Mr. Montagu Norman, and at the same time to welcome two other prominent members of the same historic institution. I refer to Sir Gordon Nairne and Mr. Travers. As you have been told, the Royal Bank of Scotland has had business relations during the whole period of its existence with the Bank of England—a wonderful record truly in banking, and one which (if I may be permitted to say so) is highly creditable to the Bank of England. (Laughter and applause.) It is therefore only fitting that representatives of our great and famous client should join with us in celebrating the two hundredth anniversary of our birth and of the year of our first business connection with the still more ancient House.

## The Royal Bank of Scotland

We are very sensible of the compliment which the Bank of England has paid us in selecting her representatives, and we bid them also a most cordial welcome to-night. (Applause.)

" Another of our distinguished guests to whose presence I must specially refer—although our Governor has already referred to it—is Sir Otto Niemeyer. Following the example of certain other successful Civil Servants, he is about to give up the post of Controller of Finance at the Treasury, in which he has rendered signal service to his country, for an appointment which, I trust, he will find equally congenial and substantially more lucrative. (Laughter.) In this case, at any rate, not even a politician could deny that the Treasury's loss will be the gain of the Bank of England. And we, who welcome so notable an accession of strength to the banking world, heartily congratulate him upon this fresh success in an already brilliant career.

" We have also with us to-night a number of other distinguished bankers and financial authorities from London who are guests indeed, but not strangers amongst us. They are of the number of those who justified the remark of the young member of the Bank who, on his return from his first business visit to London, was asked whether he did not find the southern accent rather difficult to follow. 'Indeed I didna experience ony deeficulty at a',' he replied, ' I had dealings wi' naebody but heads of depairtments.' (Laughter.)

"These men, now well-known names in banking and financial circles of London, received their early training in the service of the Royal Bank of Scotland, and we are proud to greet them once more as old friends and honoured guests.

"If I were to attempt to enumerate all those guests whose achievements entitle them to our esteem, and make their presence here an honour to those who so gladly welcome them, I should go far beyond the time allotted to me for my remarks. Finance is a bond between all professions; banks, and especially such old-established institutions as ours, serve the community in all its multifarious activities. We number, therefore, among our guests to-night, not only the General Managers of other Scottish banks—(applause)—with whom we are friendly rivals, as well as two members of the old banking House of Drummond, with whom friendly rivalry has given way to closer and more intimate relations—but also the principal office-bearers of such other important Scottish bodies and institutions as the Edinburgh Merchant Company and the Edinburgh Chamber of Commerce; the Glasgow Royal Exchange and the Glasgow Trades House; the W.S. Society; the S.S.C. Society; the Society of Accountants; the Faculty of Actuaries; and the Edinburgh

# The Royal Bank of Scotland

Stock Exchange. We have here also brilliant representatives of that other almost universal branch of human activity, the Press, together with many other friends and connections of our House—some of them from abroad. To all we extend a Scottish welcome, and feel that this unique occasion in our history is enriched by their presence.

" I have only one word more to add, and that is to say how pleased are all the members of the Board of Directors to greet the Managers and Agents and Staff of our Bank. They can scarcely be described as guests, for they are part of our organisation itself, and a part to whose loyal and devoted service is peculiarly due the continued success of the Royal Bank of Scotland. I ask them, therefore, to join with me in this toast, and call upon the Governor, Directors, and all officials and members of the Staff—all in fact who are connected with our Bank— to rise and drink to the health and prosperity of our guests. Long life to them! " (Loud applause.)

The Right Hon. LORD ALNESS, Lord Justice-Clerk, replying to the toast of " Our Guests ", said:

" My Lord Duke, my Lords and Gentlemen—As I listened to Lord Haig proposing this toast, I felt that, during the twenty-nine years or thereby which I have spent at the Bar, it had never fallen to my lot to represent so important and distinguished a body of clients as I represent to-night.

" I also feel that, in responding to a toast like this, one can hardly escape from the language of convention; and, if I assure you, the officials of the Royal Bank of Scotland, that your guests, on whose behalf I speak, are deeply grateful to you for your gracious hospitality on this interesting and, indeed, impressive occasion, then I beg you to believe that, although the words are conventional, they are none the less sincere. I have ventured to describe this as an interesting and impressive occasion. That it is interesting I think no one can gainsay, but I also think that it is impressive. It is impressive, in a world of evanescence, to contemplate something which is enduring, in a world where monarchies and ministries rise and fall, in which dynasties and even dresses rise and fall (laughter), to contemplate an institution which, if it rises, certainly never falls, which is stable as a rock, and which stands four-square to the winds that blow. Such an institution, I apprehend, is the Royal Bank of Scotland. Following upon what Sir Alexander Wright said a few moments ago, I cannot doubt that, a century hence—not, perhaps, in this room, but in some room in the city—the directors of the Bank of that day, none of whom are yet born, will entertain guests of the Bank who

## The Royal Bank of Scotland

have not yet seen the light of day. And, when that time comes, though I cannot venture to predict precisely what will happen, or to portray the exact features of the function, I am quite certain of one thing, and that is that the guests of that time will not enjoy themselves more, and will not be more grateful to their hosts on that occasion than the guests to-night when they profess to have experienced the highest enjoyment, and desire to express the deepest gratitude to their hosts for the privileges which have been theirs.

"And now, my Lord Duke, I will not multiply words. I feel certain that at this hour you will not deem me ungrateful, and that I shall best consult your convenience by merely saying, ' We thank you '." (Applause.)

The CHAIRMAN—" We don't want to be considered exclusively Edinburgh men, though Edinburgh is excellent in many ways. I have great honour and pleasure in calling upon Mr. James Morton, president of the Glasgow Chamber of Commerce."

Mr. MORTON—" My Lord Duke, Earl Haig, my Lords and Gentlemen—I desire very briefly to associate myself with the remarks which have been made by Lord Alness. When I listened to the list of distinguished people who are your guests to-night and for whom I was expected to reply, I confess I was amazed at my temerity in coming here and undertaking that very onerous duty. I had congratulated myself I was to be preceded by such an one as Lord Alness, and I therefore proposed to occupy a subordinate rôle, and I do not dream of venturing to reply for all those distinguished men—particularly those distinguished bankers from across the Border.

"I will rather deal with the position as it appeals to us in Scotland and tender the thanks more particularly of all those who are associated with the Bank, and of their guests, from the West of Scotland. We who are here to-night are merely representative of the countless friends and well-wishers of the Bank who cannot possibly be with you, and I would desire on their behalf, as well as on our own, to express the very great honour we feel it to be that the toast of our health has been proposed by Earl Haig. I desire to thank him for the kind expressions he has used regarding us, and I desire to thank you all for the manner in which you have received them.

"I confess that there are not many things for which we really envy the Capital. (Laughter.) If my Lord Alness will forgive me for so doing, I would assure him that, notwithstanding certain appearances to the contrary, even the College of Justice is not one. (Laughter.) We do, however, my Lord Duke,

## The Royal Bank of Scotland

envy the Capital that it was the cradle and nursery of the great institution over which your Grace so worthily presides. I say it was the cradle and the nursery because, as to the home of the Bank in its adult life, we, along with the whole of Scotland, claim to have our share of that. And we watch with great interest the extension of your activity into that foreign country which lies south of the Tweed. We in Glasgow and in the West of Scotland, which I particularly represent, have many connections, not all material, with the Royal Bank. The history of the Bank is the history of Scotland in epitome; in a special sense it is the history of Glasgow. In Glasgow we were fellow-adventurers in the Darien scheme, from the ashes of which the Royal Bank rose; and had much to do with the Union Parliament which opened up the English colonies to Scottish trade. We thus claim with the Bank a kinship of origin. We are proud to know that our city and your Bank rose from the same ashes, as well as to note that our money, which is the blood of commerce, continues to circulate through you as yours through us. Long may it continue to do so! (Applause.)

"The Bank and our city in the West are associated also in the high regard in which they hold the memory of David Dale. David Dale, who was instrumental in bringing the Bank to Glasgow in 1783, was one of Glasgow's greatest

## The History of

citizens. In many respects he was its greatest citizen, because he was the father of industrial Glasgow. The year in which he brought the Bank to Glasgow—1783—was a memorable year for that city, because there was a triple bond forged which was continued and has strengthened greatly from that day till now. It was the year of the Bank's first coming to Glasgow from Edinburgh; it was the year of the beginning of what is now the *Glasgow Herald*, and it was the year of the foundation of the Chamber of Commerce of Glasgow. And, among the founders of the Chamber of Commerce, we find the name of David Dale, who was responsible for bringing the Bank to Glasgow. As a boy, in an Ayrshire village, I lived within the sound of the horn of a mill which once belonged to David Dale and which now belongs to a Company, one of whose directors is an extraordinary director of this Bank.

"I was, for years, a partner of a firm of lawyers—M'Grigor Donald & Coy.—who, and their predecessors, have acted as the Bank's lawyers in Glasgow almost, if not quite, from the time it opened its branch there in 1783.

"From the personal point of view, therefore, it was with the greatest pleasure I received your invitation, and I rejoice I have the honour to bear to you the tribute of the West, and the good wishes of all for the continuance of that

## The Royal Bank of Scotland

prosperity which you have so well deserved and so fully enjoyed in the past, and for the continuance of which in the future you have so fully laid the foundation.

"My Lord Duke, I speak more particularly for those who are here from the West of Scotland. I can scarcely fulfil the higher task of replying for those eminent men who have come to honour you from across the Border, but I would again tender to Earl Haig and to you all our very best and most hearty thanks." (Applause.)

Sir GORDON NAIRNE, proposing the toast of "The Chairman", said:

"My Lords and Gentlemen — The toast which I have the honour to propose to you is one which needs no commendation to you or, indeed, to any Scottish audience. It is that of your Chairman, the Governor of the Royal Bank of Scotland, His Grace the Duke of Buccleuch.

"You have heard how closely the House of Buccleuch has been associated with the Royal Bank of Scotland through its long history. It always seems to me that it would be difficult to imagine the Royal Bank of Scotland without a Duke of Buccleuch as its Governor. Looking into the far-distant future, although 'men may come and men may go', and institutions may rise and fall, we hope that the Dukes of

## The Royal Bank of Scotland

Buccleuch and the Royal Bank of Scotland will go on for ever.

"Sir Alexander Wright—I am not quite sure whether he is to be more admired or respected or loved or feared—has told me that my words are to be few, and therefore I must, without more ado, give you the health of your Chairman, His Grace the Duke of Buccleuch." (Applause.)

The CHAIRMAN said:
"We have heard a good deal about heredity. I have always understood by reading what is commonly called the popular Press that the very worst thing in the whole of this world is heredity, but after what we have heard of a succession of Governors, Chairmen, Directors, and so forth, it only amplifies the fact that the Royal Bank of Scotland, in spite of this heredity, is still more than able to hold its own. And also I may put this to you. I know that it has been asserted that my family in the past were always rather drastic. It is entirely a delusion. They were always very peace-loving people—(laughter)—and, whether they were so or not, there is one thing Sir Walter Scott said about Scotsmen, 'If ever they got hold of anything, they never let go'. In spite of this disability, you must be thankful: you might have done worse." (Laughter.)

# LIST OF THOSE PRESENT

Chairman—His Grace THE DUKE OF BUCCLEUCH AND
QUEENSBERRY, K.T. (Governor)

*On Chairman's right*

The Rt. Hon. Alexander Stevenson (Lord Provost of Edinburgh)
The Rt. Hon. Lord Alness (Lord Justice-Clerk)
Mr. H. W. Haldane, C.A. (Director)
Sir Gordon Nairne, Baronet (Director, Bank of England)
Field-Marshal the Rt. Hon. Earl Haig of Bemersyde, K.T., etc. (Director)
Mr. James Morton (President of the Glasgow Chamber of Commerce)
Mr. George J. Scott (Treasurer, Bank of Scotland)
Mr. W. D. Graham Menzies of Hallyburton (Extraordinary Director)
Mr. William Carnegie (General Manager, National Bank of Scotland, Ltd.)
Mr. Charles W. Allan (Master of the Edinburgh Merchant Company)

*On Chairman's left*

The Rt. Hon. Montagu Collet Norman, D.S.O. (Governor, Bank of England)
The Rt. Hon. the Earl of Strathmore and Kinghorne, G.C.V.O. (Deputy Governor)
Sir Otto E. Niemeyer, K.C.B.
Sir Alexander Kemp Wright, K.B.E., D.L. (General Manager)
Mr. Robert Fleming (Extraordinary Director)
Sir Henry Cook, W.S. (Director)
Mr. Maldwin Drummond
Mr. W. C. Johnston (Deputy Keeper of the Signet)
Sir Thomas Dunlop, Baronet, G.B.E. (Director)
Mr. A. Henderson, B.Sc., J.P. (President of the Edinburgh Chamber of Commerce)
Colonel Robert M'Laren (Chairman of the Royal Exchange, Glasgow)

# The History of

*On Chairman's right*

Mr. C. E. W. Macpherson, C.A. (President of the Society of Accountants)
Mr. David Young (General Manager, Clydesdale Bank, Ltd.)
Sir Robert Bruce
Mr. E. N. Travers (Principal of Branch Banks Office, Bank of England)
Mr. M. S. S. Gubbay, C.S.I., C.I.E. (General Manager, P. & O. Banking Corporation)
Mr. R. A. Möllerson (Estonian Legation and Consulate)
Mr. C. C. Maconochie, C.B.E., K.C., of Avontoun (Director)
Mr. F. G. Milne (Secretary, General Post Office)
Mr. R. C. Wyse (Union Discount Company, Ltd.)
Mr. E. G. Baxter of Teasses (Director)

*On Chairman's left*

Mr. John Dallas (Deacon Convener, Trades House, Glasgow)
Mr. Alexander Robb (General Manager, Commercial Bank of Scotland, Ltd.)
Mr. R. Hill Stewart, F.F.A. (President of the Faculty of Actuaries)
Rev. George Christie, D.D., T.D.
Mr. Norman L. Hird (General Manager, Union Bank of Scotland, Ltd.)
Mr. Alfred A. Lawrie (of the Stock Exchange, Edinburgh)
Mr. R. H. James (President of the S.S.C. Society)
Mr. Harvey H. Smith (General Manager, North of Scotland Bank, Ltd.)
J. D. Sutherland, C.B.E., LL.D. (Forestry Commission)

*Croupiers*

The Rt. Hon. the Earl of Elgin and Kincardine, C.M.G. (Director)
Mr. G. J. Lidstone, F.I.A., F.F.A., LL.D. (Director)
Mr. James B. Adshead (Secretary)
Mr. J. F. Ferguson (Joint Superintendent of Branches)
Mr. William Whyte (Manager, London)
Mr. Thomas Lillie (Manager, Glasgow)

Mr. Q. B. Grant (Agent, Dundee)
Mr. G. F. B. Hunter (Joint Superintendent of Branches)
Mr. James Macara (Agent, St. Vincent Street, Glasgow)
Mr. R. H. Cowie (Agent, Aberdeen)
Mr. D. Speed (Accountant)
Mr. John Young (Agent, Greenock)

# The Royal Bank of Scotland

Mr. Adam Tait
Mr. William Wallace
Mr. R. N. Dundas, W.S.
Mr. Fred. H. J. Drummond
Sir T. Smith, V.D.
Mr. H. M. Bell, C.B.E.
Mr. E. F. Davies
Mr. W. Lyon Mackenzie, K.C.
Mr. Hugh R. Buchanan, LL.B., S.S.C.
Mr. C. J. Mill
Mr. David Marshall, W.S.
Mr. A. W. Kiddy
Mr. C. J. G. Paterson, C.A.
Mr. E. M. Beilby, C.A. (Auditor)
Mr. B. Bracken
Mr. Neil Munro, LL.D.
Mr. W. H. Smith
Mr. N. R. Adshead
Mr. F. H. Allan
Mr. W. Davidson
Mr. J. M. Thomson
Mr. D. H. Huie, C.A.
Mr. J. N. Noble
Mr. T. M. Guthrie
Mr. J. Harper
Mr. R. Neil
Mr. D. S. Lunan
Mr. D. Calder
Mr. D. M. Lyon
Mr. G. H. Liston Foulis
Mr. Charles Anderson
Mr. J. Taylor
Mr. John Craig
Mr. A. G. Ferguson
Mr. A. Farfor
Mr. C. Belfield
Mr. J. Johnston
Mr. J. J. Paterson
Mr. W. Grant
Mr. Jno. Kerr
Mr R. F. Robertson
Mr. Don. MacLaren
Mr. R. Short
Mr. J. Graham
Mr. T. L. Reid
Mr. R. Pate
Mr. A. J. Stewart
Mr. A. J. Young
Mr. F. Scott
Mr. W. M. Marshall
Mr. J. C. Rose
Mr. T. Russell
Mr. J. A. Smart
Mr. A. T. Wood
Mr. W. H. Kerr
Mr J. Stiven
Mr. P. Moir
Mr. T. D. Allan
Mr. J. I. Moffat
Mr. J. R. Howie
Mr. A. Auchinachie
Mr. J. M. Purvis
Mr. D. Millar
Mr. D. Jack
Mr. F. G. Johnston
Mr. D. Cormack
Mr. A. Westwater
Mr. D. W. Laurence
Mr. H. N. Robson
Mr. D. L. M'Lennan
Mr. A. L. Deans
Mr. V. H. Beattie
Mr. J. Rowland
Mr. Jas. Stewart
Mr. J. D. Falconer
Mr. T. H. Burns
Mr. J. R. Mitchell

## The History of

Mr. W. J. Paterson
Mr. R. G. Hillcoat
Mr. M. B. Anderson
Mr. J. Dunlop
Mr. W. L. Dunn
Mr. J. M. Gibson
Mr. T. P. Doughty
Mr. W. R. Gardner
Mr. J. Brownlie
Mr. R. B. Langwill
Mr. S. G. Manford
Mr. A. Wallace
Mr. W. Tytler
Mr. J. Yeaman
Mr. W. Donald
Mr. R. P. Mathewson
Mr. C. W. Anderson
Mr. J. W. Whitelaw
Mr. J. A. White
Mr. C. Jamieson
Mr. W. J. Gibson
Mr. E. E. Malcolm
Mr. H. E. T. Tew
Mr. W. Macniven
Mr. W. Stevenson
Mr. David Mitchell
Mr. P. Gifford
Mr. A. Orr
Mr. N. W. Willins
Mr. J. S. Gilmour
Mr. J. K. Selkirk
Mr. J. S. Ross
Mr. A. D. Haddon
Mr. J. Conn
Mr. A. Cameron
Mr. J. W. E. Steedman
Mr. C. S. Grace
Mr. W. Galloway
Mr. J. Hart
Mr. A. Lawson

Mr. E. G. Fisher
Mr. J. F. Johnston
Mr. T. Brown
Mr. J. M. Maitland
Mr. R. S. Sweet
Mr. A. Macfarlane
Mr. A. B. Steven
Lt.-Col. G. A. Phillips
Mr. C. Denholm
Mr. G. Bruce
Mr. J. S. Hunter
Mr. J. M. Denholm
Mr. J. Elliot
Mr. I. M. Mactaggart
Mr. K. Macdonald
Mr. J. R. Paterson
Mr. J. Bunyan
Mr. F. Will
Mr. T. W. Wilson
Mr. J. Currie
Mr. T. R. D. Prentice
Mr. J. M'Queen
Mr. W. Barrie
Mr. G. T. Hamilton
Mr. A. S. Miller
Mr. P. Mackie
Mr. R. Stanton
Mr. Robert Wright
Mr. A. C. S. Wright
Mr. J. Lothian
Mr. J. W. Martin
Mr. C. P. Leiper
Mr. R. B. Thomson
Mr. A. B. Gorman
Mr. G. Elder
Mr. W. Power
Mr. R. M. Angus
Mr. S. Cosh
Mr. D. C. Fletcher
Mr. A. Laurie

# The Royal Bank of Scotland

Mr. C. Smith
Mr. A. Dunnachie
Mr. W. J. Simpson
Mr. K. A. Hutchison
Mr. D. W. Nicholson
Mr. Geo. M'Intosh
Mr. W. Fraser
Mr. G. Rutherfurd
Mr. J. M. Bennie
Mr. J. R. M'Math
Mr. W. S. Inverarity
Mr. A. P. Smith
Mr. T. G. Fraser
Mr. W. Stirling
Mr. R. S. Cargill
Mr. A. W. Kerr
Mr. D. Melrose
Mr. D. T. Gardner
Mr. A. B. Russell
Mr. W. D. Duncan
Mr. Jas. Adam
Mr. W. W. Adam
Mr. W. J. Walker Todd (Architect)
Mr. Jno. Barrie
Mr. A. M'Cormick
Mr. A. K. H. Boyd
Mr. Jno. Paterson
Mr. J. L. Niven
Mr. W. T. Newlands
Mr. J. C. Hansen
Mr. J. Kirkaldy
Mr. J. Robson
Mr. J. M. Steel
Mr. R. S. Young
Mr. W. M. Crone
Mr. Jas. Thomson
Mr. Jno. Baldie
Mr. R. L. Mudie
Mr. A. Briggs
Mr. D. Dewar
Mr. A. Berwick
Mr. J. Kirk
Mr. J. P. Mackenzie
Mr. W. M. Brims
Mr. W. T. Moir
Mr. W. A. Buchan
Mr. A. Rogers
Mr. J. Law
Mr. T. Matthew
Mr. A. F. Peterson
Mr. W. Wilson
Mr. W. J. Deans
Mr. T. Burnet
Mr. J. T. Tweedie
Mr. D. A. Wilkie
Mr. W. A. Watt
Mr. H. K. C. Ovens
Mr. J. W. Underwood
Mr. J. P. Johnston
Mr. W. Henderson
Mr. T. M. Rankin
Mr. W. Ferguson
Mr. A. Scott
Mr. A. Brockie
Mr. C. A. O. Renwick
Mr. M. G. Greig
Mr. A. Craig
Mr. W. C. Walls
Mr. G. Melrose
Mr. J. K. Bell
Mr. W. Bishop
Mr. A. E. Anton
Mr. A. A. Imrie
Mr. W. Adams
Mr. Geo. Marshall
Mr. J. H. Rankin
Mr. Alex. Russell
Mr. H. Mitchell
Mr. George Dundas

# The Royal Bank of Scotland

## THE BANK'S POSITION FROM 1865 TO 1927

| | Capital. | Rest. | Deposits. | Advances and Bills Discounted. | | Profits. | Dividend. |
|---|---|---|---|---|---|---|---|
| | £ | £ | £ | £ | | £ | |
| 1865 | 2,000,000 | 332,437 | 8,127,791 | 8,206,984 | | 177,941 | 7½% less tax |
| 1875 | 2,000,000 | 500,000 | 10,588,334 | 10,460,163 | | 204,310 | 9½% free of tax |
| 1885 | 2,000,000 | 761,636 | 12,027,480 | 9,529,922 | | 183,992 | 9% ,, |
| 1895 | 2,000,000 | 757,638 | 13,061,341 | 9,504,961 | | 164,344 | 8% ,, |
| 1900 | 2,000,000 | 844,078 | 14,157,122 | 10,807,892 | | 226,457 | 10% ,, |
| 1905 | 2,000,000 | 933,439 | 13,606,171 | 10,684,368 | | 239,715 | 10% ,, |
| 1906 | 2,000,000 | 970,221 | 13,666,322 | 10,453,942 | | 242,781 | 10% ,, |
| 1907 | 2,000,000 | 970,221 | 14,569,781 | 11,530,598 | | 254,057 | 10% ,, |
| 1908 | 2,000,000 | 1,005,473 | 14,013,795 | 10,272,278 | | 240,252 | 10% ,, |
| 1909 | 2,000,000 | 1,030,620 | 13,861,273 | 9,885,568 | | 230,147 | 10% ,, |
| 1910 | 2,000,000 | 1,013,565 | 13,920,173 | 9,551,608 | | 237,944 | 10% less tax |
| 1911 | 2,000,000 | 1,013,565 | 14,455,195 | 9,559,492 | | 247,166 | 11% ,, |
| 1912 | 2,000,000 | 951,565 | 15,406,007 | 10,215,483 | | 267,808 | 11% ,, |
| 1913 | 2,000,000 | 960,629 | 16,654,481 | 11,247,389 | Includes British Treasury Bills. | 275,931 | 11% ,, |
| 1914 | 2,000,000 | 960,629 | 16,948,699 | 11,369,588 | £ | 266,308 | 11% ,, |
| 1915 | 2,000,000 | 800,986 | 19,144,394 | 9,294,497 | (1,564,000) | 293,731 | 10% ,, |
| 1916 | 2,000,000 | 800,986 | 21,966,710 | 12,631,734 | (5,696,000) | 338,420 | 10% ,, |
| 1917 | 2,000,000 | 914,968 | 26,177,865 | 16,798,203 | (8,090,000) | 303,981 | 10% ,, |
| 1918 | 2,000,000 | 1,030,470 | 29,202,380 | 18,537,438 | (9,650,000) | 310,502 | 10% ,, |
| 1919 | 2,000,000 | 1,082,276 | 35,548,823 | 19,438,362 | (6,087,000) | 325,805 | 10% ,, |
| 1920 | 2,000,000 | 1,082,276 | 39,114,127 | 25,353,227 | (6,930,000) | 375,138 | 11% ,, |
| 1921 | 2,000,000 | 1,241,777 | 40,749,031 | 25,084,687 | (8,640,000) | 377,500 | 11% ,, |
| 1922 | 2,000,000 | 1,403,735 | 40,265,016 | 21,077,516 | (4,030,000) | 401,958 | 12% ,, |
| 1923 | 2,000,000 | 1,565,961 | 37,880,518 | 19,682,831 | (2,690,000) | 426,225 | 13% ,, |
| 1924 | 2,500,000 | 2,347,393 | 39,719,331 | 20,357,120 | (1,870,000) | 452,369 | 14% ,, |
| 1925 | 2,500,000 | 2,464,704 | 40,790,229 | 22,828,676 | (1,835,000) | 472,622 | 14½% ,, |
| 1926 | 2,500,000 | 2,571,249 | 40,457,710 | 23,388,561 | (1,770,000) | 476,545 | 15½% ,, |
| 1927 | 2,500,000 | 2,683,226 | 44,186,574 | 26,453,671 | (2,525,000) | 481,977 | 16% and Bicentenary Bonus of 5% less tax |

# THE BANK'S REPORT AND BALANCE SHEET AS AT 8TH OCTOBER 1927

# REPORT TO THE ANNUAL GENERAL COURT OF PROPRIETORS, HELD ON 30TH NOVEMBER 1927

The Directors now submit to the Proprietors the annexed Abstract Statement of the Affairs of the Bank at the Second Saturday of October 1927, with relative Profit and Loss Account, certified by the Auditors.

|  |  |  |
|---|---|---|
| The net Profits of the year, after providing for all bad and doubtful debts, amounted to | £481,977 3 11 | |
| *Add*—From sums set aside as provision for depreciation on Investments not now required | 100,000 0 0 | |
| | £581,977 3 11 | |
| The Midsummer Dividend, at the rate of 16 per cent per annum, required £200,000 : 0 : 0. *Less* Income Tax £40,000 : 0 : 0 | £160,000 0 0 | |
| It is now proposed to pay a Dividend at Christmas, at the rate of 16 per cent per annum, which will require £200,000 : 0 : 0. *Less* Income Tax £40,000 : 0 : 0 | 160,000 0 0 | |
| And also to pay a Special Bicentenary Bonus at 5 per cent requiring £125,000 : 0 : 0. *Less* Income Tax £25,000 : 0 : 0 | 100,000 0 0 | |
| There has been written off expenditure on Bank Buildings and Heritable Property | 20,000 0 0 | |
| Carried to Pension Reserve Fund | 30,000 0 0 | |
| And added to Rest, the balance of | 111,977 3 11 | |
| | £581,977 3 11 | |

With the above addition, the REST now amounts to £2,683,226, 15 : 5.

All the Bank's investments are valued in the annexed State of Affairs at or under the prices ruling at the date of the Balance.

The Bank attained its BICENTENARY on 31st May 1927. In recognition of the event a Bonus was paid to the Staff.

The Directors record with regret that owing to the state of his health Mr. Edward Gorrel Baxter, who was appointed an Ordinary Director in 1895, and has always taken a warm interest in the affairs of the Bank, has found it necessary to retire. In virtue of the Powers conferred upon them by the Royal Bank of Scotland Act, 1873, the Directors elected Mr. Thomas Middleton Murray, Writer to the Signet, Edinburgh, as an Ordinary Director. Mr. Murray holds office until this Annual General Court only, but is eligible for re-election. In exercise of these Powers, the Directors also elected Captain George Ilay Campbell, Younger of Succoth, as an Extraordinary Director.

The Governor, the Deputy Governor, the Extraordinary Directors, and the Senior Ordinary Director (Mr. Lidstone) all retire at this time, but are eligible for re-election.

Auditors also fall to be appointed for the ensuing year, and Mr. J. Maxtone Graham, C.A., and Mr. Eric M. Beilby, C.A., offer themselves for re-election.

By Order of the Court of Directors,

A. K. WRIGHT,
*Cashier and General Manager.*

# ABSTRACT STATE OF AFFAIRS AT 8TH OCTOBER 1927

## LIABILITIES

| | | |
|---|---:|---:|
| 1. DEPOSITS with accrued Interest | £44,186,574 | 8 4 |
| 2. NOTES in Circulation | 2,707,112 | 0 0 |
| 3. DRAFTS OUTSTANDING | 687,421 | 17 5 |
| 4. ACCEPTANCES and INDORSEMENTS of Foreign Bills | 1,134,343 | 17 7 |
| | £48,715,452 | 3 4 |
| 5. CAPITAL  £2,500,000 0 0 | | |
| 6. REST  2,683,226 15 5 | | |
| 7. Proposed Half-year's DIVIDEND and Special Bicentenary BONUS payable at Christmas (*less* Income Tax)  260,000 0 0 | | |
| | 5,443,226 | 15 5 |
| TOTAL LIABILITIES | £54,158,678 | 18 9 |

## ASSETS

| | | |
|---|---:|---:|
| 1. GOLD and SILVER COIN, CURRENCY NOTES, NOTES of other Banks, and CASH with Bank of England and other London Bankers  £5,062,621 19 5 | | |
| 2. MONEY in London at Call and short notice, and Cheques, etc., payable on demand, in hand, and *in transitu*  6,620,857 5 1 | | |
| 3. BRITISH GOVERNMENT SECURITIES (*War Loans, Conversion Loans, Exchequer Bonds, National War Bonds and Treasury Bonds*)  12,490,540 16 10 | | |
| 4. COLONIAL GOVERNMENT SECURITIES, BANK OF ENGLAND STOCK and CORPORATION STOCKS  1,071,700 16 0 | | |
| 5. Other Marketable Securities  320,861 4 10 | | |
| | £25,566,582 | 2 2 |
| 6. BILLS discounted (of which £2,525,000 British Treasury Bills)  £5,019,087 19 2 | | |
| 7. ADVANCES on Cash Credit and Current Accounts  19,642,525 12 7 | | |
| 8. LOANS on Stocks and Securities  1,792,057 15 0 | | |
| 9. BANKING CORRESPONDENTS and other Customers for Acceptances and Indorsements, *per contra*  1,134,343 17 7 | | |
| 10. BANK BUILDINGS (partly yielding rent)  357,977 10 2 | | |
| 11. PROPERTY yielding rent  171,104 2 1 | | |
| 12. FREEHOLD PROPERTIES in London (partly occupied by Bank and partly yielding rent)  475,000 0 0 | | |
| | 28,592,096 | 16 7 |
| TOTAL ASSETS | £54,158,678 | 18 9 |

## PROFIT AND LOSS ACCOUNT

| | | | |
|---|---:|---|---:|
| To Expenditure on Bank Buildings and Property written off  £20,000 0 0 | | By Rest at 9th October 1926  £2,571,249 11 6 | |
| ,, Pension Reserve Fund  30,000 0 0 | | ,, From Investments Account  100,000 0 0 | |
| ,, Dividend for half-year, paid at Midsummer, *less* Income Tax  160,000 0 0 | | | £2,671,249 11 6 |
| ,, Dividend and Special Bicentenary Bonus to be paid at Christmas, *less* Income Tax  260,000 0 0 | | By Net Profits after deducting expenses of Management at Head Office and 224 Branch Establishments, allowing for rebate on Bills Current and Income Tax, and providing for all bad and doubtful debts  481,977 3 11 | |
| ,, Balance, being free Rest or undivided Profits, carried forward  2,683,226 15 5 | | | |
| £3,153,226 15 5 | | £3,153,226 15 5 | |

D. SPEED, *Accountant*.

## AUDITORS' REPORT

As Auditors appointed by the Proprietors of THE ROYAL BANK OF SCOTLAND, we have checked the Cash on hand at Head Office, Glasgow and London (City Office), verified the Cash with London Bankers, the Securities for money at call and short notice, the Government Securities and other Investments, and examined the details of the other Assets and of the Liabilities set forth in the foregoing Abstract State of Affairs; and we now certify that in our opinion said Abstract State is a full and fair Balance Sheet, properly drawn up, and exhibits a true and correct view of the state of the Bank's Affairs, as shown by the books, at 8th October 1927.

EDINBURGH, 14*th November* 1927.

J. MAXTONE GRAHAM, C.A., *Auditor*.
E. M. BEILBY, C.A., *Auditor*.

# THE ROYAL BANK OF SCOTLAND
*INCORPORATED BY ROYAL CHARTER 1727*

GOVERNOR

His Grace the DUKE OF BUCCLEUCH
AND QUEENSBERRY, K.T.

DEPUTY GOVERNOR

The Right Hon. the EARL OF STRATHMORE
AND KINGHORNE, G.C.V.O.

ORDINARY DIRECTORS

Sir Thomas Dunlop, Baronet, G.B.E., Glasgow.
Field-Marshal The Right Hon. Earl Haig of Bemersyde, K.T., G.C.B., O.M., G.C.V.O., K.C.I.E.
Herbert William Haldane, Chartered Accountant, Edinburgh.
Sir Henry Cook, Writer to the Signet, Edinburgh.
Charles C. Maconochie, C.B.E., K.C., of Avontoun, Linlithgow.
The Right Hon. The Earl of Elgin and Kincardine, C.M.G.
Robert William Dundas, M.C., Writer to the Signet, Edinburgh.
Thomas Middleton Murray, Writer to the Signet, Edinburgh.
George James Lidstone, F.I.A., F.F.A., LL.D., Edinburgh.

EXTRAORDINARY DIRECTORS

Sir Hugh Shaw Stewart of Greenock and Blackhall, Baronet, C.B.
Robert Fleming, 8 Crosby Square, Bishopsgate, London.
The Right Hon. Viscount Inchcape, G.C.S.I., G.C.M.G., K.C.I.E.
William D. Graham Menzies of Hallyburton, Coupar-Angus.
The Right Hon. The Earl of Airlie, M.C.
George Henry Drummond, 49 Charing Cross, London.
Sir Arthur Worley, C.B.E., 61 Threadneedle Street, London.
James Finlay Muir, 22 West Nile Street, Glasgow.
Captain George Ilay Campbell, Younger of Succoth.

## HEAD OFFICE: EDINBURGH

*Cashier and General Manager*—Sir ALEXANDER KEMP WRIGHT, K.B.E., D.L.
*Secretary*—J. B. ADSHEAD.

## BRANCHES

GLASGOW (CHIEF) OFFICE (Royal Exchange Square and Buchanan Street)
THOMAS LILLIE, *Manager*.   W. DONALD, *Sub-Manager*.

ABERDEEN.
   Do.   MARKET.
AIRDRIE.
ALLOA.
ALYTH.
ANNAN.
ARBROATH.
ARDROSSAN.
ARMADALE.
ARROCHAR.
   Sub Branch to Helensburgh.
AUCHINLECK.
   Sub Branch to Cumnock.
AYR.
AYTON.
BALLACHULISH.
   Sub Branch to Kinlochleven.
BARR.
   Sub Branch to Girvan.
BATHGATE.
BELLSHILL.
BIGGAR.
BLAIRGOWRIE.
BOAT OF GARTEN.
   Sub Branch to Grantown-on-Spey.
BO'NESS.
BOWMORE.
BRECHIN.
BRODICK (Arran).
BROUGHTY FERRY.
BUCKHAVEN.
BUCKIE.
CALLANDER.
CAMPBELTOWN.
CAMPSIE.
CARDENDEN.
   Sub Branch to Cowdenbeath.
CARR BRIDGE.
   Sub Branch to Grantown-on-Spey.
CARSPHAIRN.
   Sub Branch to Dalmellington.
CASTLE DOUGLAS.
CATHCART.
CATRINE.
CHAPELTON.
   Sub Branch to Strathaven.
CLYDEBANK.
COATBRIDGE.
COCKENZIE.
COLDINGHAM.
   Sub Branch to Ayton.
CORSTORPHINE.
COWDENBEATH.
CUMBERNAULD.
CUMNOCK.
CUPAR.
DAILLY.
   Sub Branch to Girvan.
DALKEITH.
DALMELLINGTON.
DALMUIR.
DAVIDSON'S MAINS.
   Sub Branch to West End, Edinburgh.

DENHOLM.
   Sub Branch to Hawick.
DINGWALL.
DRYMEN.
DUMFRIES.
DUNDEE.
   Do.   HILLTOWN.
   Do.   KING STREET.
   Do.   MURRAYGATE.
   Do.   PERTH ROAD.
   Do.   WEST PORT.
DUNFERMLINE.
DUNS.
DUNURE.
   Sub Branch to Ayr.
ECCLEFECHAN.
EDINBURGH.
   Do.   BLACKFORD.
   Do.   BROUGHTON DISTRICT.
   Do.   CASTLE STREET.
   Do.   FORREST ROAD.
   Do.   GILMERTON.
      Sub Branch to Newington.
   Do.   GORGIE.
   Do.   GRANGE.
   Do.   HAYMARKET.
   Do.   HUNTER SQ.
   Do.   LEVEN STREET.
   Do.   MARKETS.
      Sub Branch to West End.
   Do.   MAYFIELD.
      Sub Branch to Newington.
   Do.   MORNINGSIDE.
   Do.   SOUTH MORNINGSIDE.
   Do.   NEWINGTON.
   Do.   PITT STREET.
   Do.   ST. PATRICK SQ.
   Do.   SAUGHTONHALL.
      Sub Branch to Corstorphine.
   Do.   STOCKBRIDGE.
   Do.   WEST END.
ELGIN.
EYEMOUTH.
FAIRLIE.   Sub Branch to Largs.
FALKIRK.
FORFAR.
   Do.   MARKET.
      Sub Branch to Forfar.
FORRES.
FORT WILLIAM.
GALASHIELS.
GIRVAN.
GLAMIS.
GLASGOW.
   Do.   ALEXANDRA PARADE.
   Do.   ANDERSTON.
   Do.   CALTON AND BRIDGETON.
   Do.   CHARING CROSS.
   Do.   COWCADDENS.
   Do.   DOWANHILL.
   Do.   DUKE STREET.
   Do.   EASTPARK.
   Do.   GALLOWGATE.

GLASGOW (*contd.*).
    Do.    GARSCUBE CROSS.
    Do.    HOPE STREET.
    Do.    HUTCHESONTOWN.
    Do.    IBROX.
    Do.    JAMAICA STREET.
    Do.    NORTH WOODSIDE.
    Do.    PLANTATION.
    Do.    POLLOKSHIELDS.
    Do.    POSSILPARK.
    Do.    RIDDRIE.
        Sub Branch to Alexandra Parade.
    Do.    ST. ROLLOX.
    Do.    ST. VINCENT ST.
    Do.    SAUCHIEHALL ST.
    Do.    SHAWLANDS.
    Do.    SPRINGBURN.
    Do.    TRADESTON.
    Do.    TRONGATE.
GOVAN.
GRANGEMOUTH.
GRANTON (Edinburgh).
GRANTOWN-ON-SPEY.
GRANT'S HOUSE.
    Sub Branch to Ayton.
GREENLAW (Berwickshire).
GREENOCK.
    Do.    WEST END.
HADDINGTON.
HAMILTON.
HAWICK.
HELENSBURGH.
HUNTLY.
INVERNESS.
IRVINE.
JEDBURGH.
JOHNSTONE.
KEITH.
KELSO.
KELTY.
    Sub Branch to Cowdenbeath.
KILMACOLM.
KILMARNOCK.
KILSYTH.
KILWINNING.
KINLOCHLEVEN.
KINROSS.
KIRKCALDY.
KIRKINTILLOCH.
KIRKLISTON.
    Sub Branch to Corstorphine.
KIRKWALL.
KIRRIEMUIR.
LANARK.
LARGS.
LARKHALL.
LEITH.
    Do.    LEITH WALK.
    Do.    NORTH LEITH.
LEITHOLM.
    Sub Branch to Duns.
LESMAHAGOW.
LEVEN.
LOCHEE.
LOCKERBIE.
LONGNIDDRY.
    Sub Branch to Haddington.

MARKINCH.
MARYHILL.
MAYBOLE.
MEIGLE.
MELROSE.
METHIL.
MILNGAVIE.
MONIFIETH.
MONTROSE.
MOTHERWELL.
MUNLOCHY.
MUSSELBURGH.
NAIRN.
NETHY BRIDGE.
    Sub Branch to Grantown-on-Spey.
NEWHAVEN (Edinburgh).
NEWMILNS.
NEWTON STEWART.
NEWTOWN (St. Boswells).
    Sub Branch to Melrose.
NEWTYLE.
    Sub Branch to Meigle.
OBAN.
ORMISTON.
    Sub Branch to Tranent.
PAISLEY.
PARTICK.
PERTH.
PINWHERRY.
    Sub Branch to Girvan.
PORT ELLEN.
PORT GLASGOW.
PORTOBELLO.
PORTPATRICK.
    Sub Branch to Stranraer.
PRESTONPANS.
PRESTWICK.
RATHO.
    Sub Branch to Corstorphine.
RENFREW.
ROTHESAY.
RUTHERGLEN.
ST. ABBS.
    Sub Branch to Ayton.
ST. ANDREWS.
ST. BOSWELLS.
    Sub Branch to Melrose.
SALTCOATS.
SANQUHAR.
SELKIRK.
SHETTLESTON.
STEPPS.
STEVENSTON.
    Sub Branch to Saltcoats.
STEWARTON.
STIRLING.
STRANRAER.
STRATHAVEN.
STRATHBLANE (Netherton).
    Sub Branch to Milngavie.
SWINTON.
    Sub Branch to Duns.
THURSO.
TIGHNABRUAICH.
TRANENT.
WEST KILBRIDE.
WHITING BAY.
WISHAW.

LONDON (CITY) OFFICE (3 Bishopsgate, E.C.2)
WILLIAM WHYTE, *Manager.*    JOHN ROBB, *Deputy Manager.*

LONDON: DRUMMONDS' BRANCH, 49 Charing Cross, London, S.W.1.
Under the charge of the Messrs Drummond.—W. H. SMITH, *Manager.*

# GOVERNORS, DEPUTY GOVERNORS, DIRECTORS, AND CASHIERS SINCE THE INCORPORATION OF THE BANK IN 1727

## I. GOVERNORS

| | |
|---|---|
| Ilay, Archibald, Earl of | 1727–1737 |
| Lant, Mathew, Lord Chief Baron, Court of Exchequer | 1737–1742 |
| Lant, Robert, of Putney | 1742–1743 |
| Hotham, Beaumont, Commissioner of Customs | 1743–1750 |
| Montrose, Duke of | 1750–1756 |
| Hotham, Beaumont, Commissioner of Customs | 1756–1761 |
| Edwards, John, Merchant, London | 1761–1764 |
| Dundas, Sir Lawrence, of Kerse | 1764–1777 |
| Buccleuch and Queensberry, Duke of | 1777–1812 |
| Buccleuch and Queensberry, Duke of | 1812–1819 |
| Hopetoun, Earl of | 1820–1824 |
| Dalhousie, Earl of | 1824–1838 |
| Buccleuch and Queensberry, Duke of | 1838–1884 |
| Buccleuch and Queensberry, Duke of | 1884–1914 |
| Buccleuch and Queensberry, Duke of | 1914– |

The History of

## II. DEPUTY GOVERNORS

| | |
|---|---|
| Dalrymple, Sir Hew, Lord President of Session | 1727–1737 |
| Fletcher, Andrew (Lord Milnton), Lord Justice-Clerk | 1737–1766 |
| Pringle, Andrew (Lord Alemoor) | 1766–1776 |
| Veitch, James (Lord Elliock) | 1776–1794 |
| Innes, Gilbert, of Stow | 1794–1837 |
| Buccleuch and Queensberry, Duke of | 1832–1838 |
| Hope, Sir John, of Craighall, Baronet | 1839–1854 |
| Drummond, H. Home, of Blair Drummond | 1854–1858 |
| Craig, Sir William Gibson, of Riccarton, Baronet | 1858–1878 |
| Strathmore and Kinghorne, Earl of | 1878–1903 |
| Elgin and Kincardine, The Right Hon. The Earl of, K.G. | 1904–1917 |
| Strathmore and Kinghorne, The Right Hon. The Earl of | 1917– |

## III. ORDINARY DIRECTORS

| | |
|---|---|
| Alexander, William, Merchant and Lord Provost of Edinburgh | 1730–1760 |
| Anderson, David, Writer to the Signet | 1763–1784 |
| Anderson, John, Writer to the Signet | 1784–1788 |
| Allan, Robert | 1799–1802 |
| Allan, William, of Glen | 1826–1833 |
| Bogle, James, Solicitor | 1742–1743 |
| Buchan, George, of Kello, Clerk to Commissioners of Teinds | 1752–1761 |

# The Royal Bank of Scotland

| | |
|---|---|
| Brown, George, Commissioner of Excise | 1762–1779 |
| Brown, Charles, Writer to the Signet | 1770–1777 |
| Brown, George, of Ellieston | 1779–1787 |
| Bonar, Andrew, Banker in Edinburgh | 1792–1805 |
| Bonar, Alexander | 1798–1818 |
| Bruce, James | 1806–1826 |
| Burnley, William Frederick, Edinburgh | 1880–1891 |
| Baxter, Edward Gorrel, of Teasses | 1895–1927 |
| | |
| Campbell, Patrick, of Monzie (Lord Monzie) | 1727–1751 |
| Craufurd, Patrick, Senior | 1727–1735 |
| Coutts, John, Lord Provost of Edinburgh | 1744–1751 |
| Chalmers, George, Writer to the Signet | 1751–1758 |
| Colston, Lord | 1761–1763 |
| Craufurd, Ronald, Writer to the Signet | 1762–1763 |
| Campbell, John, Writer to the Signet | 1781–1799 |
| Campbell, John, Writer to the Signet | 1803–1810 |
| Cockburn, Baron Archibald | 1792–1796 |
| Campbell, John, Receiver-General of Customs | 1794–1798 |
| Campbell, John, Receiver-General of Customs | 1800–1820 |
| Connell, Sir John | 1822–1831 |
| Craig, Sir William Gibson, of Riccarton, Baronet | 1854–1858 |
| Clark, Andrew Rutherford, Advocate | 1861–1869 |
| Colonsay, Lord, *see* Duncan McNeill. | |
| Crichton, James Arthur, Advocate | 1888–1891 |
| Cook, Sir Henry, Writer to the Signet | 1891–1928 |
| Carlow, Charles, Coalmaster, Edinburgh | 1898–1923 |
| Carmichael, Sir Thomas D. Gibson, of Skirling, Baronet | 1900–1908 |

# The History of

| | |
|---|---|
| Drummond, George, Lord Provost of Edinburgh | 1727–1745 |
| Drummond, George | 1759–1765 |
| Dowdeswell, Richard | 1727–1758 |
| Davidson, John, Writer to the Signet | 1779–1790 |
| Dalrymple, John, Ex-Lord Provost of Edinburgh | 1773–1779 |
| Dundas, Robert, Solicitor-General | 1787–1789 |
| Duncan, Alexander, Writer to the Signet | 1798–1818 |
| Dundas, James, Writer to the Signet | 1796–1831 |
| Davidson, Henry | 1799–1802 |
| Drummond, H. Home, of Blair Drummond | 1835–1854 |
| Dundas, John, Clerk to the Signet | 1845–1873 |
| Dundas, Ralph, Clerk to the Signet | 1880–1895 1896–1911 |
| Dickson, Leonard Walter, C.A., Edinburgh | 1906–1919 |
| Davidson, Ernest Archibald, Edinburgh | 1908–1919 |
| Dunlop, Sir Thomas, Baronet, G.B.E., Glasgow | 1917– |
| Dundas, Robert William, M.C., W.S., Edinburgh | 1919– |
| | |
| Elliock, Lord, *see* James Veitch. | |
| Erskine, David, Clerk to the Signet | 1790–1792 |
| Elder, Thomas, of Forneth | 1793–1796 |
| Elgin and Kincardine, The Right Hon. The Earl of | 1892–1894 1900–1902 |
| Elgin and Kincardine, The Right Hon. The Earl of, C.M.G. | 1926– |
| | |
| Fletcher, Andrew, Lord Justice-Clerk (Lord Milnton) | 1727–1736 |
| Fordyce, John, Merchant | 1759–1761 |

[ 400 ]

# The Royal Bank of Scotland

| | |
|---|---|
| Fairholme, Adam, Merchant . . | 1760–1761 |
| Fullerton, William, of Carstairs . | 1778–1780 |
| Ferrier, James . . . . | 1815–1821 |
| Ferrier, John, Writer to the Signet . | 1822–1844 |
| Fleming, James Alexander, K.C., Edinburgh | 1911–1926 |
| | |
| Gray, Alexander, Writer in Edinburgh . | 1762–1768 |
| Guthrie, James, Merchant in Edinburgh . | 1767–1772 |
| Gladstone, John, of Fasque . . | 1834–1837 |
| Gibson, Alexander, Edinburgh . | 1886–1896 |
| | 1896–1898 |
| | |
| Hotham, Beaumont, Commissioner of Customs | 1737–1743 |
| Hamilton, John, Writer to the Signet . | 1740–1756 |
| Hope, Sir Archibald, of Craighall . | 1778–1794 |
| Hope, Sir John, of Craighall . . | 1821–1839 |
| Horne, Archibald, Accountant, Edinburgh . | 1838–1862 |
| Hay, James, Merchant, Leith . . | 1849–1880 |
| Hozier, James, of Newlands . . | 1850–1874 |
| | 1876–1878 |
| Hamilton, John Glencairn Carter, of Dalzell | 1875–1885 |
| Harrison, George, Lord Provost of Edinburgh | 1883–1885 |
| Haldane, James, C.A., Edinburgh . | 1901–1906 |
| Haldane, Herbert William, C.A., Edinburgh | 1917– |
| Haig, Field-Marshal The Right Hon. Earl, K.T., G.C.B., O.M., G.C.V.O., K.C.I.E. . | 1923–1928 |
| | |
| Irving, George, of Newton . . | 1727–1737 |
| Innes, Gilbert, of Stow . . . | 1787–1793 |
| Innes, William Mitchell, of Parsons Green . | 1841–1853 |
| Innes, William Mitchell, of Ayton Castle . | 1853–1859 |
| Innes, George Mitchell, of Bangour . | 1860–1884 |
| | 1885–1886 |

## The History of

| | |
|---|---|
| Jollie, Alexander, Writer, Edinburgh . | 1743–1744 |
| Jardine, Sir Henry, King's Remembrancer | 1816–1848 |
| Jamieson, George Auldjo, Accountant, Edinburgh . . . . . | 1868–1879 |
| | 1880–1892 |
| | 1893–1900 |
| Johnston, Henry, K.C., Sheriff of Forfarshire | 1902–1904 |
| | |
| Kinloch, David, of Gilmerton . . . | 1762–1777 |
| | |
| Laurie, Gilbert, Lord Provost of Edinburgh . | 1767–1787 |
| Learmonth, John, of Dean, Lord Provost of Edinburgh . . . . . | 1830–1858 |
| L'Amy, James, Advocate, of Dunkenny | 1832–1853 |
| Lindsay, William, Merchant, Leith . . | 1839–1842 |
| Lindsay, Donald, Accountant, Edinburgh | 1843–1867 |
| Lidstone, George James, F.I.A., F.F.A., LL.D., Edinburgh . . . | 1919– |
| | |
| Milnton, Lord, see Andrew Fletcher. | |
| Monzie, Lord, see Patrick Campbell. | |
| Mansfield, James, Merchant, Edinburgh . | 1752–1753 |
| Muir, George, Writer to the Signet . . | 1763–1777 |
| Murray, Colonel Robert, Receiver-General of Customs . . . . . | 1764–1770 |
| Meason, Gilbert, Merchant in Edinburgh . | 1776–1779 |
| Miller, William, of Barskimming . . | 1780–1788 |
| Miller, Sir William, of Glenlee . . | 1788–1791 |
| Moncrieff, Robert Scott . . . | 1806–1814 |
| Mitchell, William, of Parsons Green . . | 1840–1841 |
| Murray, James Thomas, Writer to the Signet | 1855–1857 |
| Maitland, Sir Alexander Gibson, of Barnton and Cliftonhall, Baronet . . . | 1864–1875 |

# The Royal Bank of Scotland

| | |
|---|---|
| Menzies, Graham, Distiller, Edinburgh . | 1877–1880 |
| Moncrieff, Hon. Henry James, Advocate . | 1882–1888 |
| Murray, Thomas Middleton, Writer to the Signet . . . . . | 1927– |
| McKenzie, John, of Delvin, Writer to the Signet . . . . . | 1773–1778 |
| McQueen, Robert, Lord Justice-Clerk (Lord Braxfield) . . . . . | 1789–1799 |
| McDonald, William . . . . | 1799–1806 |
| McNeill, Duncan, Lord Advocate (Lord Colonsay) . . . . . | 1841–1849 |
| Maconochie, Charles Cornelius, C.B.E., K.C. | 1905– |
| | |
| Nimmo, James, Receiver-General of the Excise | 1728–1758 |
| | |
| Philp, John . . . . . | 1727–1751 |
| Paterson, James, one of the Commissaries of Edinburgh . . . . . | 1727–1728 |
| | |
| Rosebery, Earl of . . . . | 1759–1760 |
| Russell, John, Jr., Clerk to the Signet . | 1778–1780 |
| Ramsay, William, of Barnton, Merchant, Edinburgh . . . . . | 1781–1822 |
| Ramsay, George, Banker, Edinburgh . . | 1804–1809 |
| Rae, Sir William, Lord Advocate, Baronet . | 1816–1843 |
| Russell, Claud . . . . . | 1822–1828 |
| Rattray, Hon. Baron Clerk . . . | 1829–1830 |
| Ramsay, William, of Barnton . . . | 1832–1834 |
| Robertson, James, Writer to the Signet . | 1859–1864 |
| Richardson, Thomas, of Ralston, Merchant, Glasgow . . . . . | 1871–1872 |

# The History of

| | |
|---|---|
| Somervell, Hugh, Writer to the Signet | 1727–1738 |
| Shairp, Alexander, Merchant, Edinburgh | 1743–1772 |
| Stirling, James, Merchant, Edinburgh | 1779–1790 |
| Stirling, Sir James, Lord Provost of Edinburgh | 1792–1804 |
| Selkrig, Charles, Accountant | 1810–1837 |
| Scott, John Corse, of Sinton | 1816–1839 |
| Stirling, John, of Kippendavie | 1857–1882 |
| Stirling, Patrick, of Kippendavie | 1890–1896 |
| Thomson, William Thomas, Actuary, Edinburgh | 1857–1883 |
| Turnbull, Andrew Hugh, Actuary, Edinburgh | 1884–1893 1894–1917 |
| Veitch, James (Lord Elliock) | 1768–1776 |
| Whitefoord, Allan, Receiver-General of Land Tax | 1745–1761 |
| Watson, John, Writer to the Signet | 1753–1762 |
| Warrender, Hugh, Writer in Edinburgh | 1791–1821 |
| Walker, James, of Dalry | 1838–1857 |
| Warrender, Sir George, of Lochend | 1866–1877 1878–1888 1889–1900 |
| Wilson, William, Clerk to the Signet, Edinburgh | 1873–1880 |
| Walker, James, of Dalry | 1879–1890 1891–1900 |
| Wright, John Patrick, Writer to the Signet | 1886–1898 1898–1917 |
| Young, John | 1761–1765 |

# The Royal Bank of Scotland

## IV. EXTRAORDINARY DIRECTORS

| | |
|---|---|
| Areskine, Charles, of Tinwald (Lord Tinwald) | 1727–1763 |
| Alexander, William, Merchant, Edinburgh . | 1728–1729 |
| Alva, Lord . . . . . | 1773–1789 |
| Advocates, Dean of Faculty of (Hon. Henry Erskine) . . . . . | 1795–1796 |
| Allan, Robert . . . . . | 1796–1798 |
| Allan, Thomas . . . . . | 1816–1832 |
| Allan, William, of Glen . . . | 1823–1826 |
| | 1834–1840 |
| Aitchison, William, of Drummore . . | 1844–1845 |
| Abbott, Francis, Moray Place, Edinburgh . | 1865–1869 |
| Aberdeen, Earl of . . . . | 1873–1880 |
| Aberdeen, Earl of . . . . | 1881–1889 |
| | 1891–1898 |
| | 1899–1915 |
| Aitken, Thomas, of Nivingston . . | 1900–1906 |
| Allan, Hugh Andrew, Shipowner, Glasgow . | 1909–1919 |
| Airlie, The Right Hon. The Earl of, M.C. . . | 1921– |
| | |
| Baillie, George, of Jerviswood . . | 1727–1730 |
| Buchan, George, of Kello, Clerk to Commissioners of Teinds . . . | 1736–1751 |
| Bell, John, Merchant, Edinburgh . . | 1738–1739 |
| Bogle, James, Solicitor to the Court of Exchequer . . . . . | 1739–1743 |
| Burges, George . . . . . | 1759–1772 |
| Brown, George, Commissioner of Excise . | 1761–1762 |
| Baillie, George, of Jerviswood . . . | 1762–1777 |
| | 1782–1785 |
| Buchan, John, of Letham . . . | 1762–1777 |

## The History of

| | |
|---|---|
| Brown, Charles, Writer to the Signet . . | 1764–1770 |
| Barjarg, Lord . . . . . | 1765–1772 |
| Braxfield, Lord . . . . . | 1778–1787 |
| Blair, James Hunter, Merchant, Edinburgh . | 1779–1781 |
| Bonar, Andrew, Banker in Edinburgh . | 1791–1792 |
| | 1798–1799 |
| Bonar, Alexander . . . . | 1794–1796 |
| Bonar, John . . . . . | 1797–1799 |
| Bruce, James . . . . . | 1799–1805 |
| | 1814–1815 |
| | 1820–1821 |
| Balfour, James, of Whittingehame . . | 1839–1844 |
| Brown, John, of Parkhead . . . | 1849–1851 |
| Brown, John, of Marlie . . . | 1851–1858 |
| Bell, John Montgomerie, Sheriff of Kincardine | 1859–1863 |
| Bolton, Joseph Cheney, of Carbrook . . | 1874–1881 |
| Balfour, John Blair, Advocate, latterly Lord Kinross . . . . . | 1880–1888 |
| | 1889–1897 |
| | 1898–1904 |
| Brand, James, of Messrs. Harvey, Brand & Co., London . . . . . | 1889–1894 |
| Burnley, William Frederick, Edinburgh . | 1891–1897 |
| Boase, William Lindsay, Merchant, Dundee . | 1901–1910 |
| Bilsland, Sir William, Baronet, LL.D., Glasgow . . . . . | 1913–1921 |
| | |
| Clerk, Sir John, Baron of Court of Exchequer | 1727–1728 |
| Cathcart, Lord, Receiver-General for Scotland | 1727–1740 |
| Campbell, Patrick, Jr., Merchant, Edinburgh | 1728–1735 |
| Craig, James, Writer to the Signet . . | 1731–1743 |
| Coutts, John, Lord Provost of Edinburgh . | 1743–1744 |
| Campbell, Patrick, Younger of Monzie . | 1752–1757 |

# The Royal Bank of Scotland

| | |
|---|---|
| Cheap, George . . . . | 1752–1763 |
| Craufurd, Patrick, of Aiknamis . | 1755–1758 |
| | 1767–1768 |
| Chalmers, George, Merchant, Edinburgh . | 1758–1760 |
| Crauford, Ronald, Writer to the Signet . | 1761–1762 |
| Colston, Lord . . . . . | 1764–1767 |
| | 1772–1777 |
| Campbell, Colonel Robert . . | 1773–1790 |
| Campbell, General Henry . . | 1778–1780 |
| Campbell, Ilay, Advocate . . | 1779–1789 |
| Cockburn, Baron Archibald . . | 1789–1791 |
| Campbell, John, Receiver-General of Customs | 1791–1793 |
| | 1799–1800 |
| Campbell, Colonel, of Monzie . . | 1794–1795 |
| Creech, William, Lord Provost . | 1812–1814 |
| Connell, Sir John . . . | 1821–1822 |
| Cockburn, Patrick . . . | 1825–1831 |
| Campbell, Colin, of Jura . . | 1843–1848 |
| Craig, James T. Gibson, Writer to the Signet | 1846–1866 |
| Cunningham, James, Writer to the Signet . | 1849–1855 |
| Campbell, Sir Archibald Ilay, of Succoth, Baronet . . . . . | 1862–1867 |
| Clark, Andrew Rutherford, Advocate, Solicitor-General . . . . . | 1870–1879 |
| | 1880–1887 |
| | 1888–1895 |
| Crichton, James Arthur, Advocate . . | 1883–1888 |
| Carmichael, Sir Thomas D. Gibson, of Skirling, Baronet, M.P. . . . | 1898–1900 |
| Campbell, George Ilay, Younger of Succoth | 1927– |
| Dalrymple, Hew, one of the Senators of College of Justice . . . . | 1727–1728 |
| Drummore, Lord . . . . | 1727–1735 |

# The History of

| | |
|---|---|
| Dundas, Thomas, of Fingask . . . | 1741–1754 |
| Douglas, Sir James . . . . | 1768–1778 |
| Davidson, John, Writer to the Signet . . | 1772–1778 |
| Duncan, Alexander, Writer to the Signet . | 1791–1793 |
| | 1796–1798 |
| Dundas, James, Writer to the Signet . . | 1792–1795 |
| Dunn, William, of Duntocher . . . | 1832–1849 |
| Drummond, H. Home, of Blair Drummond | 1842–1843 |
| | 1850–1851 |
| Dunn, Alexander, of Duntocher . . | 1850–1856 |
| Duthie, Walter, Writer to the Signet . . | 1851–1864 |
| Dundas, John, Clerk to the Signet . . | 1853–1854 |
| | 1866–1867 |
| Drummond, George Stirling Home, of Blair Drummond . . . . | 1865–1870 |
| | 1874–1876 |
| Dundas, Ralph, Clerk to the Signet . . | 1895–1896 |
| Dundas, The Hon. Lord . . . | 1905–1917 |
| Dundas, William John, LL.D., C.S., Edinburgh | 1917–1921 |
| Drummond, George Henry, London . . | 1924– |

| | |
|---|---|
| Erskine, James, one of the Senators of College of Justice . . . . . | 1727–1728 |
| Elibank, Lord . . . . . | 1777–1778 |
| Erskine, David, Clerk to the Signet . . | 1785–1788 |
| Erskine, Hon. Henry . . . . | 1789–1791 |
| | 1796–1798 |
| | 1810–1818 |
| Elgin and Kincardine, The Right Hon. The Earl of . . . . . | 1894–1900 |
| | 1902–1904 |
| Elgin and Kincardine, The Right Hon. The Earl of, C.M.G. . . . . | 1919–1926 |

# The Royal Bank of Scotland

| | |
|---|---|
| Forbes, William, City Clerk of Edinburgh | 1743–1754 |
| Finlay, Robert, of Drummore | 1767–1777 |
| Fletcher, General Henry, of Saltoun | 1780–1788 |
| Ferguson, William, of Raith | 1794–1796 |
| Ferrier, James | 1803–1814 |
| Free, Peter | 1811–1827 |
| Finlay, Kirkman, Merchant, Glasgow | 1821–1842 |
| Ferrier, John, Writer to the Signet | 1836–1837 |
| Fleming, Robert, Merchant, London | 1907– |
| | |
| Grange, Lord | 1729–1730 |
| Graham, John, Writer in Edinburgh | 1736–1737 |
| Grant, William (Lord Prestongrange) | 1740–1764 |
| Garden, Alexander, of Troop | 1755–1767 |
| Gordon, Baron | 1792–1794, 1796–1799 |
| Gardner, John, Banker, Edinburgh | 1792–1793 |
| Grant, William | 1794–1796, 1799–1806 |
| Gordon, John | 1797–1803, 1805–1809 |
| Glassford, Henry | 1814–1819 |
| Goddard, William | 1826–1831 |
| Gladstone, John, of Fasque | 1837–1838 |
| Graham, William, of Lancefield | 1855–1856 |
| Graham, John, of Lancefield | 1863–1877, 1878–1884, 1885–1886 |
| Glasgow, Earl of | 1870–1878, 1879–1886 |
| Graham, Sir John Hatt Noble, of Larbert, Baronet | 1894–1924 |
| Gibson, Alexander, Edinburgh | 1896–1898 |

# The History of

| | |
|---|---|
| Hamilton, John, Writer to the Signet . . | 1730–1739 |
| Hotham, Beaumont, Commissioner of Customs | 1731–1736 |
| Hathorn, Hugh, Merchant, Edinburgh . | 1744–1755 |
| Home, Patrick, of Billie, Advocate . . | 1756–1772 |
| Hope, Sir Archibald, of Craighall, Baronet . | 1790–1791 |
| Hepburn, Baron . . . . . | 1803–1806 |
| | 1808–1812 |
| Hopkirk, James . . . . . | 1807–1821 |
| Hepburn, Sir George Buchan, Baronet . | 1815–1818 |
| Haig, James, of Lochrin . . . | 1831–1834 |
| Hozier, William, of Newlands . . . | 1832–1838 |
| Hodgson, John, Merchant, London . . | 1834–1848 |
| Hay, James, Merchant, Leith . . . | 1845–1849 |
| Hozier, James, of Newlands . . . | 1846–1850 |
| | 1862–1863 |
| | 1875–1876 |
| Handasyde, The Hon. Lord . . . | 1857–1858 |
| Horne, Archibald, Accountant . . | 1862–1863 |
| Hozier, Lieutenant-Colonel William Wallace, of Newlands . . . . | 1878–1885 |
| Hamilton, John Glencairn Carter, of Dalzell (Lord Hamilton) . . . . | 1885–1892 |
| | 1893–1898 |
| Haig, Hugh Veitch, of Ramornie . . | 1900–1902 |
| Haldane, James, C.A., Edinburgh . . | 1900–1901 |
| Innes, George Mitchell, of Bangour . . | 1859–1860 |
| | 1884–1885 |
| Inchcape, The Right Hon. Lord, G.C.M.G., K.C.S.I., K.C.I.E. . . . | 1916– |
| Jollie, Alexander, Writer, Edinburgh . . | 1737–1742 |
| Jamieson, Robert . . . . | 1799–1802 |

# The Royal Bank of Scotland

| | |
|---|---|
| Jeffrey, Hon. Francis, Lord Advocate | 1832–1841 |
| Jardine, Sir Henry, King's Remembrancer | 1841–1842 |
| Jamieson, George Auldjo, Accountant, Edinburgh | 1867–1868 |
| | 1879–1880 |
| | 1892–1893 |
| Johnston, The Hon. Lord | 1909–1917 |
| | |
| Keir, William, Baxter in Edinburgh | 1743–1751 |
| Kinnear, Hon. Lord, LL.D. | 1887–1892 |
| Kincairney, Hon. Lord | 1902–1909 |
| | |
| Lant, Mathew, Lord Chief Baron of Court of Exchequer | 1727–1736 |
| L'Amy, James, Advocate, of Dunkenny | 1826–1831 |
| Learmonth, John, of Dean, Lord Provost of Edinburgh | 1840–1841 |
| Lindsay, Donald, Accountant, Edinburgh | 1842–1843 |
| | 1851–1852 |
| | 1864–1865 |
| | 1867–1870 |
| | |
| Mansfield, James, Merchant, Edinburgh | 1744–1751 |
| Mansfield, John, Merchant | 1760–1761 |
| Murray, Sir Robert | 1771–1772 |
| Moncrieff, Baron Stewart, of Moredun | 1778–1790 |
| Montrose, Duke of | 1779–1793 |
| Montague, Duke of | 1785–1790 |
| Macdonald, William | 1822–1829 |
| Moncrieff, William Scott | 1824–1831 |
| Melville, J. T. Leslie, Banker, London | 1829–1849 |
| Murray, James Thomas, Writer to the Signet | 1849–1855 |
| Maitland, Sir Alexander C. Gibson, of Barnton, etc. | 1863–1864 |

## The History of

| | |
|---|---|
| Molison, Francis, of Errol, Dundee . . | 1864–1877 |
| Muir, John, of Deanston, Merchant, Glasgow | 1887–1894 |
| | 1896–1902 |
| Moncrieff, The Hon. Lord . . . | 1897–1909 |
| Menzies, William D. Graham, of Halliburton, Coupar-Angus . . . . | 1917– |
| Muir, James Finlay, Glasgow . . . | 1926– |
| Maconochie, Allan, Advocate . . . | 1790–1792 |
| McCall, John . . . . . | 1827–1832 |
| McCall, James, of Daldowie . . . | 1833–1867 |
| McNeill, Duncan (Lord Colonsay) . . | 1849–1853 |
| | 1872–1873 |
| McNeill, Sir John, G.C.B. . . . | 1853–1875 |
| | 1877–1883 |
| Macdonald, W. Macdonald, of St. Martins . | 1867–1872 |
| Nimmo, James, Receiver-General of the Excise | 1727–1728 |
| Newton, James, Writer to the Signet . . | 1860–1861 |
| Oswald, Roger, Writer, Edinburgh . . | 1737–1739 |
| Prestongrange, Lord, *see* William Grant. | |
| Pringle, John, of Haining . . . | 1777–1778 |
| | 1782–1784 |
| " President, The Lord " (Ilay Campbell) . | 1790–1791 |
| Pillans, James . . . . . | 1819–1824 |
| Paul, Sir George M., D.K.S., LL.D., Edinburgh . . . . . | 1921–1926 |
| Ross, George, Commissioner of Excise . | 1727–1754 |
| Russell, John, Jr., Clerk to the Signet . | 1755–1778 |
| Ramsay, George, Banker, Edinburgh . . | 1792–1794 |
| | 1797–1803 |

# The Royal Bank of Scotland

| | |
|---|---|
| Ramsay, David . . . . | 1799–1806 |
| Ramsay, William Ramsay, of Barnton | 1806–1808 |
| | 1834–1843 |
| Rae, Sir William, Lord Advocate . | 1809–1814 |
| Rutherford, Lord . . . | 1839–1854 |
| Ryburn, John, Merchant, Glasgow . | 1843–1844 |
| Rose, Sir John, Baronet, G.C.M.G. . | 1886–1889 |
| Reid, James Alexander, LL.D., Writer, Glasgow . . . . | 1910–1913 |
| Robertson, Sir William, Lord-Lieutenant of the County of Fife . . | 1917–1923 |
| | |
| Shairp, Alexander, Merchant, Edinburgh . | 1740–1742 |
| Somervill, Lord . . . . | 1752–1759 |
| Stirling, Sir James, Lord Provost of Edinburgh | 1791–1792 |
| Selkrig, Charles, Accountant . . | 1808–1810 |
| Smith, Alexander . . . | 1821–1827 |
| Stirling, Sir Gilbert, Baronet . . | 1841–1843 |
| Steuart, Lieutenant-General George Mackenzie . . . . | 1855–1856 |
| Stewart, Sir Michael Robert Shaw, Baronet . | 1867–1873 |
| | 1876–1882 |
| | 1883–1890 |
| | 1893–1899 |
| | 1900–1903 |
| Strathmore and Kinghorne, Earl of . | 1868–1874 |
| | 1876–1878 |
| Strathmore and Kinghorne, Earl of, G.C.V.O. | 1904– |
| Stirling, John, of Kippendavie . . | 1882–1882 |
| Stirling, Patrick, of Kippendavie . | 1897–1900 |
| Stewart, Sir Hugh Shaw, of Greenock and Blackhall, Baronet, C.B. . . | 1904– |

Tinwald, Lord, *see* Charles Areskine.

# The History of

| | |
|---|---|
| Thornton, Henry, Banker in Edinburgh | 1791–1796 |
| | 1798–1810 |
| Tawse, John . . . . | 1815–1821 |
| Torrance, George McMiken, of Threave | 1856–1861 |
| Thomson, William Thomas . . | 1869–1883 |
| Warrender, Hugh, Writer, Edinburgh | 1796–1797 |
| | 1802–1803 |
| | 1811–1812 |
| Warrender, Sir George, Baronet . | 1822–1828 |
| Walker, James, of Dalry . . | 1844–1845 |
| | 1852–1853 |
| Walker, James, Writer to the Signet . | 1856–1863 |
| Wilson, Robert Sym, of Woodburn . | 1858–1863 |
| Wilson, William, Clerk to the Signet . | 1860–1867 |
| Watson, William, LL.D., Dean of the Faculty of Advocates (Lord Watson) | 1876–1883 |
| | 1884–1891 |
| Warrender, Sir George, of Lochend, Baronet | 1877–1878 |
| | 1888–1889 |
| Walker, James, of Dalry . . | 1878–1879 |
| | 1890–1891 |
| Wellwood, The Hon. Lord, one of the Senators of the College of Justice | 1889–1894 |
| Wright, John Patrick, W.S., Edinburgh | 1898–1898 |
| Worley, Sir Arthur, Baronet, C.B.E., London | 1925– |

## V. CASHIERS

| | | |
|---|---|---|
| Allan Whitefoord | . . . | 1727–1734 |
| Allan Whitefoord | First | 1734–1745 |
| John Campbell . | Second | |
| John Campbell . | First | 1745–1777 |
| George Innes | Second | |

# The Royal Bank of Scotland

| | | |
|---|---|---|
| George Innes | First | } 1777–1780 |
| William Simpson | Second | |
| William Simpson | . | 1780–1808 |
| George Mitchell | First | } 1808–1816 |
| William Mitchell | Second | |
| William Mitchell | . | 1816–1825 |
| William Mitchell | } Joint | 1825–1827 |
| Andrew Bogle | | |
| John Thomson | . | 1827–1845 |
| Robert Sym Wilson | . | 1845–1856 |
| Laurence Robertson | . | 1856–1871 |
| James Simpson Fleming, Cashier and General Manager | . | 1871–1891 |
| David Robertson Williamson Huie, Cashier and General Manager | . | 1892–1907 |
| Adam Tait, Cashier and General Manager | . | 1907–1917 |
| Sir Alexander Kemp Wright, K.B.E., D.L., Cashier and General Manager (now known as General Manager) | . | 1917– |

# THE GREAT WAR

## ROLL OF THE FALLEN

Andrew Aitken
James Stewart Allison
Peter Harper Anderson
Thomas Elliot Armour
Peter Edwin Beatton
John Berwick
John Birrell
Alexander Mercer Brittain
Robert Cecil Brockie
Harold Cellars Brown
James Tod Brown
Robert Nisbet Brown
John Burt
George Storrie Campbell
David Shand Cant
Charles George Cheyne
Henry Nicolson Craigie
William John Kirton Cullen
Alexander Donald
Fredk. Montague Watson Duncan
Robert Hunter Dunn
Bertram Thomas Alexr. Forrest
William Stewart Fraser
George Wood Galloway
Alexander Scott Gibson
Frank Hamilton
Alexander Hay
Arthur Orr Hay
Frederick Hayworth
Lorimer Headley
Archibald Deans Henderson
James Fyfe Holmes, M.C.
Archibald Houston
William Wyllie Howat
Henry William Richard Huie
David Lumsden Hunter
David Imrie
Robert Prentice Innes
Charles Johnston
Robert Willis Johnston
Robert Brown Johnstone
William Ker
Alexander Lawrie
James M'Kercher Lawson
Arthur Justice Loutit.
John M'Cord
George Lyall Macdonald
William Henry Macintosh
Angus Norman Mackay
John Roddan Mackenzie
Samuel M'Knight
Thomas M'Lean
Duncan Macleay
Alexander Macniven
Alexander Mactaggart

THE WAR MEMORIAL AT THE HEAD OFFICE

# The Royal Bank of Scotland

Murdoch Archd. Mactaggart
John Mann
George Brownlee Mungall
Charles Paterson
John Robert Payne
George Horne Pirie
David Porter
Andrew Jack Prentice
Charles Dickson Reid
William Matheson Ross
David Sharpe
James Randolph Stedman Sidey
Peter Thomson Simpson
Harold Henderson Smith
James Smith
Donald Stewart
John Macalister Stewart
James Hampton Strachan
James Neil Sutherland
William Lachlan Sutherland
David Swan
David Borthwick Tait
James M'Gill Talman
John Taylor
William Thomson
Thomas Watson
Wm. George Douglas Watson
William Roberton Weir
Alfred Cairns Wilson, M.C.

THE END

www.ingramcontent.com/pod-product-compliance
Lightning Source LLC
Chambersburg PA
CBHW050247170426
43202CB00011B/1586